Great American Homes

EXPLORE AMERICA

Great American Homes

Reader's
Digest

THE READER'S DIGEST ASSOCIATION, INC.
Pleasantville, New York / Montreal

GREAT AMERICAN HOMES was created and produced by ST. REMY MULTIMEDIA INC.

STAFF FOR GREAT AMERICAN HOMES
Series Editor: Elizabeth Cameron
Art Director: Solange Laberge
Editor: E.W. Lewis
Assistant Editor: Neale McDevitt
Photo Researcher: Linda Castle
Cartography: Hélène Dion, David Widgington
Designer: Anne-Marie Lemay
Research Editor: Robert B. Ronald
Contributing Researcher: Olga Dzatko
Copy Editor: Joan Page McKenna
Index: Linda Cardella Cournoyer
Production Coordinator: Dominique Gagné
System Coordinator: Éric Beaulieu
Technical Support: Mathieu Raymond-Beaubien, Jean Sirois
Scanner Operators: Martin Francoeur, Sara Grynspan

ST. REMY STAFF
PRESIDENT, CHIEF EXECUTIVE OFFICER: Fernand Lecoq
PRESIDENT, CHIEF OPERATING OFFICER: Pierre Léveillé
VICE PRESIDENT, FINANCE: Natalie Watanabe
MANAGING EDITOR: Carolyn Jackson
MANAGING ART DIRECTOR: Diane Denoncourt
PRODUCTION MANAGER: Michelle Turbide

Writers: Rod Gragg—Biltmore Estate, The White House
Susan Hart—The Moss Mansion
Jim Henderson—San Francisco Plantation
Rose Houk—Taliesin West
Steven Krolak—Hearst Castle
E.W. Lewis—Mark Twain's House
Margaret Locklair—Monticello
Neale McDevitt—Winterthur
Allan Seiden—Iolani Palace

Contributing Writers: Adriana Barton, Jacquie Charlton,
Patricia McDevitt, Paul Serralheiro

Address any comments about *Great American Homes*
to U.S. Editor, General Books, c/o Customer Service,
Reader's Digest, Pleasantville, NY 10570

READER'S DIGEST STAFF
Editor: Kathryn Bonomi
Art Editor: Eleanor Kostyk
Production Supervisor: Mike Gallo
Editorial Assistant: Mary Jo McLean

READER'S DIGEST GENERAL BOOKS
Editor-in-Chief, Books and Home
Entertainment: Barbara J. Morgan
Editor, U.S. General Books: David Palmer
Executive Editor: Gayla Visalli
Managing Editor: Christopher Cavanaugh

Opening photographs
Cover: The Mount, Massachusetts
Back Cover: Monticello, Virginia
Page 2: Drayton Hall, South Carolina
Page 5: Marland Mansion and Estate, Oklahoma

Library of Congress Cataloging in Publication Data

Great american homes.
        p.   cm.—(Explore America)
    Includes index.
    ISBN 0-89577-964-1
    1. Mansions—United States—Guidebooks.   2. Dwellings—United
States—Guidebooks.   3. United States—Guidebooks.   4. Architecture,
Domestic—United States—Guidebooks.   I. Reader's Digest
Association.   II. Series.
    E159.G66   1997
    917.304'929—dc21   97-20746

CONTENTS

MARK TWAIN'S HOUSE ▪ *Connecticut*	8
WINTERTHUR ▪ *Delaware*	20
THE WHITE HOUSE ▪ *District of Columbia*	30
MONTICELLO ▪ *Virginia*	42
BILTMORE ESTATE ▪ *North Carolina*	54
SAN FRANCISCO PLANTATION ▪ *Louisiana*	66
THE MOSS MANSION ▪ *Montana*	76
TALIESIN WEST ▪ *Arizona*	86
HEARST CASTLE ▪ *California*	96
IOLANI PALACE ▪ *Hawaii*	108
GAZETTEER: *Traveler's Guide to Great American Homes*	118
INDEX	142
CREDITS AND ACKNOWLEDGMENTS	144

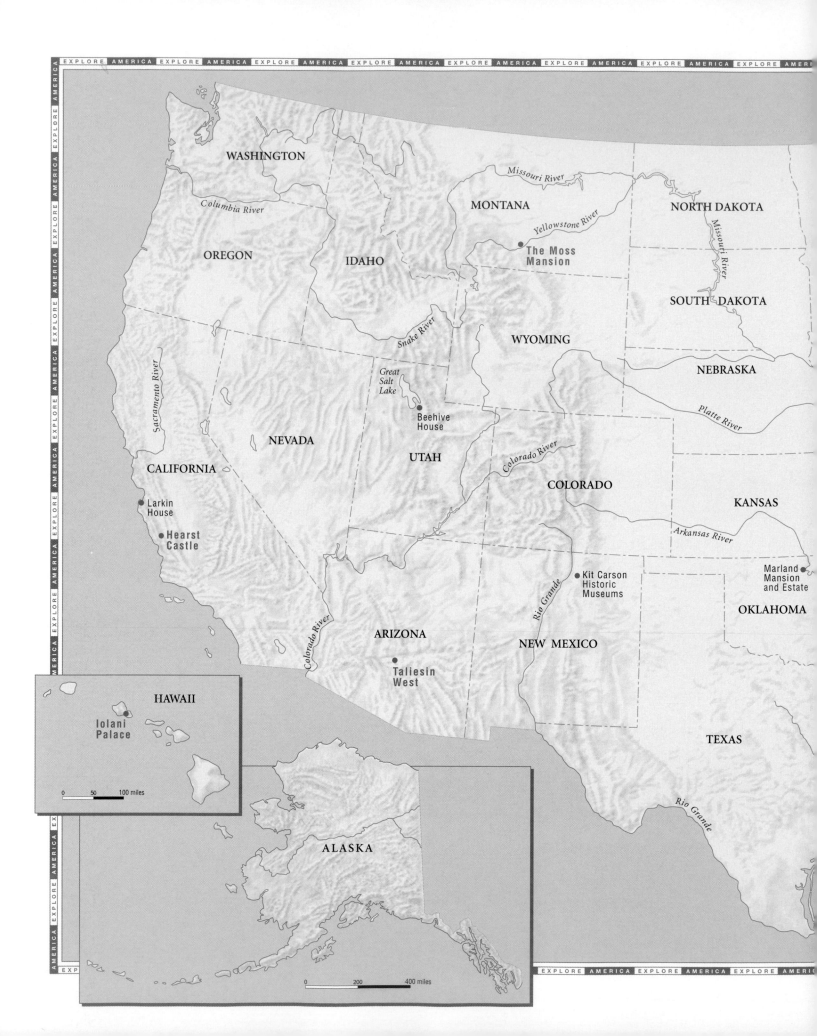

WASHINGTON

Columbia River

Missouri River

MONTANA

NORTH DAKOTA

OREGON

IDAHO

Yellowstone River

The Moss
Mansion

Missouri River

SOUTH DAKOTA

Snake River

WYOMING

Sacramento River

*Great
Salt
Lake*

NEBRASKA

Platte River

Beehive
House

NEVADA

UTAH

Colorado River

COLORADO

CALIFORNIA

KANSAS

Larkin
House

Arkansas River

Hearst
Castle

Kit Carson
Historic
Museums

Marland
Mansion
and Estate

Rio Grande

OKLAHOMA

Colorado River

ARIZONA

NEW MEXICO

Taliesin
West

TEXAS

HAWAII

Iolani
Palace

Rio Grande

0   50   100 miles

ALASKA

0   200   400 miles

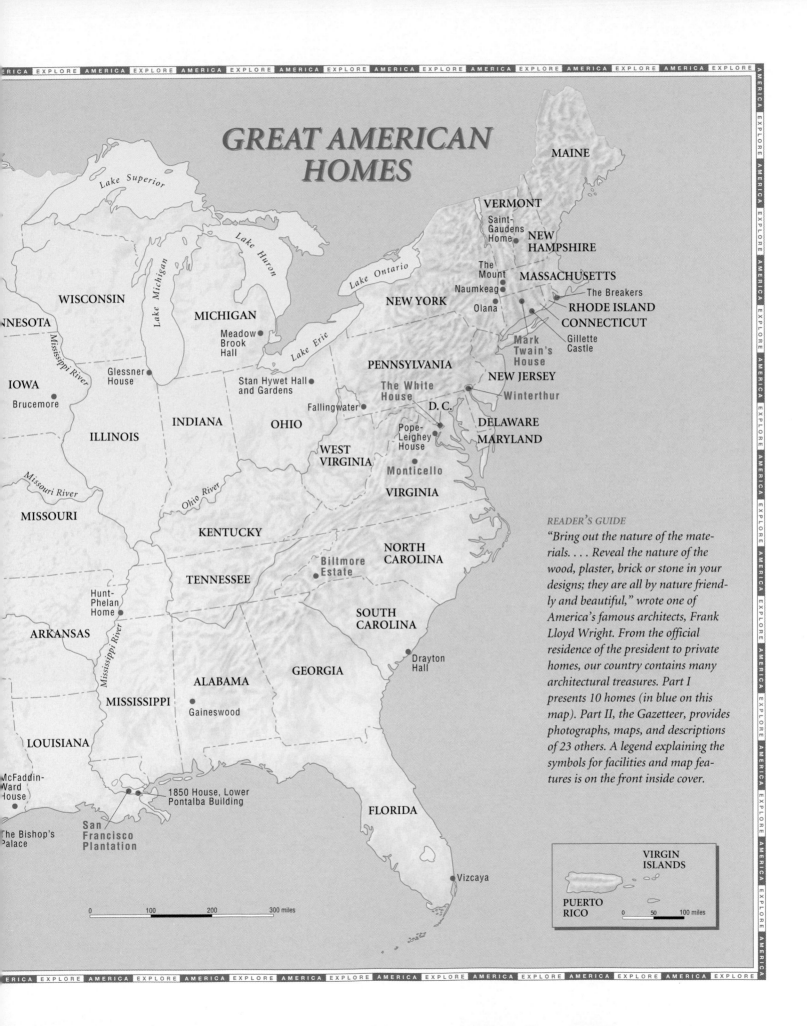

GREAT AMERICAN HOMES

MAINE

VERMONT

Saint-Gaudens Home

NEW HAMPSHIRE

The Mount

MASSACHUSETTS

Naumkeag

The Breakers

Olana

RHODE ISLAND

CONNECTICUT

Mark Twain's House

Gillette Castle

Lake Superior

Lake Huron

Lake Michigan

Lake Ontario

Lake Erie

WISCONSIN

MICHIGAN

NNESOTA

Meadow Brook Hall

NEW YORK

PENNSYLVANIA

NEW JERSEY

The White House

Winterthur

D. C.

DELAWARE

MARYLAND

Glessner House

Stan Hywet Hall and Gardens

Fallingwater

IOWA

INDIANA

OHIO

Brucemore

ILLINOIS

WEST VIRGINIA

Pope-Leighey House

Monticello

VIRGINIA

Missouri River

Mississippi River

Ohio River

MISSOURI

KENTUCKY

NORTH CAROLINA

Biltmore Estate

TENNESSEE

SOUTH CAROLINA

Hunt-Phelan Home

ARKANSAS

Drayton Hall

GEORGIA

Mississippi River

ALABAMA

MISSISSIPPI

Gaineswood

LOUISIANA

McFaddin-Ward House

1850 House, Lower Pontalba Building

The Bishop's Palace

San Francisco Plantation

FLORIDA

Vizcaya

VIRGIN ISLANDS

PUERTO RICO

0   50   100 miles

0   100   200   300 miles

MARK TWAIN'S HOUSE

*The Victorian exuberance of
Mark Twain's home in Hartford
was once looked on as avant-garde.*

On March 23, 1874, a reporter working for *The Hartford Daily Times* gave a detailed description of the residence that was rising on a lot beside Farmington Avenue in Hartford, Connecticut: "The novelty displayed in the architecture of the building, the oddity of its internal arrangement, and the fame of its owner, will all conspire to make it a house of note for a long time to come." The house in question belonged to Samuel Langhorne Clemens, known to the world by his pen name, Mark Twain. More than 120 years after its construction, visitors come to see the rooms in which the American humorist and writer spent some of the happiest days of his life.

The building stands on a hill above a wide thoroughfare in the once affluent neighborhood of Nook Farm. Three stories high and made of red brick, it imparts a feeling of prosperous, upper-middle-class comfort. Yet visitors are quick to notice its fanciful exterior design elements,

CHILDREN'S HAVEN
The younger two Clemens girls, Clara, born 1874, and Jean, born 1880, slept in the nursery on the second floor, right. The eldest daughter, Susy, who was two years old when the Clemenses moved into the house on Farmington Avenue, had her own room next door. Sam and Livy's firstborn, Langdon, died of diphtheria in 1872.

JOY OF READING
Overleaf: Mark Twain described the library in 1892 when he wrote of "the perfect taste of this ground floor, with its delicious dream of harmonious color, and its all-pervading spirit of peace and serenity and deep contentments." The room was the center of the Clemenses' family life and now contains their memorabilia, including an oil sketch of Olivia Clemens with her daughter Jean. The bookshelves overflow with Twain's more than 4,000 volumes.

which include a whimsical collection of Victorian gables, turrets, and porches, woodwork in purplish brown hues, and bricks painted black and orange (or, as Twain preferred to call the color, vermilion) to form a diamond pattern echoing the design of the steep slate roofs.

HOME OF AN AMERICAN ICON

Since the day Mark Twain's home was built, people have poked fun at its eccentric architectural features. Perhaps the first person to mock it in print was a reporter from *The Hartford Daily Times,* who found the house "one of the oddest looking buildings in the State ever designed for a dwelling, if not in the whole country." Others appreciated the building's uniqueness. In Justin Kaplan's 1983 biography of Mark Twain, the house is described as "permanent polychrome and gingerbread Gothic . . . part steamboat, part medieval stronghold and part cuckoo clock."

Its architect, Edward Tuckerman Potter, had studied with Richard Upjohn, who was known for his Revival Gothic–style churches, including Trinity Church in New York City. For Samuel Clemens' home, Potter chose an architectural style known as Picturesque, which was popular in England in the 1840's and had begun to make its appearance in

America in the 1850's. The style incorporated a medley of colors, textures, and irregular silhouettes to mimic the variety of shapes found in the natural landscape. The development of the style was described by Uvedale Price in his *Essays on the Picturesque* (1794), who wrote that the architecture is "neither grand nor beautiful" but it possesses "the two opposite qualities of roughness and sudden variation, joined to that of irregularity." The felicitous exterior of the Mark Twain House is in perfect harmony with the gentle, forested terrain of Nook Farm.

Named for the bend, or nook, formed by the Park River as it cut through Samuel Clemens' property, Nook Farm counted some of Hartford's most influential citizens among its residents, including lawyers, business leaders, politicians, and writers. Harriet Beecher Stowe, author of *Uncle Tom's Cabin* (1851) and *The Minister's Wooing* (1859), lived next door, and Charles Dudley Warner, who collaborated with Mark Twain in the writing of *The Gilded Age* (1873), was also a neighbor.

When Clemens and his wife of four years, the former Olivia "Livy" Langdon, moved into their newly built house in Nook Farm, the Civil War had been over for nine years. Sam was 39 years old, and he had already achieved moderate fame as the author of *The Innocents Abroad* (1869) and

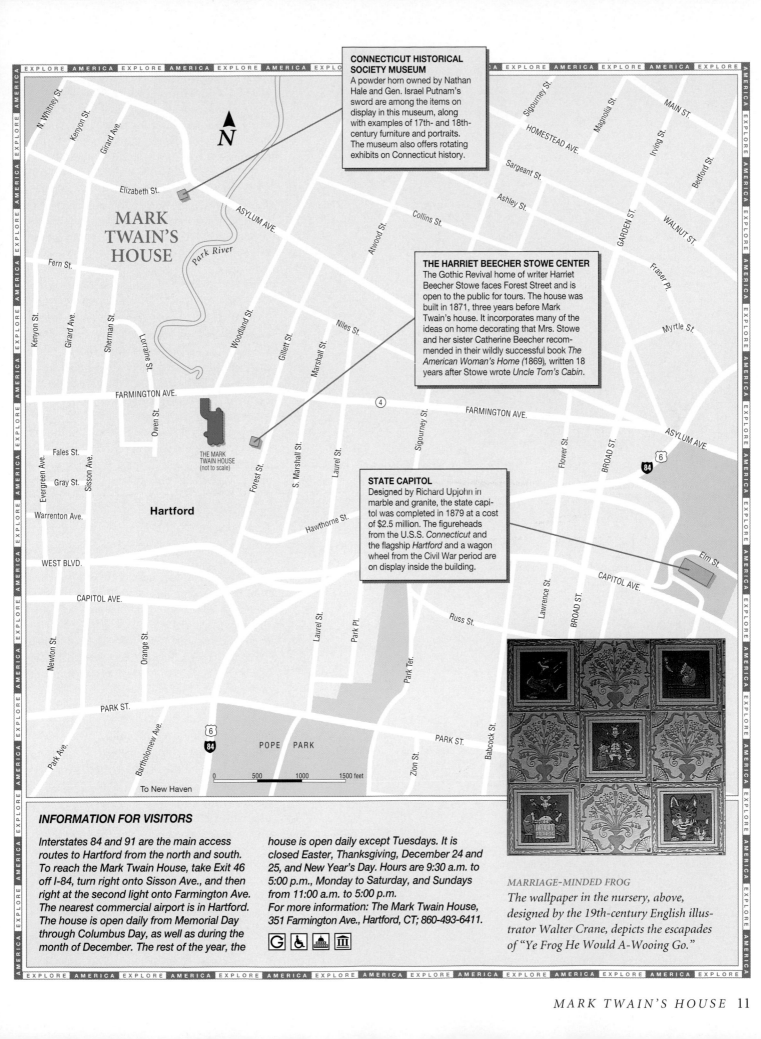

CONNECTICUT HISTORICAL SOCIETY MUSEUM

A powder horn owned by Nathan Hale and Gen. Israel Putnam's sword are among the items on display in this museum, along with examples of 17th- and 18th-century furniture and portraits. The museum also offers rotating exhibits on Connecticut history.

MARK TWAIN'S HOUSE

THE HARRIET BEECHER STOWE CENTER

The Gothic Revival home of writer Harriet Beecher Stowe faces Forest Street and is open to the public for tours. The house was built in 1871, three years before Mark Twain's house. It incorporates many of the ideas on home decorating that Mrs. Stowe and her sister Catherine Beecher recommended in their wildly successful book *The American Woman's Home* (1869), written 18 years after Stowe wrote *Uncle Tom's Cabin*.

THE MARK TWAIN HOUSE (not to scale)

Hartford

STATE CAPITOL

Designed by Richard Upjohn in marble and granite, the state capitol was completed in 1879 at a cost of $2.5 million. The figureheads from the U.S.S. *Connecticut* and the flagship *Hartford* and a wagon wheel from the Civil War period are on display inside the building.

POPE PARK

0   500   1000   1500 feet

To New Haven

INFORMATION FOR VISITORS

Interstates 84 and 91 are the main access routes to Hartford from the north and south. To reach the Mark Twain House, take Exit 46 off I-84, turn right onto Sisson Ave., and then right at the second light onto Farmington Ave. The nearest commercial airport is in Hartford. The house is open daily from Memorial Day through Columbus Day, as well as during the month of December. The rest of the year, the house is open daily except Tuesdays. It is closed Easter, Thanksgiving, December 24 and 25, and New Year's Day. Hours are 9:30 a.m. to 5:00 p.m., Monday to Saturday, and Sundays from 11:00 a.m. to 5:00 p.m.
For more information: The Mark Twain House, 351 Farmington Ave., Hartford, CT; 860-493-6411.

MARRIAGE-MINDED FROG
The wallpaper in the nursery, above, designed by the 19th-century English illustrator Walter Crane, depicts the escapades of "Ye Frog He Would A-Wooing Go."

Roughing It (1872). His best work, however, was ahead of him. From 1874 to 1891, a period when the Clemenses generally spent 10 months out of the year here, the author published two travel books, numerous essays, and five novels, including his masterpiece, *Adventures of Huckleberry Finn* (1884). They also raised their three daughters, Susy, Clara, and Jean, in Hartford. Looking back, Mark Twain wrote of the house: "We never came home from an absence that its face did not light up and speak out its eloquent welcome—and we could not enter it unmoved."

NOURISHING THE MYTH The guides at the Mark Twain House enjoy recounting amusing stories about its owner, as one might expect of guides to the house of a great American humorist. Some of these are documented, others apocryphal, but they all give texture to the life of the house and to the events that took place here.

Guided tours begin outside the front entrance, which is distinguished by an elaborately decorated carriage porch, or porte cochere. The house was designed to face away from Farmington Avenue and toward the home of Harriet Beecher Stowe, whose habit of wandering over to pick flowers in the Clemenses' greenhouse alternately amused and irritated Sam. The greenhouse was torn down in 1909 after the Clemenses had sold the house.

Behind the house the land slopes down to the floodplain for the Park River, which is now covered over with an aqueduct. In the 1870's and 1880's the river created a pretty sight as it flowed through the meadow. In winter the water froze over, and Sam taught his girls to ice-skate there.

When E. T. Potter undertook to design the home, one of the first things Livy did was give him a sketch of the layout of the rooms: she wanted to incorporate numerous windows into the design so that the family would have views of the countryside from as many rooms as possible. Perhaps that is why the house has seven balconies: six on the third floor and one off the master bedroom on the second floor. A large porch was added to the ground floor. Evidently Mr. Clemens found the balconies useful in evading unwanted visitors. According to one story, when such visitors came calling, Sam would make a hasty exit onto an upstairs balcony so that his butler, George Griffin—who hated to lie—could say, truthfully, "I'm sorry, Mr. Clemens has just stepped out."

Sam left many of the details of the construction and decoration to Livy. In a letter to his mother-in-law he wrote: "I have been bullyragged all day by the builder, by his foreman, by the architect, by the tapestry devil who is to upholster the furniture, by

WRITER'S REC ROOM
The ceiling of the billiard room and study, left, is painted with symbols of Mark Twain's pleasures, including pipes, cigars, and billiard cues. The twin marble windows at the far end are similarly decorated with the addition of champagne flutes and beer steins.

RENAISSANCE REVIVAL
Olivia Clemens chose Renaissance Revival furnishings for the drawing room, far left. The room was used for formal social occasions, such as afternoon teas. The marble bust is of Olivia Clemens.

the idiot who is putting down the carpets, by the scoundrel who is setting up the billiard table (and has left the balls in New York) . . . by a book agent, whose body is in the back yard and the coroner notified . . . and I am a man who loathes details with all my heart!"

The money—some $45,000—to purchase the land and build the house came out of Livy's inheritance from her father's thriving coal business. Unfortunately, expenses quickly exceeded their budget, forcing the Clemenses to leave many of the walls unpainted and unpapered for some time.

Livy delighted in the challenge of creating a home that would suit her temperamental husband. She realized that "Youth," as she called Sam, yearned for, and even gloried in, the security that an extravagant house could bestow. Like his fashionable sealskin hat and coat, their new house—which required at least seven servants to run smoothly—gave Twain a certain cachet.

The house also allowed him to indulge in a passion for gadgets and inventions: Twain had already patented a self-pasting scrapbook and he would devise a specially designed bed clamp to secure his children's sheets and blankets in place (it never worked). He had his house equipped with seven modern bathrooms and its rooms were heated by hot-air registers linked to a coal-burning furnace

—amenities that were practically unheard of at that time. A network of speaking tubes and bells was hooked up to the servants' wing and a telephone was installed in 1879 in a closet off the entrance hall. One of the few private wires in Hartford, its erratic operation was the source of much aggravation to Twain, whose curses could be heard all over the house when it acted up. He

TOO COLD FOR COMFORT
Icicles fringe the large wraparound veranda, or ombra, (Italian for shadow), below, on the first floor of the Mark Twain House. In warmer weather the Clemens family often relaxed and entertained their friends here.

Louis Comfort Tiffany and Associated Artists drew on the in-house talents of American artists Lockwood de Forest, Samuel Colman, Candace Thurber Wheeler, and Louis Comfort Tiffany—the famed designer of stained-glass windows and lamps, and son of the founder of the New York jewelry firm. These artists, who were at the fore-front of American decorative art at the time, sought to go beyond the conventions of European styles to develop a distinctly American tradition. Their designs incorporated non-Western motifs of Native American, Middle Eastern, Indian, and North African origin. Another aspect of their artistry was the use of reflective materials such as glass, exotically patterned tile work, and metallic paints. The distinctive touch of this team is perhaps most evident in the paneling employed in the entrance room, where Moorish designs have been stenciled in silver metallic paint on stained walnut to create the illusion of inlaid mother-of-pearl.

RESTORED AND REFURNISHED

Mark Twain's home, the only house decorated by Associated Artists that is open to the public, has been carefully restored. The Mark Twain Memorial undertook the restoration in the 1950's, aided by Clara Clemens Samossoud, the middle daughter, who sketched a layout of the rooms indicating the position of the furniture. Some of the pieces on display represent a sampling of the Renaissance Revival, Colonial Revival, and Aesthetic styles and were owned by the Clemenses. These include a billiard table, an ornate double bed from Venice, and a full-length mirror that hangs in the front parlor. Other furnishings, such as a 19th-century Steinway piano and a medieval-style tapestry, displayed on the third floor above the staircase, are similar to items once owned by the family.

When the restorers got to work, the lighting in the house had long since been converted from gas to electricity, so to achieve the dim lighting typical of the Victorian period, they ingeniously covered the bulbs with gas mantles, and installed dimmer switches to control the intensity of the light.

Most people who visit the Mark Twain House have a favorite room. Some prefer the dining room, where Sam enjoyed gazing through the window above the fireplace and watching the snowflakes fall. The room also features several unusual items, such as an Indian screen with inlaid ivory and an upright piano that was converted into a cabinet for crystal glassware. Some of the most brilliant minds and wits in the nation dined at the large table, including actor Edwin Booth (brother of Lincoln's assassin, John Wilkes Booth); humorist Petroleum Nasby; fellow author Bret Harte; and

ONE OF A KIND
The Clemens home in Hartford, above, was considered quite modern by local residents, who would come to gawk as the house took shape. In the summer the Clemenses traveled to Europe or, more often, to the Langdon family home in New York State. After Mr. Clemens sold his house in 1903, it passed through numerous hands until, in 1929, it was rescued from demolition by the Mark Twain Memorial. Restoration efforts began in the 1950's and were largely completed by 1974, the year of the house's 100th anniversary.

WELCOMING SPIRIT
A brass shield mounted on the library fireplace, right, is inscribed with the words, "The ornament of a house is the friends who frequent it." This spirit of hospitality reigns in the grand entrance hall as well, far right, whose sweeping walnut staircase seems to draw visitors into the house.

rated the instrument's performance and tacked the grades on the wall by the phone: a plus sign for "artillery can be heard" in the phone lines, two plus signs for "thunder can be heard." Yet such was his admiration for technology that he installed a second line in his billiard room/study.

In 1881, the same year that Mr. Clemens had a second phone added to the house, Livy and Sam hired Alfred H. Thorp, who had worked on the house with E. T. Potter, to extend the kitchen and servants' quarters. They hired the decorating firm Louis Comfort Tiffany and Associated Artists to decorate the first floor and front entrance hall. Firms that specialized in interior decorating were only beginning to emerge in the 1880's.

two celebrated editors of the *Atlantic Monthly*, novelist William D. Howells and the short story writer, Thomas Bailey Aldrich.

ENTERTAIN-
ING HOST

Mark Twain was a restless person by nature and during dinner parties he often paced the floor between the different courses. According to legend, his butler would wait hidden from view behind a screen by the pantry door until it was time for him to serve, listening as Twain amused his guests with his tales. Sometimes Griffin would anticipate Mark Twain's best lines and burst into laughter ahead of the dinner guests.

Some visitors linger in Mark Twain's third-floor haunt, the billiard room, where he could work in peace away from the hustle and bustle of the rest of the house. To keep his restless mind focused on writing, he faced his desk away from the window. Twain's original study was located on the second floor, but he found he got little work done because its large windows offered such pleasant views of Park River and the lawns and trees of Nook Farm. So Twain retreated to the top floor of the house where he could work—and play the occasional game of billiards with his cronies—undisturbed. Visitors have little trouble conjuring up the sight of Twain puffing on one of the 20 or more large cigars he smoked each day, as he leaned on his cue stick and waited for his opponent to finish his turn—all the while talking in a measured, emphatic way.

For some visitors the most evocative room in the house is the library, which is located on the ground floor. The firm of Associated Artists originally painted the walls in peacock blue and stenciled them with delicate gold metallic designs. The restorers have carefully replicated their work. Blue silk draperies decorate the windows, and the shelves overflow with Twain's collection of books.

ANGEL BED

The Clemenses slept in an ornate bed, below right, which they had bought on a trip to Venice in 1878. Sam called it his "angel bed" because of the figures on the 16th-century bedposts, above, right. He described the bed as "the most comfortable bedstead that ever was, with space enough in it for a family, and carved angels enough . . . to bring peace to the sleepers, and pleasant dreams."

The Clemens girls staged theatrical productions in the library, including one of *The Prince and the Pauper* adapted by Livy, and Sam spent many evenings here reading his manuscripts aloud to his wife, whose advice he trusted completely. On one occasion Livy, who didn't like her husband to use profane language, suggested that Huck Finn not be "combed all to hell," as Twain originally wrote it, but instead, "all to thunder."

At one end of the library is a conservatory that features a fountain and Chinese lanterns. The idea for the greenhouse came from their neighbor Harriet Beecher Stowe. Flowering vines, callas, and other water-loving lilies once grew in such profusion here that it became the perfect jungle setting for the Clemens girls' games, in which Griffin was cast as the wild beast. An 1896 sketch of the conservatory by the American Impressionist Childe Hassam hangs on the library wall.

Dominating the center of one wall in the library is an oak fireplace mantel, bought from the aristocratic proprietors of a Scottish castle outside Edinburgh. Unfortunately, the mantel was too tall and its crest had to be removed. The crest was affixed above the doorway to the dining room.

When the library was first opened for public viewing in the 1950's, the mantel was missing because Mr. Clemens had removed it at the time the house was sold in 1903. But as luck would have it, one day a visitor on a tour of the house observed that the mantelpiece described by the guide sounded very similar to one that his father had stored in his barn. Museum staff inspected the mantel and found it to be the Clemenses' original. They rescued and reinstalled the piece in the house in 1958.

| TWAIN'S NEMESIS | One of the first things visitors notice when they enter the bookstore in the basement of the Mark Twain House is a |

large piece of equipment that squats, ugly and immovable, in the corner. It is a Paige Compositor, a typesetting machine with 18,000 moving parts that promised to revolutionize the printing industry. Clemens invested in its development, hoping to make his fortune. Unfortunately, the venture bankrupted him, forcing the family to leave the house they loved so much and move to Europe in 1891, where they could live more cheaply. During the nine years that Clemens invested in the typesetter, he lost more than $200,000—the equivalent of about $1,000,000 today. This ruinous loss, plus the failure in 1894 of his business, the Webster Publishing Company may be expressed in Twain's ironic aphorism: "There are two times in a man's life when he should not speculate: when he can't afford it, and when he can."

The Clemenses never lived in the house as a family after 1891. In 1896 the eldest daughter, Susy, fell ill with spinal meningitis while Livy, Sam, and Clara were in Europe. Susy moved back into the house to convalesce, and died several days later.

Twain wrote of the Hartford home: "To us, our house was not unsentient matter—it had a heart, and a soul, eyes to see with; approvals, and solicitudes, and deep sympathies; it was of us, and we were in its confidence, and lived in its grace and in the peace of its benediction." The Mark Twain House conveys the vital spirit of the family that once lived there.

HEIGHT OF FASHION
The Clemenses' interior design team, Associated Artists, chose a color scheme favored by the Aesthetic art movement when they stenciled the drawing room's salmon pink walls with silver patterns, above.

Nearby Sites & Attractions

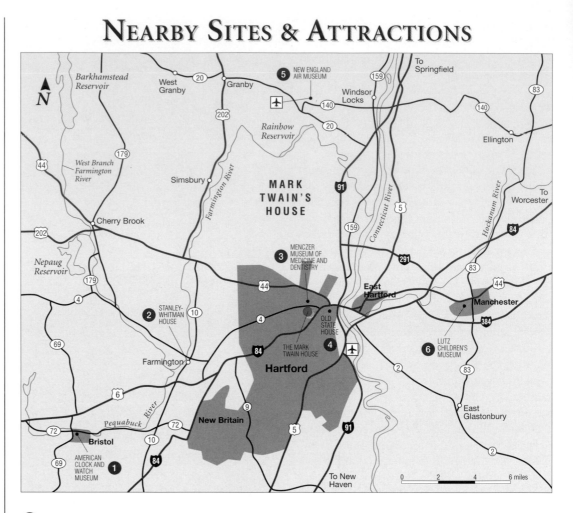

The long table in the Old State House, below, accommodates 18 and was the setting for many important governmental meetings.

1 AMERICAN CLOCK AND WATCH MUSEUM

This museum, which was established in 1952 to honor the work of Connecticut clock makers, displays more than 3,400 timepieces, including the finest mass-produced American clocks in the world. The museum is housed in a historic 1801 Colonial homestead, complete with its original oak and chestnut interior paneling. Among the more than 1,700 clocks and 1,600 watches on display is a clock dating back to 1680, a 1595 watch, and a grandfather clock, notable for its 10-foot stature. One room displays 18th-century tallcase clocks, some of which were designed by Thomas Harland and Simon Willard. Another room, set up as an 1890 Victorian clock-making shop, exhibits the early tools of the trade. Located at 100 Maple St. in Bristol.

2 STANLEY-WHITMAN HOUSE

This building was constructed by Deacon John Stanley in 1720. Considered the finest example of New England framed architecture in the state, the house displays several architectural details, including a massive central chimney and diamond-paned windows. The second floor of the house is 18 inches wider than the ground floor, an overhang that may have been introduced to save on British property taxes, which were determined by the size of the ground floor. A lean-to was added to the back of the house, giving it the shape of a New England saltbox house. The interior is furnished with primitive country pieces and 17th- and 18th-century Queen Anne furniture made of solid wood with simple brass accessories. Other displays focus on 18th-century Farmington and on the Stanley, Smith, and Whitman families, who were the owners of the house during the Colonial period. The museum hosts demonstrations of candle making, spinning, open hearth cooking, and weaving. The gardens have been restored to reflect the Colonial period and include plots for medicinal and culinary plants; there is also a flower garden. The house was opened as a museum in 1935 and declared a National Historic Landmark in 1961. Located at 37 High St. in Farmington.

③ MENCZER MUSEUM OF MEDICINE AND DENTISTRY

The history of American medicine and dentistry from the Revolutionary War to the present is the highlight of this museum in the Hunt Memorial Building. Medical artifacts on display include portraits of physicians and antique medical instruments with handles made of ivory, rosewood, mother-of-pearl, and snakewood. One room in the museum is devoted to the professional contributions of Horace Wells, who was a world-renowned Hartford dentist and anesthetist in the 19th century. Another room re-creates a 1919 dentist's office, including the foot-powered drills of the era. More than 20 doctor's bags of the 19th and early 20th century—once the trademark of doctors who made house calls—are on display. Located at 230 Scarborough St. in Hartford.

④ OLD STATE HOUSE

Designed by Charles Bulfinch and constructed in 1796, this Federal-style building is the oldest state house in the nation and one of the most historically significant sites in Connecticut. Once a day cannon-fire booms across the grounds, commemorating the 1780 meeting that took place here between George Washington and the Comte de Rochambeau as they planned their strategy to defeat the British at Yorktown. Prominent guests at the Old State House included Charles Dickens, Samuel Colt, Mark Twain, Harriet Beecher Stowe, and P. T. Barnum, who served for a time in the Connecticut legislature. Presidents Andrew Jackson and James Monroe spoke before the Connecticut Congress and the Marquis de Lafayette was granted American citizenship in this building. Guides in period costumes lead visitors on tours that begin in the grand foyer, which has been refurbished to its 1920's appearance. The Senate Chamber has been restored to look as it did in 1796, complete with the original yellow walls and cream-colored woodwork. One of the famous portraits of George Washington by the 18th-century artist Gilbert Stuart adorns a wall in the Senate Chamber. It is the only portrait of Washington that is still displayed in its original setting. The state house's Council Chamber is decorated in the Victorian style typical of 1878 to 1915, when it served as Hartford City Hall. Design elements include stenciling, wide floorboards, a chandelier, and period desks. A year after the Old State House opened in 1796, local artist Joseph Steward was given permission to set up his studio in the building. Now known as Mr. Steward's Museum, the studio is open to the public. His paintings and a collection of stuffed and mounted game animals, including a Bengal tiger and a nine-foot-long alligator, are some of the objects on display. The state house grounds are bordered by an 1834 wrought-iron fence. Axes bound in sheaths of wheat—a Roman symbol of health, power, and authority—decorate the fence. The grounds are lit by gas lanterns. Located at 800 Main St. in Hartford.

⑤ NEW ENGLAND AIR MUSEUM

Seventy-five historic aircraft are displayed in two hangars at the Bradley International Airport. The aircraft range from World War I biplanes and triplanes to modern fighters and commercial craft. The oldest example is the 1909 Bleriot monoplane. World War II aircraft include a Hellcat, B-25 Mitchell bomber, and several World War II fighter planes painted with the images of snarling animals on their fuselages. The Link trainer, used to train thousands of American pilots during World War II, and Bell Huey helicopters and Phantom jets from the Vietnamese War also belong to the collection. A highlight of the museum is the exhibition on the aircraft races of the 1920's and 1930's. Located three miles west of Windsor Locks.

⑥ LUTZ CHILDREN'S MUSEUM

This museum on history, art, and natural science caters to the interests of children. Young visitors can put on their own shows in the puppet theater and play with a miniature train set. But the star attractions are the natural-history displays of insects and live snakes, turtles, woodchucks, and owls. A variety of programs, such as craft workshops and field trips, also are offered by the museum and there are special storytelling and arts and crafts sessions for preschoolers. The Oak Grove Nature Center adjacent to the museum encompasses more than 53 acres of swamps, woodlands, and fields. Located at 247 South Main St. in Manchester.

An 1890 timepiece, above, by E. H. Howard Watch & Clock Company of Boston, stands outside the American Clock and Watch Museum. The Stanley-Whitman House, below, provides a glimpse of 17th-century Connecticut.

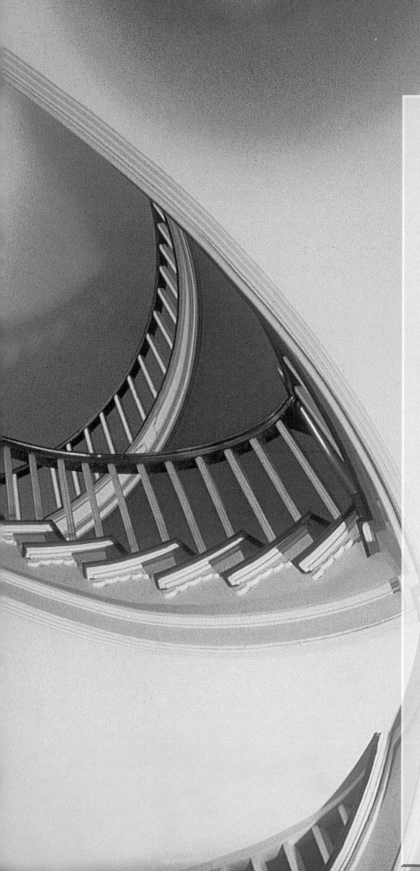

WINTERTHUR

*A delightful mix of man-made and
natural splendors, Winterthur
serves up a feast for the senses.*

On the ledger sheet, the Winterthur Museum, Garden and Library looks imposing in scope. More than 89,000 American items dating from 1640 to 1860—including furniture, textiles, paintings, silverware, clocks, and pewter—are displayed in this 175-room mansion-turned-museum and its three exhibition galleries. To top it off, the resplendent collection of American decorative arts is set within a 983-acre estate of lush woodlands, pasturelands, and a 60-acre garden blooming with native and exotic plants.

Impressive as the numbers may be, Winterthur is more than a repository for valuable antiques and horticultural marvels—it is a unique place where the past clasps hands with the present, and the natural and the man-made complement and magnify one another.

Designed so that no one part upsets the organic balance of the whole, Winterthur's mansion, exhibition spaces, and grounds are testaments to the rare esthetic sensibility and personal philosophy of their creator, Henry Francis du Pont.

Du Pont—who lived at Winterthur from 1880 until his death in 1969—was always quick to point

EARLY BLOOMERS

Witch hazel and crocuses speckle Winterthur's East Terrace, below. These harbingers of spring flower on the estate in late winter.

SWIRLING VIEW

Overleaf: The elegant curves of the Montmorenci spiral staircase wind up four flights. The free-hanging staircase came from a house in Shocco Springs, North Carolina.

out that three generations of his family had tended this parcel of land before he exerted any influence on it. In fact, the estate is a living monument to the Delaware clan that made its fortune in the Brandywine Valley in the 19th century by producing everything from gunpowder and wheat to prize sheep and cows. The du Pont family has deep roots in the region. They go back to 1802, when Henry Francis' great-grandfather, Eleuthère Irénée du Pont, set up a farm and gunpowder mill along Brandywine Creek.

From 1810 to 1818, Irénée purchased a series of adjoining plots that would eventually make up the Winterthur estate. The original Greek Revival mansion, which had three stories, was completed in 1839 by Irénée's daughter Evelina and her husband, Jacques Antoine Bidermann. Two years after Bidermann's death in 1865, Irénée's son Gen. Henry du Pont bought the Winterthur estate. By the time his son Henry Algernon, inherited Winterthur some 33 years later, it had blossomed into a 1,000-acre estate that included a profitable dairy-cow operation, a large woodland area, and an extensive garden. Henry Francis du Pont was born in this verdant paradise in 1880.

Given free reign of the grounds, Henry Francis, his sister, Louise, and the children of the workers who lived on the estate enjoyed a fairy-tale existence. When Henry and Louise weren't helping their mother, Pauline, plant flowers and vegetables in the ever-expanding garden, they spent hours exploring their kingdom. On these excursions, young du Pont amassed a large store of tiny, colored bird eggs, the delicate shards of which are still preserved at Winterthur. A passion for collecting would burn in him throughout his life.

Enrolling at Harvard in 1901, du Pont took courses in agriculture and horticulture. While at the university he developed a friendship with Marian Cruger Coffin, a talented young landscape architect whose unerring sense of balance, proportion, and harmony would exert a lasting influence on the development of the Winterthur estate

grounds. Coffin would go on to design 50 East Coast estate gardens and a number of university campuses, but her work at Winterthur would stand as the highlight of her brilliant career.

The following year du Pont's mother died of cancer, a tragedy that cut short Henry's studies. However, with her death came a new chapter for Winterthur. After returning home to be at his grieving father's side, du Pont assumed the responsibilities of the day-to-day operation of the estate, duties that included overseeing the family's renowned Holstein dairy farm and his mother's beloved garden. The theoretical principles of horticulture he had acquired at school, his passionate love of the land—learned at his mother's knee—and his own innate sense of artistry came together, and du Pont began the construction of his living masterpiece.

ARTIST'S TOUCH

A long, leisurely walk through the grounds of the estate allows visitors a true appreciation of du Pont's genius. In a concerted effort to preserve the "peace and great calm" that Winterthur inspired in him, du Pont tampered little with the topography of the land. There are no rigid boundaries separating Winterthur's garden from agricultural areas and woodland. Indeed, each part of the terrain blends naturally with the next to create a unified landscape. Walking along the paved pathways through the garden area, visitors come upon eye-pleasing vistas of open meadows and hilly farm country, dotted with ponds that are populated by resident flocks of Canada geese.

Flying in the face of horticultural formalism, du Pont held that a garden should be an uncluttered showcase for nature. As a result, there are few man-made structures in the Winterthur garden: no Greek statues on pedestals; no ostentatious fountains; no box hedges trimmed in geometric shapes. Any architectural elements are artfully hidden away and fully integrated with the surrounding terrain so as not to detract from it.

The sweet fragrance of epaulette trees fills the air where visitors stroll through the riotous yellow, red, and pink of the Peony Garden. A delicate lattice archway marks the endpoint of this section. Overlooking the Sundial Garden are benches such as the one tucked beneath the outstretched branches of a blue atlas cedar. This peaceful spot allows visitors to contemplate the scenery in private.

Following the natural undulations of the land, pathways slip in and out of sight. In some areas the concrete ends, and visitors walk across plush lawn to a bench about 20 yards away. Perhaps this was du Pont's way of giving them a chance to experience the intimacy with nature he felt as a boy running free through this enchanted land.

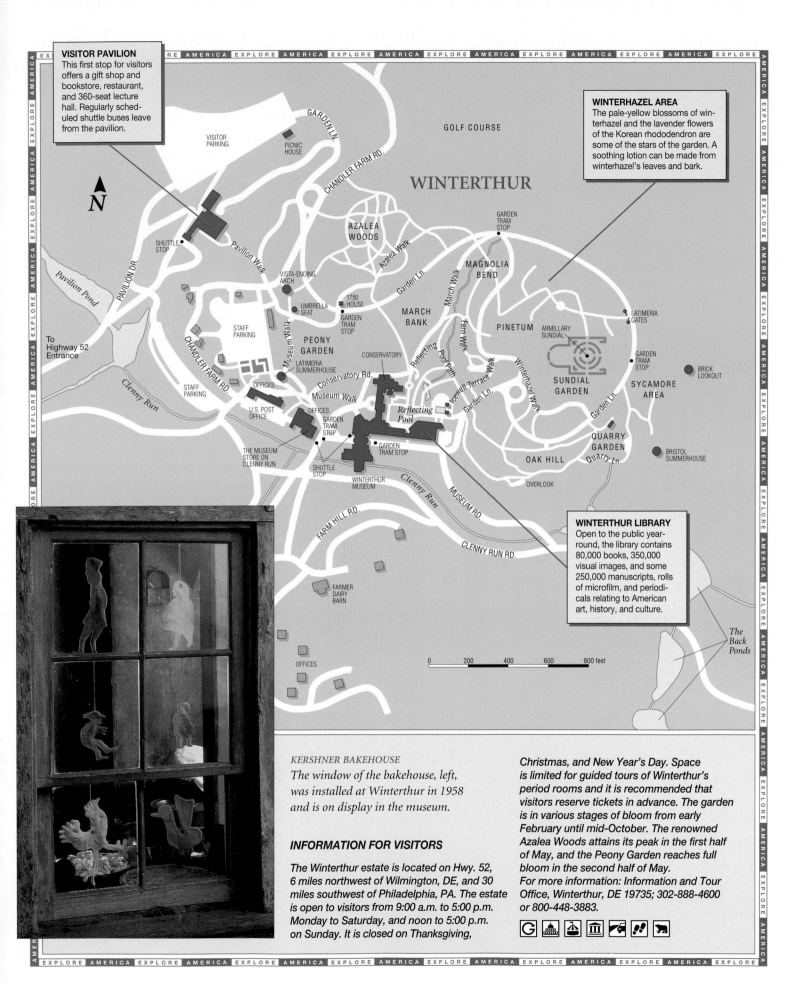

VISITOR PAVILION
This first stop for visitors offers a gift shop and bookstore, restaurant, and 360-seat lecture hall. Regularly scheduled shuttle buses leave from the pavilion.

WINTERHAZEL AREA
The pale-yellow blossoms of winterhazel and the lavender flowers of the Korean rhododendron are some of the stars of the garden. A soothing lotion can be made from winterhazel's leaves and bark.

WINTERTHUR LIBRARY
Open to the public year-round, the library contains 80,000 books, 350,000 visual images, and some 250,000 manuscripts, rolls of microfilm, and periodicals relating to American art, history, and culture.

GOLF COURSE

WINTERTHUR

N

VISITOR PARKING

GARDEN LN.

PICNIC HOUSE

CHANDLER FARM RD.

SHUTTLE STOP

Pavilion Walk

GARDEN TRAM STOP

Pavilion Pond

PAVILION DR.

To Highway 52 Entrance

AZALEA WOODS

Azalea Walk

VISTA-ENDING ARCH

Garden Ln.

MAGNOLIA BEND

March Walk

LATIMERIA GATES

CHANDLER FARM RD.

Clenny Run

STAFF PARKING

1750 HOUSE

UMBRELLA SEAT

GARDEN TRAM STOP

MARCH BANK

PINETUM

ARMILLARY SUNDIAL

PEONY GARDEN

Museum Walk

CONSERVATORY

Conservatory Rd.

Fern Walk

Reflecting Pool Path

SUNDIAL GARDEN

GARDEN TRAM STOP

BRICK LOOKOUT

SYCAMORE AREA

LATIMERIA SUMMERHOUSE

STAFF PARKING

OFFICES

Museum Walk

Icewell Terrace

Garden Ln.

Garden Ln.

U.S. POST OFFICE

OFFICES

GARDEN TRAM STOP

Reflecting Pool

Winterhazel Walk

QUARRY GARDEN

BRISTOL SUMMERHOUSE

THE MUSEUM STORE ON CLENNY RUN

SHUTTLE STOP

GARDEN TRAM STOP

WINTERTHUR MUSEUM

OAK HILL

Quarry Ln.

OVERLOOK

Clenny Run

MUSEUM RD.

FARM HILL RD.

CLENNY RUN RD.

FARMER DAIRY BARN

OFFICES

OFFICES

The Back Ponds

0   200   400   600   800 feet

KERSHNER BAKEHOUSE
The window of the bakehouse, left, was installed at Winterthur in 1958 and is on display in the museum.

INFORMATION FOR VISITORS

The Winterthur estate is located on Hwy. 52, 6 miles northwest of Wilmington, DE, and 30 miles southwest of Philadelphia, PA. The estate is open to visitors from 9:00 a.m. to 5:00 p.m. Monday to Saturday, and noon to 5:00 p.m. on Sunday. It is closed on Thanksgiving, Christmas, and New Year's Day. Space is limited for guided tours of Winterthur's period rooms and it is recommended that visitors reserve tickets in advance. The garden is in various stages of bloom from early February until mid-October. The renowned Azalea Woods attains its peak in the first half of May, and the Peony Garden reaches full bloom in the second half of May.
For more information: Information and Tour Office, Winterthur, DE 19735; 302-888-4600 or 800-448-3883.

Viewing the garden as his artist's canvas, du Pont paid particular attention to the hue of each plant's petals and the time of year that it bloomed. He kept meticulous notes on each plant genus and laid out the garden so that every section in it exhibited a succession of blooms and the entire garden would flower throughout the spring and summer.

Strolling along the March Bank in early February, visitors delight in spotting Winterthur's earliest blossoms: the white snowdrop. In a matter of weeks, this delicate flower gives way to yellow winter aconite, which in turn yields to the lavender of crocuses in early March. Finally, a wave of yellow and blue washes over the scene as glory-of-the-snow and cornelian cherries burst forth. It wasn't until horticulturalists studied du Pont's papers for the restoration of Winterthur's garden that they realized he had designed it to bloom in a series of stages away from the house, creating an effect like a bold stroke by a giant paintbrush. The living canvas changes from one week to the next so that no matter the time of year, visitors are ensured of beholding the garden's splendor.

In wielding his brush, du Pont loved to bring the terrain to life with wide swatches of the same color. The eight-acre Azalea Woods reaches its peak bloom in the first half of May with a dazzling array of fragrant pink blossoms. In places throughout this spectacular display, du Pont dabbed playful flecks of lavender, orange, and deep red blossoms, providing a tonal counterpoint.

LABOR OF LOVE

Du Pont's interest in Winterthur's grounds and gardens also extended to the decoration of the house. This gentleman farmer, so fond of traipsing across his family's land, was also an early champion of American-made furniture and decorative arts.

At the turn of the 20th century, collectors and museum curators saw little merit in the decorative arts and fine furniture produced in America. They placed a premium instead on items from Europe. In the 1920's, however, a wave of postwar nationalism swept the country, sending ripples through the art world. By the next decade, a group of collectors began to seek out finely crafted American-made pieces that were also of historical value.

Du Pont was at the forefront of this surge in American collecting. Although he started off modestly enough—buying a single Pennsylvania walnut chest with a date of 1737 inlaid on the top drawer—it wasn't long before he embraced collecting with the same all-consuming fervor that he brought to his garden. However, unlike du Pont's guardianship of the land, which he inherited from his parents, this project was his alone. With the purchase of this chest in 1923, du Pont embarked on a personal odyssey that, in his own words, sought to preserve the "country's rich tradition of craftsmanship in architecture and household arts."

Du Pont spent the better part of 30 years scouring private homes and dusty antique shops for American treasures. He originally intended to stock only his summer home on Long Island with his purchases, but du Pont's zeal—and his feeling that if one antique Windsor chair was worth saving, certainly they all were—quickly compelled him to enlarge his plans. In 1931 he completed a new wing for the Winterthur mansion, effectively doubling its size to accommodate his prized collection. Over the next three decades, the rhythms of carpenters' saws and hammers became the background music to life on the estate as the constantly expanding collection demanded more space.

PRESERVING
A WAY
OF LIFE

But du Pont was not content to collect only fine furniture: he wanted to preserve entire eras. To find representatives of the esthetic values and sensibilities of various periods and regions, he crossed the country, buying entire rooms, including their furniture, fireplaces, wallpaper, and wood paneling. The rooms were dismantled and transported to Winterthur, where they were reconstructed.

Du Pont even turned his cherished indoor badminton court into a cobblestoned street scene made up of the facades of three houses and a tavern called the Red Lion Inn. Upon walking through the door of the ale hall, visitors enter an imaginatively reconstructed interior, complete with backgammon games, handmade pipes, and cock spurs used to arm fighting roosters strewn on the benches and the mantelpiece. Close inspection of one mug reveals that inside it sits a green-glazed ceramic

frog: when the glass is drained, the frog appears—no doubt the source of laughter at the expense of unsuspecting patrons.

Visitors can take guided tours of Winterthur's period rooms, ranging from one-hour introductory tours to comprehensive two-hour tours that focus on specialized subjects. The enthusiastic guides take great pleasure in revealing Winterthur's many hidden treasures, pointing out easily overlooked details such as the feet of Chippendale furniture made to resemble lions' paws, and the carved heads of presidents of the United States that stare out from rococo revival chairs and sofas.

DUCKS IN A CHINA SHOP
China masterpieces from the delicate to the ungainly fill the reconstructed China Shop, below, at Winterthur. Most of the store's decor dates to 1800 and came from the Bond Apothecary Shop in Fredericksburg, Virginia.

Guides also recount stories about some of the lighter moments that took place at Winterthur. On a stroll through the Chinese Parlor, for instance, visitors learn that this was where du Pont's daughter received guests on her wedding day. Out of concern that people might scuff or otherwise damage the room's exquisite hand-painted wallpaper, du Pont—never one to erect formal barricades—came up with an ingenious plan: he constructed a four-foot-thick barrier of flowers along the wall.

PERFECT BALANCE

In adherence with the tenets of of the neoclassical style, du Pont insisted on symmetry in the layout of each room and ensured that no single piece of furniture dominated. He struck a happy balance between luxurious objects and everyday items. Alongside the more

FOUR HORSEPOWER
A team of four Appaloosa horses pulls an antique carriage, above, during the Carriage Parade of the annual Winterthur Point-to-Point, held in early May. The day-long festivities include a variety of equestrian events, most notably races over post-and-rail fences.

SUNNY HUES
The gold and yellow tones of the Port Royal Parlor, right, match the yellow witch hazel that blooms outside on the East Terrace in March.

lavish pieces, such as silver tankards worked by Paul Revere and George Washington's 66-piece Chinese porcelain dinner service, are ordinary straight razors, combs, wire-frame glasses, and other unremarkable—although equally historic—objects. More than one teenager has paid special attention to the antique samplers on the walls, whose delicate embroidered signatures and dates reveal that they were created about 200 years ago by someone their own age.

Winterthur represents not just a time or a place in history, but also the people who lived there as well. The house is not a sterile showcase: the curators have given as much thought and care to a room's opulent four-poster bed, including the three-step stool required to reach the high mattress, as to a snuffbox, inkstand, and other personal items on display in many of the rooms.

MASTER BEDROOM
The Cecil Bedroom, above, is the epitome of style and grace. Once the bedroom of Henry Francis du Pont, Winterthur's premier creator and landscaper, the room is painted a muted green. The four-poster bed's covering and canopy are decorated in a floral needlework pattern.

Not surprisingly, given du Pont's unifying vision for the estate, many of the rooms have been decorated to complement the flower beds and shrubbery that bloom just outside the windows. Du Pont coordinated the curtains, slipcovers, and other accessories in each room to mirror the view from the window. For example, the Patauxent Room, with its green walls and textiles, looks out upon the lush upper lawns and a canopy of trees.

TRIBUTE TO GREATNESS

Despite Winterthur's imposing size, it does not dominate the landscape. Nestled in a thickly wooded glen, much of the building is camouflaged by greenery. From a distance, occasional breaks in the foliage provide tantalizing views of the mansion where Henry du Pont brought together man and nature, fine art and utilitarian objects, past and present.

NEARBY SITES & ATTRACTIONS

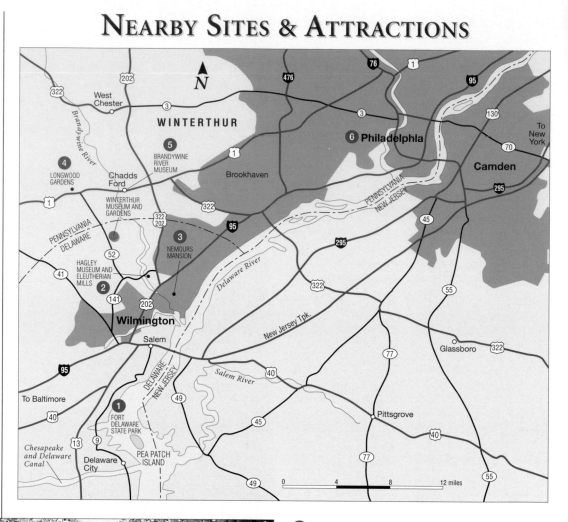

Five generations of the du Pont family lived at Eleutherian Mills, below, in Wilmington, Delaware. The designer of the Georgian-style residence is unknown.

① FORT DELAWARE STATE PARK, DELAWARE

Visitors to this state park on Pea Patch Island can tour Fort Delaware and explore the island's wildlife sanctuary. Fort Delaware was originally built to protect the harbors of Philadelphia and Wilmington. The pentagonal fortress, completed in 1859, was constructed of brick and granite. It served as a prisoner-of-war camp during the Civil War for more than 12,000 Confederate soldiers. During the summer, living history programs demonstrate musket firing and typical day-to-day activities at the early fort. There are craft demonstrations as well. The parade ground, officers' quarters, and enlisted men's barracks are open to the public. Mudflats on the island attract nine species of herons, including black-crowned night herons and great blue herons, and more than 9,000 pairs nest here. The flats also attract great and snowy egrets, and glossy ibises. An observation tower provides visitors with an excellent vantage point for viewing the island's natural treasures. Located on Pea Patch Island.

② HAGLEY MUSEUM AND ELEUTHERIAN MILLS, DELAWARE

Several early 19th-century industrial mills have been preserved at this 235-acre indoor and outdoor museum, a tribute to American industrial development of the 19th century. Displays include early

28

More than 2,700 Confederate soldiers died of yellow fever and smallpox at Fort Delaware, left, during the Civil War. The fort is listed on the National Register of Historic Places.

19th-century mills, a worker's cottage, and a school, all of which provide glimpses of the living conditions of 19th-century workers. An 1814 cotton mill is now a visitor center with exhibits on early industries in the Brandywine Valley. The Eleutherian Mills estate, erected in 1802 by Eleuthère Irénée du Pont, was the first residence of the du Pont family in the United States. A tour of the house includes the first floor and its furnishings acquired by Mrs. Crowninshield, the last du Pont to live here. The second-floor bedrooms contain items dating from 1803 to the 1830's. Portraits, clothing, and other family memorabilia are displayed on both floors. The restored front garden was originally planted in 1803. Located on Hwy. 141 in Wilmington.

③ NEMOURS MANSION, DELAWARE

The architectural design of this 102-room mansion is a tribute to the French ancestors of Alfred Irénée du Pont. Completed in 1910, the mansion combines elements of a Louis XVI chateau and a Southern plantation home. Nemours is surrounded by 300 acres of natural woodlands, as well as landscaped gardens with fountains and ponds. The front of the mansion is graced by a cast-iron gate that once belonged to Russian czarina Catherine the Great, and an English gate from Wimbledon Manor that was given to one of Henry VIII's wives, Catherine Parr, in 1543. The interior of the house features a treasure trove of European art and furniture, offset by ornate wall tapestries, and an impressive collection of 17th-century Dutch paintings. Alfred du Pont's grave on the estate is marked by a granite bell tower. Located on Rockland Rd. in Wilmington.

④ LONGWOOD GARDENS, PENNSYLVANIA

Encompassing more than 1,000 acres in the Brandywine Valley, the former estate of Pierre du Pont displays 11,000 species of plants that grow in formal gardens, natural woodlands, and meadows. Elaborate greenhouses take up more than three and a half acres of the estate. Longwood Gardens hosts a number of events, including the Festival of Fountains, a fireworks and fountain show presented during the summer. Poinsettias take center stage during the Christmas Conservatory Display, and the grounds are illuminated with 400,000 decorative lights. In addition to 20 indoor gardens, the conservatory features a ballroom with crystal chandeliers, walnut parquet floors, and an organ equipped with 10,010 pipes. The nearby Peirce–du Pont House was built in 1730 and purchased by Pierre du Pont in 1906. A tour of the house includes du Pont's den, where brass and ivory drafting tools, laboratory equipment, and the desk from his office in the Empire State Building are displayed. Located 30 miles west of Philadelphia on Hwy. 1.

⑤ BRANDYWINE RIVER MUSEUM, PENNSYLVANIA

A gristmill that dates from the Civil War era was restored and converted into a museum devoted to the Brandywine Valley in 1971. The mill's wide floorboards and ceiling beams have been carefully preserved, and the museum displays one of the largest and most impressive collections of works by the artists N.C., Andrew, and James Wyeth. Also on display are works by Howard Pyle, the first noted American illustrator, and 19th-century landscape paintings, including Jasper Cropsey's *Autumn on the Brandywine* and William Trost Richards' *The Valley of the Brandywine, Chester County.* Located in Chadds Ford.

⑥ PHILADELPHIA, PENNSYLVANIA

The city of Philadelphia was founded in 1682 by Quaker William Penn and designed with wide streets and five public squares. Twenty-six historic sites comprise Independence National Historical Park, site of Independence Hall, which was constructed between 1732 and 1757. Independence Hall served as the Pennsylvania State House, and the Declaration of Independence was signed here on July 4, 1776. The park is also the home of the 2,080-pound Liberty Bell, which was made in England in 1752. From 1790 to 1800 the U.S. Congress convened at Congress Hall, built between 1787 and 1789. George Washington gave his farewell address from Congress Hall, which also served as the venue for John Adams' induction as the nation's second president in 1796. Located on Hwy. 95; the visitor center is at Third and Chestnut streets.

Showy chrysanthemums and petunias encircle a quiet pool at Longwood Gardens, below.

THE WHITE HOUSE

Home to 40 of the 41 American presidents, this is the most visited house in the nation.

George Washington did not sleep here. In fact, he is the only American president never to have spent a night in the White House. During the 19th century, America's most famous house was called the Executive Mansion and even the Presidential Palace, but President Washington (1789–97), a direct and forthright man, wanted it called the President's House—plain and simple. Although time and tradition denied him his wish, Washington has cast a lasting influence on 1600 Pennsylvania Avenue in Washington, D.C.

America's first president—who made his personal fortune in land speculation—chose the site for the White House in 1791, once he had determined that the young republic's new capital would be built on the banks of the Potomac River. He served on the jury that selected Irish-born architect James Hoban as the winner of the federally sponsored contest for the design of the house. Hoban won a gold medal and cash totaling $500 for his simple, elegant plan, inspired by the Irish Parliament building in Dublin. The jury rejected

a classically inspired plan that was submitted anonymously but is believed to have been the work of Thomas Jefferson (1801–09).

MEMORY LANE

The present White House is a far cry from Hoban's 20-room building, which lacked running water, baths, and electricity. Two centuries of renovation and expansion have transformed the original sandstone residence into an imposing building with more than 130 rooms. Most of the working and residential White House is closed to the public, including the president's second-floor living quarters, the Cabinet Room, the Situation Room, private dining room, family movie theater, and the Oval Office.

Despite modern security measures and myriad changes to the structure over the years, the White House has scrupulously maintained its links to the past and preserved the imprints of the presidents and first ladies who have lived here.

The White House is set within the 18-acre President's Park, whose every tree and garden has some historical significance. A scarlet oak planted by Benjamin Harrison (1889–93) flourishes in the northeast corner; south of the East Entrance is

Dwight D. Eisenhower's (1953–61) northern red oak; and near the South Portico is a magnolia contributed by Andrew Jackson (1829–37). Richard Nixon (1969–74) planted birch trees; Woodrow Wilson (1913–21) proudly donated an American elm; and Calvin Coolidge (1923–29) added a European white birch near the fence of the South Lawn. Among the gardens are the Jacqueline Kennedy Garden, a peaceful sanctuary used as an informal reception area by first ladies, and the famous Rose Garden, which is laid out west of the South Portico within sight of the Oval Office. This garden is used for formal events, such as the 1971 wedding of Tricia Nixon and Edward Cox.

Most of the presidents have bestowed on the White House some physical reminder of their time, but perhaps none has altered the mansion as dramatically as Pres. Harry S. Truman (1945–53). In 1948 Truman had a balcony built onto the South Portico—a move that was decried by critics who felt it was an architectural blight—so that he and Mrs. Truman could sit outside during the city's humid summers. Later, in response to a warning that the mansion was teetering on the verge of collapse, a four-year renovation plan was implemented. The house was gutted and rebuilt. In the

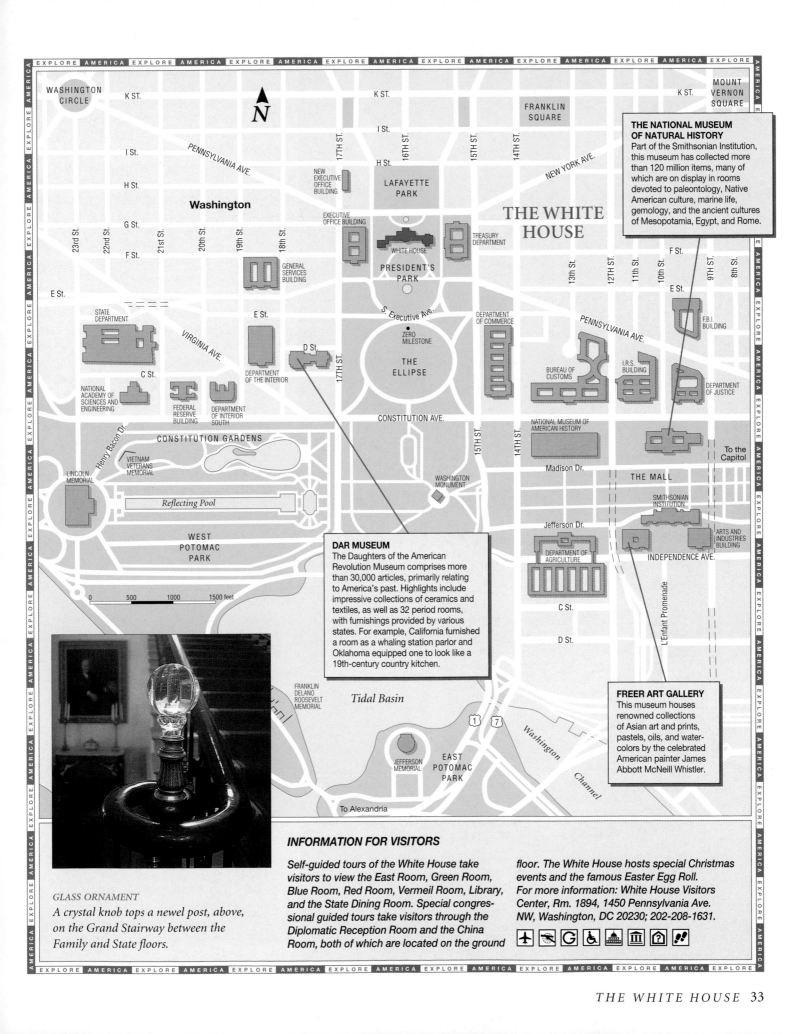

WASHINGTON CIRCLE

K ST.

I St.

PENNSYLVANIA AVE.

H St.

Washington

G St.

F St.

23rd St. 22nd St. 21st St. 20th St. 19th St. 18th St.

E St.

STATE DEPARTMENT

VIRGINIA AVE.

C St.

NATIONAL ACADEMY OF SCIENCES AND ENGINEERING

FEDERAL RESERVE BUILDING

DEPARTMENT OF INTERIOR SOUTH

E St.

DEPARTMENT OF THE INTERIOR

D St.

17TH ST.

NEW EXECUTIVE OFFICE BUILDING

K ST.

I St.

H St.

17TH ST. 16TH ST. 15TH ST. 14TH ST.

LAFAYETTE PARK

EXECUTIVE OFFICE BUILDING

GENERAL SERVICES BUILDING

WHITE HOUSE

PRESIDENT'S PARK

S. Executive Ave.

ZERO MILESTONE

THE ELLIPSE

CONSTITUTION AVE.

NEW YORK AVE.

THE WHITE HOUSE

TREASURY DEPARTMENT

FRANKLIN SQUARE

MOUNT VERNON SQUARE

K ST.

13th St. 12th St. 11th St. 10th St. 9th St. 8th St.

F St.

E St.

PENNSYLVANIA AVE.

F.B.I. BUILDING

DEPARTMENT OF COMMERCE

BUREAU OF CUSTOMS

I.R.S. BUILDING

DEPARTMENT OF JUSTICE

THE NATIONAL MUSEUM OF NATURAL HISTORY
Part of the Smithsonian Institution, this museum has collected more than 120 million items, many of which are on display in rooms devoted to paleontology, Native American culture, marine life, gemology, and the ancient cultures of Mesopotamia, Egypt, and Rome.

Henry Bacon Dr.

CONSTITUTION GARDENS

VIETNAM VETERANS MEMORIAL

LINCOLN MEMORIAL

Reflecting Pool

WEST POTOMAC PARK

0   500   1000   1500 feet

NATIONAL MUSEUM OF AMERICAN HISTORY

15TH ST. 14TH ST.

Madison Dr.

WASHINGTON MONUMENT

THE MALL

To the Capitol

SMITHSONIAN INSTITUTION

ARTS AND INDUSTRIES BUILDING

Jefferson Dr.

DEPARTMENT OF AGRICULTURE

INDEPENDENCE AVE.

C St.

D St.

L'Enfant Promenade

DAR MUSEUM
The Daughters of the American Revolution Museum comprises more than 30,000 articles, primarily relating to America's past. Highlights include impressive collections of ceramics and textiles, as well as 32 period rooms, with furnishings provided by various states. For example, California furnished a room as a whaling station parlor and Oklahoma equipped one to look like a 19th-century country kitchen.

FRANKLIN DELANO ROOSEVELT MEMORIAL

Tidal Basin

JEFFERSON MEMORIAL

EAST POTOMAC PARK

1   7

Washington Channel

To Alexandria

FREER ART GALLERY
This museum houses renowned collections of Asian art and prints, pastels, oils, and watercolors by the celebrated American painter James Abbott McNeill Whistler.

GLASS ORNAMENT
A crystal knob tops a newel post, above, on the Grand Stairway between the Family and State floors.

INFORMATION FOR VISITORS

Self-guided tours of the White House take visitors to view the East Room, Green Room, Blue Room, Red Room, Vermeil Room, Library, and the State Dining Room. Special congressional guided tours take visitors through the Diplomatic Reception Room and the China Room, both of which are located on the ground floor. The White House hosts special Christmas events and the famous Easter Egg Roll. For more information: White House Visitors Center, Rm. 1894, 1450 Pennsylvania Ave. NW, Washington, DC 20230; 202-208-1631.

NEOCLASSICAL DETAIL
Pillars with ornate Ionic capitals support the south-facing oval portico, right, which was added to the house by James Hoban in 1824.

PANORAMA OF THE PAST
One of three oval rooms in the White House, the Diplomatic Reception Room, below, was redecorated by Jacqueline Kennedy, who added the unique panoramic wallpaper. Originally printed in 1834, the wallpaper depicts favorite American scenes and settings, such as West Point, Niagara Falls, and Virginia's Natural Bridge.

meantime the Trumans lived in Blair House, the presidential guest house across the street. When the renovations were completed in 1952, the White House had been reinforced with concrete and steel, a complete third story had been added, and the basement had been expanded.

The renovations brought to light charred timbers that historians date to August 24, 1814, during the War of 1812, when British troops marched into Washington and set fire to the White House. President James Madison (1809–17) was absent with the army, so First Lady Dolley Madison was forced to flee without him, taking as many White House treasures as she could carry.

It took almost three years to rebuild the fire-ravaged mansion. James Hoban was called in to supervise the restoration. In 1824 the South Portico was added; the North Portico was built six years later. By the late 19th century the mansion was again in sore need of repair and upgrading. Both Grover Cleveland (1885–89 and 1893–97) and William McKinley (1897–1901) complained about the unstable flooring, unsanitary plumbing, dangerously obsolete wiring, and the sprawling, unsightly greenhouses on the mansion's west side. But to no avail.

When the extremely popular Theodore Roosevelt (1901–09) became president and took to his bully pulpit, however, the White House received the necessary appropriation. "Smash the glass houses!" ordered the former Rough Rider during the Spanish-American War, and soon America's most prominent architects were hard at work renovating and updating the White House to suit Teddy's taste and afford his rambunctious family some privacy. During her husband's presidential tenure, Eleanor Roosevelt was an energetic first lady who raised six children and an endless variety of pets, including raccoons, snakes, a bear, and a pony.

TELEVISED WHITE HOUSE TOUR

After the Truman overhaul, there were no significant renovations at the White House until 1961, when First Lady Jacqueline Kennedy appointed a fine arts committee to undertake an ambitious restoration of parts of the mansion's interior. Sixty million viewers tuned in for Mrs. Kennedy's television tour of the restoration. The work was interrupted the following year by Pres. John F. Kennedy's (1961–63) assassination, but it was resumed in the 1970's under the direction of First Lady Patricia Nixon.

As they lead visitors through the White House, knowledgeable guides tell the story of its evolution. Tours enter the house through the East Wing —a World War II addition lined with portraits of

presidents and first ladies—and then go through a glass-enclosed colonnade to the White House Ground Floor. Hoban designed the vaulted ceiling and groined archways of the Ground Floor Corridor, which were restored in Truman's time. Today the corridor is lit by three bronze and crystal Regency chandeliers and portraits of several recent first ladies adorn the walls.

PRESIDENTS' LIBRARY

Visitors on guided tours can view the Library. Originally a basement laundry, the room was transformed into a gentlemen's smoking room by Pres. Theodore Roosevelt in 1902. In 1935 it was remodeled as a library; and during the Kennedy administration a program was launched to stock the shelves with a wide-ranging selection of works representative of American thought and tradition. Furnished in the style of the late Federal period, the room features the work of the famed New York cabinetmaker Duncan Phyfe, and a gilded chandelier that once belonged to the family of James Fenimore Cooper, the 19th-century author of *The Last of the Mohicans*. The comfortable room is now primarily used for intimate presidential teas and receptions.

Across the corridor is the Vermeil Room, named for its collection of vermeil, or gilded silver, which includes pieces that date to the Renaissance. The collection was bequeathed to the White House during Dwight D. Eisenhower's administration by Philadelphia socialite Margaret Thompson Biddle. Hanging on the walls are the portraits of four first ladies, including Aaron Shikler's depictions of Jacqueline Bouvier Kennedy and Nancy Davis Reagan. There is also an unusual 1949 painting of Eleanor Roosevelt by Douglas Chandor, done as a montage of his subject's moods and expressions during the course of her busy day.

Adjacent to the Vermeil Room is the China Room, named for its collection of presidential china. Early presidents auctioned off old china to help fund new purchases, and damaged dinnerware was discarded or given away. In 1889, however, First Lady Caroline Harrison, the wife of Benjamin Harrison, started a collection of White House china. The collection was greatly enhanced by Mrs. Theodore Roosevelt, who ended the practice of selling or giving away presidential china. She also located pieces from earlier presidencies that no longer belonged to the White House. President Woodrow Wilson established a precedent of purchasing American-made instead of European-made services; his china service was manufactured by Lenox of New Jersey. Lyndon B. Johnson's (1963–69) 200-piece service ranks among the most extensive of the sets, while Rutherford B. Hayes' (1877–81) china features a game platter painted with the image of a strutting turkey, certainly the most flamboyant piece in the collection.

The wallpaper in the president's second-floor dining room, above, depicts real and imagined scenes from the American Revolution. On the left below the mirror is a rendering of George Washington's 1776 triumphant entry into Boston, and an imaginary battle near Virginia's Natural Bridge is displayed between the windows. The dining room is closed to public tours.

EXTERIOR FEATURES

The north-facing facade features White House architect James Hoban's alternating curved and triangular pediments above the windows, right.

The oval-shaped Diplomatic Reception Room, which opens onto the White House South Lawn, is often used to greet visiting dignitaries. It was once the site of the White House furnace, but Franklin Delano Roosevelt (1933–45) made the room his library. During the difficult years of the Great Depression and World War II, FDR broadcast his famous fireside chats over the radio from here. (Assistants reportedly crumpled paper in the background to simulate the sound of a crackling fire.)

After the war, the room was refurbished by Mamie Eisenhower and later it was redecorated by Jacqueline Kennedy, who added the panoramic wallpaper. The president and his aides frequently pass through this room on the way to and from the presidential helicopter, which uses the South Lawn as its landing pad.

WARTIME ACTIVITIES

The neighboring Map Room, which is closed to the public, contains an interesting collection of maps donated by the National Geographic Society, but the room's name refers to its use as a situation room. During World War II, Pres. Franklin D. Roosevelt plotted the course of the war here. It is not hard to imagine what it must have been like: the ringing telephones, hurrying aides, army and navy officers poring over fresh dispatches, and Roosevelt, in his wheelchair, conferring with Gen. George Marshall.

The largest room in the White House is located upstairs on the State Floor (also referred to as the First Floor): the East Room is 79 feet long and almost 37 feet wide. Today the spacious room looks as it did after Theodore Roosevelt's renovations. Cut-glass chandeliers, wall panels decorated with scenes from Greek and Roman mythology, and a parquet oak floor, which reportedly provided a smooth surface for the roller-skating antics of Teddy's children, are still here. The history of the room is remarkably eventful. Unfinished when John Adams (1797–1801) took office, it first served as a place to hang the presidential laundry. Thomas Jefferson set up an office here for his secretary, Meriwether Lewis, who later co-led the Lewis and Clark expedition. James Madison's cabinet met in the room until it was severely damaged by the fire in 1814. Gilbert Stuart's famous painting of George Washington, which hung in the room at that time, was cut from its frame when Dolley Madison insisted that it be saved from the invading British army.

Upon taking office in 1829, President Jackson had the room redecorated at a cost of more than $9,000. At the time he was in mourning for Rachel, his wife of 38 years, who had died of a heart attack shortly after he was elected. Jackson always believed that her death was precipitated by the revival during the campaign of the scandal that surrounded their marriage: after two years of marriage the couple had found out that Rachel's divorce from her first husband, Lewis Robards, had never been granted. The Jacksons quickly remarried in 1794.

That incident was one of many controversies that plagued Old Hickory. The father of Jacksonian democracy elicited criticism again when he asserted that the White House literally belonged to the people and threw open the doors to the public after the inauguration. A disorderly mob took up his invitation and nearly wrecked the mansion, forcing Jackson to spend his first night as president in a Washington boardinghouse. "Ladies fainted, men were seen with bloody noses," reported one eyewitness to the event.

EAST ROOM MEMORIES

As visitors to the White House enter the East Room, many pause to pay their respects to presidents who died while in office. In April of 1865, the East Room was draped in black as Pres. Abraham Lincoln's (1861–65) body lay in state. On November 24, 1963, John F. Kennedy's body was laid out in the East Room until it was moved to the state capitol for public mourning. All together, the bodies of seven U.S. presidents have laid in state here.

Happy occasions have also been celebrated in the East Room. When John Quincy Adams was president (1825–29), he held New Year's Day receptions for the public here, and when Pres. Ulysses S. Grant's (1869–77) daughter, Nellie, was married in 1874, the room was the site of her lavish wedding ceremony and reception.

When the White House was rebuilt following the fire of 1814, Pres. James Monroe (1816–24) ordered green silk for the draperies and upholstery in the room next to the East Room and turned it into a card room. The green color scheme gave the room its name. Refurbished in 1977 by First Lady Patricia Nixon, the walls were again covered with green silk, acquired in 1962 by Mrs. Kennedy. The Green Room features furnishings of the first decade of the 19th century, including pieces by Duncan Phyfe and period furnishings influenced by British designer Thomas Sheraton. Among the portraits on the walls is one of Benjamin Franklin painted by the 18th-century Scottish artist David Martin.

The tradition of naming a room for its primary color scheme was maintained for the oval-shaped

AUGUST COMPANY
A bird's-eye view of the White House shows its position in relation to the Potomac River, the obelisk of the Washington Monument, and the domed Jefferson Memorial.

Blue Room next door. President Monroe decorated the room in the Empire style, an eclectic mixture of Greek, Roman, and Egyptian-style furnishings, favored by Napoleon Bonaparte. President Martin Van Buren (1837–41) chose blue as the color for the room's upholstery and draperies.

Over the sofa in the Blue Room hangs an 1859 portrait of John Tyler (1841–45), who oversaw the annexation of Texas as a state in 1845. To the right of the center window hangs Rembrandt Peale's portrait of Jefferson, painted when he was vice president. It may be a familiar picture to visitors because of the many engravings that later were made from the portrait.

When Jefferson became president, he retained Benjamin Henry Latrobe, one of America's first professional architects, to replace the mansion's roof and design the North and South porticoes. He also made it clear from the start that the White House would not function as a palace. He shocked the diplomatic corps by refusing to seat diplomats according to rank or privilege, and he occasionally greeted official callers in his house slippers.

During the turbulent years of the Civil War, the Blue Room served as the setting for numerous receptions in honor of military officers, congressmen, senators, cabinet officials, foreign diplomats, abolitionists, and business tycoons—all hosted by Abraham Lincoln and his fashion-conscious and mercurial wife, Mary Todd Lincoln. Generations earlier, the sounds of a pianoforte and guitars accompanied the lighthearted receptions held by Dolley Madison in this room. Here guests invariably displayed—as one observer put it—"fashion, fame, beauty, wealth or talents."

THE RED ROOM

The next room on the tour has been called at various times the president's Antechamber, the Washington Parlor, and the Yellow Drawing Room. Now known as the Red Room, it features Empire-style furniture, a gilded chandelier, and signature walls of red satin twill. The room was decorated during the Kennedy and Nixon administrations. Dominating the decor is an enormous portrait of President Van Buren's daughter-in-law, the beautiful Angelica Van Buren, who served as official hostess for the widower president. Also adorning the Red Room is another Gilbert Stuart portrait, this one of Dolley Madison.

In the late 19th century, presidential entertaining became more elaborate, and it became apparent that the State Dining Room had to be enlarged. During Theodore Roosevelt's administration, a

staircase was removed to create a stately hall in the Georgian style of late 18th-century English homes. The president, who was an enthusiastic hunter, mounted trophy heads on the walls and installed a marble mantel with carved bisons' heads. During his renovation, Truman removed the trophies and replaced the mantel with a simple, black marble version. A marble reproduction of Teddy's mantel was put in during the Kennedy administration.

A portrait of Abraham Lincoln also hangs in this room. It was painted by George P. A. Healy four years after Lincoln's assassination. Carved into the mantel is a presidential prayer that was excerpted from a letter written by John Adams on his second night in the White House: "I Pray Heaven to Bestow the Best of Blessings on THIS HOUSE and on All that shall hereafter Inhabit it. May none but Honest and Wise Men ever rule under this roof."

VITAL REMINDER

From the State Dining Room, tour guests are escorted along the Cross Hall and the North Entrance Hall to the exit at the North Portico. The Cross Hall contains English chandeliers crafted in 1790, and portraits of Kennedy, Eisenhower, Truman, Wilson, and other presidents are displayed on the marble walls. Presidents often walk through the Cross Hall to the East Room for nationally telecast news conferences or to meet with visiting heads of state. Visitors who cast a backward glance as they exit will see the doorway to the Blue Room, flanked by the United States flag and the presidential flag and topped by the president's seal. It is a fitting last image that brings to mind Franklin D. Roosevelt's observation: "I never forget that I live in a house owned by all the American people."

DESIGNER PRESIDENT
James Monroe chose French Empire–style decor for the Blue Room, above, in 1817. To the right of the mantel hangs a portrait of his wife, Elizabeth Kortright Monroe, which still belongs to the Monroe estate. On the mantel is Monroe's Hannibal clock, so named because it displays the figure of the famous Carthaginian general who, in 218 B.C., led elephants and troops across the Alps to fight the Romans.

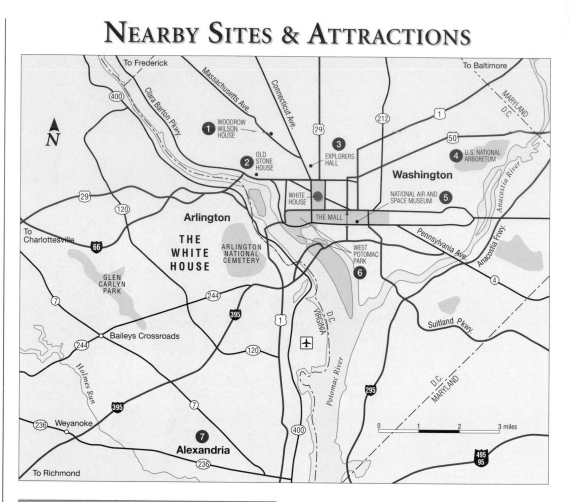

A bonsai tree, right, from the National Bonsai Collection at the U.S. National Arboretum, was one of several bonsai given as gifts to the arboretum by Japan on the occasion of the U.S. Bicentennial.

① WOODROW WILSON HOUSE, DISTRICT OF COLUMBIA

Located along Embassy Row in the nation's capital, the red-brick Georgian Revival town house was the home of Woodrow Wilson, the 28th president, from 1921 until his death in 1924. Wilson bought the house with the money he received from his 1919 Nobel Peace Prize, and gave it to his second wife, Edith Bolling Wilson, in 1920. Wilson was the only president to continue living in the capital after completing his term in office and he received many notable guests here, including Georges Clemenceau and David Lloyd George. After her husband's death, Mrs. Wilson continued to reside here until she died in 1961. She left the house to the National Trust for

Historic Preservation. Tours highlight Wilson's career as a university professor and his contributions as the nation's president, with special attention paid to his efforts to establish the League of Nations. Located at 2340 S St.

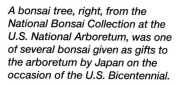

② OLD STONE HOUSE, DISTRICT OF COLUMBIA

This house, built by the cabinetmaker Christopher Layman in 1764, is the capital's oldest surviving building. Located in Georgetown, the historic house displays 18th-century furnishings and artifacts, offering a glimpse into the daily life of a middle-class family in pre–Revolutionary America. At one time it was erroneously believed that George Washington had stayed at the house when he was looking for a site for the nation's capital in 1791. The carpentry shop on the first floor and the parlors, bedrooms, and kitchen on the second floor have been restored. Located at 3051 M St.

③ EXPLORERS HALL, DISTRICT OF COLUMBIA

The National Geographic Society's museum of geography takes visitors on an interactive trip through a wealth of information on earth and space exploration. Earth Station One is a 72-foot-high amphitheater that introduces audiences to some of the planet's geographical data through the use of an 11-foot-diameter globe. Exhibits chronicle milestones in geographic research, ranging from discoveries by and about early humans to the research of 20th-century undersea explorers. Remote-controlled microscopes bring tarantulas, lizards, and other creatures into view; an interactive holographic aquarium teaches visitors about fish; and a live satellite hookup provides up-to-date weather conditions from around the world. Located at 1145 17th St.

④ U.S. NATIONAL ARBORETUM, DISTRICT OF COLUMBIA

Established in 1927, the arboretum is a research facility and a living museum encompassing 444 acres of plant collections, historical monuments, and gardens. A two-and-a-half-acre herb garden includes 800 species; an English garden contains 200 varieties of roses; and the bonsai gardens are designed in the Japanese, Chinese, and American styles. Some of the arboretum's most popular displays are of azaleas, hollies, and magnolias. The conifer collection includes the largest stand of dwarf and slow-growing conifers in North America. Walkways wind through the arboretum and several pathways lead to the top of Mount Hamilton, where visitors are afforded a view of Washington. Located at 3501 New York Ave.

⑤ NATIONAL AIR AND SPACE MUSEUM, DISTRICT OF COLUMBIA

The world's largest and most complete collection of historic aircraft and spacecraft displays everything from the Wright brothers' 1903 Flyer and Charles Lindbergh's *Spirit of St. Louis* to a North American P-51 Mustang, a Messerschmitt 262, and the front

fuselage of the *Enola Gay,* the B-52 that dropped the atomic bomb on Hiroshima in 1945. Many of the airplanes are suspended from the ceiling in the central exhibition hall. The Space Hall displays a Minuteman ICBM, a German V-2 rocket, and a Hubble telescope. The U.S. space program has lent the museum the *Apollo 11* command module, which brought the U.S. astronauts back from the moon in 1969. Located on 6th St. and Independence Ave.

⑥ WEST POTOMAC PARK, DISTRICT OF COLUMBIA

This large, urban green space on the Potomac River is best known for its memorials and monuments, which include the domed Lincoln Memorial with its 36 Doric columns for each of the 36 states in Lincoln's time; the Vietnam Veterans Memorial, a long V-shaped wall of polished black granite listing the more than 58,000 Americans who died in the war; and the Washington Monument, which at 555 feet is the tallest freestanding masonry structure in the world. The park also has facilities for picnicking, walking, and golfing. Located on Ohio Dr.

⑦ ALEXANDRIA, VIRGINIA

In the 18th century Alexandria was a flourishing tobacco port and many of the buildings from that era are still standing within the town's 100-block historic district. One of the oldest is the 1752 Carlyle House, a Palladian-style mansion that was the site of a critical meeting between Gen. Edward Braddock and five Colonial governors during the French and Indian War. General Robert E. Lee, a onetime resident of Alexandria, attended the city's Christ Church, built in 1773, as did George Washington and his family. The Friendship Fire Company Museum displays a replica of a fire engine that was given to the company in 1774 by Washington, who was one of its founding members. Located on Hwy. 95.

The distinctive colonnaded and domed Jefferson Memorial, above, is visible from West Potomac Park. The walls of the monument are inscribed with excerpts from the Declaration of Independence and the Virginia Statute for Religious Freedom.

Eighteenth-century wooden town houses, left, grace the streets of Alexandria. In 1748, the 16-year-old George Washington helped lay out the city's street plan, which was based on a grid pattern.

MONTICELLO

A Renaissance man, Thomas Jefferson made this mountaintop retreat one of his finest creations.

For 19 days, Thomas Jefferson wrote nothing. The dedicated letter writer had taken his bride, Martha, to the South Pavilion, their honeymoon cottage, in late January of 1772. This tiny brick building was but a single room at that time, 18 feet square, built over a ground-level kitchen.

Martha peered out at the rolling Virginia mountains and venturing outside, looked down on the tiny village of Charlottesville. From her small abode, she could assess the progress on the construction of a much larger brick structure that was taking shape nearby. This grand architectural experiment on Jefferson's mountaintop took 40 years to complete. Unfortunately Martha would not live to see the final masterpiece: she died just 10 years after she married.

Monticello, Italian for "little mountain," is a description that might have been contested by those who climbed its 867 feet hauling stone and timber. Other Virginia planters built their houses in the well-watered lowlands, not on peaks that required slave labor to level the ground by hand. Lacking the professional services of classically trained architects, most planters chose to adhere

Jefferson's initials are emblazoned on a crest, right, at the family cemetery, where both he and his beloved Martha are buried. Martha died in the 10th year of their marriage from complications that arose after the birth of her sixth child. Only two of her children lived to adulthood. Her gravestone reads, "Torn from me by death." Jefferson wrote his own epitaph: "Here was buried Thomas Jefferson Author of the Declaration of Independence Of the Statute of Virginia for Religious Freedom and Father of the University of Virginia."

to conventional floor plans with rectangular rooms and small rectangular windows. Monticello, on the other hand, reflected the many talents of its owner, a lawyer by profession with an intense and consuming interest in architecture. Nothing like it had ever been built in America.

A SPECIAL PLACE

Visitors ascend the mountain along much of the same route that Jefferson's guests took to Monticello. The restored house is the only one in the United States that is included on the United Nations' World Heritage List of International Treasures. About 60 percent of its furnishings are believed to be original.

Even if the property and house were merely ordinary, they would merit attention simply because they were designed by Thomas Jefferson, author of the Declaration of Independence. His achievements are indeed impressive: governor of Virginia, minister to France, America's first secretary of state, second vice president, and third president. He also sponsored the Lewis and Clark expedition and nearly doubled the nation's land holdings with the Louisiana Purchase.

A long, winding walkway leads from the West Front, which is depicted on the American nickel, to the entrance of the house. The original pathway was revealed when researchers shone their headlights across the grass at night. In accordance with

Jefferson's hand-drawn design, each side of the walkway has been planted with a profusion of flowers that blossom from April through October. Twenty oval beds, each planted with a variety of species, surround the house.

"I remember well when he first returned to Monticello," wrote Jefferson's granddaughter Ellen Randolph, "how immediately he began to prepare new beds for his flowers. . . . The roots arrived,

STATELY MONTICELLO

Overleaf: Among Monticello's most outstanding neoclassical features are its portico with Doric columns supporting a triangular pediment, and a central dome based on the designs of the 16th-century Italian architect Andrea Palladio. A bird's-eye view of the house, right, shows it nestled amid the forested surroundings of the Virginia countryside.

44

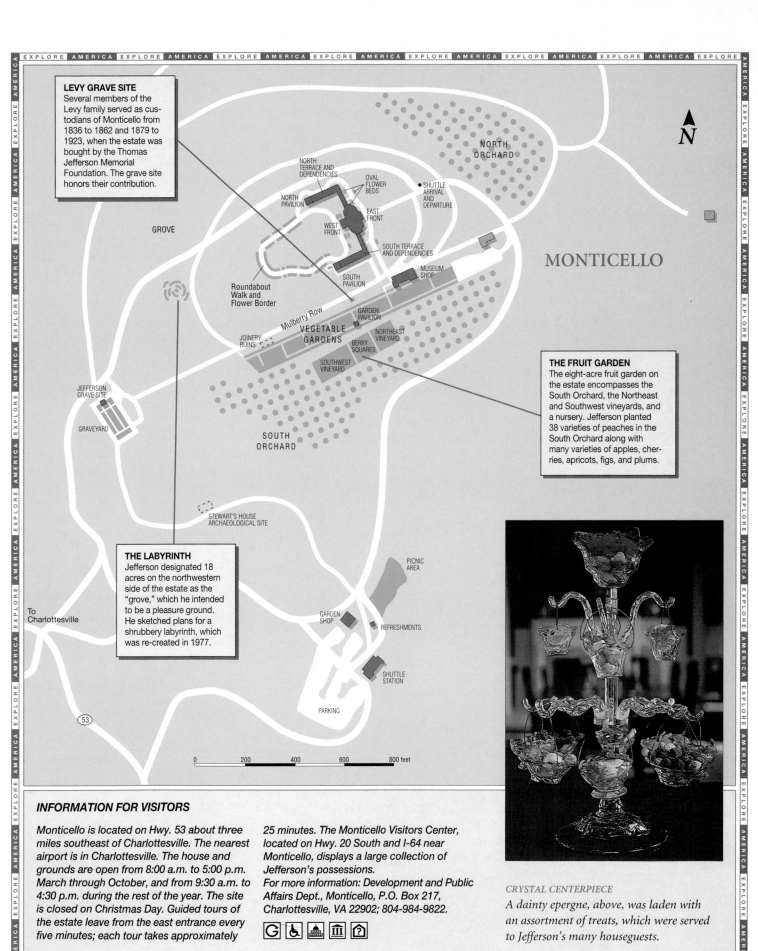

N

MONTICELLO

LEVY GRAVE SITE
Several members of the Levy family served as custodians of Monticello from 1836 to 1862 and 1879 to 1923, when the estate was bought by the Thomas Jefferson Memorial Foundation. The grave site honors their contribution.

GROVE

NORTH ORCHARD

NORTH TERRACE AND DEPENDENCIES

OVAL FLOWER BEDS

• SHUTTLE ARRIVAL AND DEPARTURE

NORTH PAVILION

EAST FRONT

WEST FRONT

SOUTH TERRACE AND DEPENDENCIES

MUSEUM SHOP

Roundabout Walk and Flower Border

SOUTH PAVILION

GARDEN PAVILION

Mulberry Row

JOINERY RUINS

VEGETABLE GARDENS

NORTHEAST VINEYARD

BERRY SQUARES

SOUTHWEST VINEYARD

JEFFERSON GRAVE SITE

GRAVEYARD

SOUTH ORCHARD

THE FRUIT GARDEN
The eight-acre fruit garden on the estate encompasses the South Orchard, the Northeast and Southwest vineyards, and a nursery. Jefferson planted 38 varieties of peaches in the South Orchard along with many varieties of apples, cherries, apricots, figs, and plums.

STEWART'S HOUSE ARCHAEOLOGICAL SITE

THE LABYRINTH
Jefferson designated 18 acres on the northwestern side of the estate as the "grove," which he intended to be a pleasure ground. He sketched plans for a shrubbery labyrinth, which was re-created in 1977.

PICNIC AREA

To Charlottesville

GARDEN SHOP

REFRESHMENTS

SHUTTLE STATION

PARKING

53

0   200   400   600   800 feet

INFORMATION FOR VISITORS

Monticello is located on Hwy. 53 about three miles southeast of Charlottesville. The nearest airport is in Charlottesville. The house and grounds are open from 8:00 a.m. to 5:00 p.m. March through October, and from 9:30 a.m. to 4:30 p.m. during the rest of the year. The site is closed on Christmas Day. Guided tours of the estate leave from the east entrance every five minutes; each tour takes approximately 25 minutes. The Monticello Visitors Center, located on Hwy. 20 South and I-64 near Monticello, displays a large collection of Jefferson's possessions.
For more information: Development and Public Affairs Dept., Monticello, P.O. Box 217, Charlottesville, VA 22902; 804-984-9822.

CRYSTAL CENTERPIECE
A dainty epergne, above, was laden with an assortment of treats, which were served to Jefferson's many houseguests.

CHRISTMAS COLORS

CHRISTMAS COLORS

Jefferson planned every detail of Monticello, including the bright red holly berries, right, that continue to thrive on the estate and still evoke the spirit of the Christmas season.

THE FAMILY PARLOR

Jefferson liked to spend time with his family in the parlor, below, reading and playing games. The room was the setting for christenings, musical recitals, and for his daughter Mary's marriage to John Wayles Eppes in 1797. More than 35 portraits are on display, as is an elegant pianoforte made of mahogany and inlaid with satinwood and other veneers. The instrument dates to about 1800 and was made by Astor & Co. of London. One of Jefferson's daughters, named Martha after her mother, often gave family recitals on the pianoforte.

labeled each with a fancy name. There was Marcus Aurelius, and the King of the Gold Mine, the Roman Empress, and the Queen of the Amazons, Psyche, and God of Love. . . . What joy it was for one of us to discover the tender green breaking through the mould, and run to grandpapa . . . how he would sympathize in our admiration."

Fonder of eating vegetables than meat, Jefferson maintained an extensive vegetable garden, that, seen today from the air, resembles a 1,000-foot length of train track, neatly segmented into plots for fruits and for vegetables. His was both a garden and a laboratory, because Jefferson imported seeds from Europe and the other parts of the New World, declaring that one of the greatest services a person could render to his country was to "add a useful plant to its culture." At Monticello he experimented with 250 known varieties of more than 70 species, keeping extensive records on how well they adapted to the climate and soil. Many of these plants are still cultivated in the re-created garden.

Jefferson grew American as well as imported specimens in his orchards, vineyards, and fruit gardens. Monticello's lofty site proved to be especially beneficial to the fruit trees because the cold air that settled in the bottomlands caused warmer air to rise over the mountain, protecting the blossoms from frosts. The Fruitery enjoyed a southeastern exposure and fruits that normally thrive in sunny places grew well here. Jefferson was particularly proud of the peaches, grapes, almonds, and pomegranates he was able to cultivate on his estate. Today visitors can wander among the restored orchards.

RECORD KEEPER Fascinated by the weather, Jefferson rose with the sun and immediately checked the outdoor temperature, which he calculated to be consistently coldest at dawn. At about 4:00 p.m.—the hottest part of the day, by his measurements—he took a second reading. He

also noted levels of precipitation and the direction and speed of the wind, recording them all in pencil in a fanlike notebook made of thin slips of ivory, which he carried in his pocket constantly. Later he copied all of his readings and other observations related to a host of subjects into permanent record books. It was easy to erase the pencil markings from the ivory pages, and Jefferson was able to reuse his notebook like a slate blackboard. He hoped his recordings would become part of a national meteorological database; today his weather memorandum book that dates from 1776 to 1820 is part of the permanent collection of the Library of Congress in Washington, D.C.

His design and furnishings for Monticello showed Jefferson to be one of the most talented men to gain national prominence. He had both inherited and married into sizable estates that included many slaves, affording him the land, manpower, and freedom to explore his remarkably broad interests and gifts. "Determine never to be idle," he once wrote to his 11-year-old daughter. "It is wonderful how much may be done if we are always doing." To the end of his days, Jefferson pursued knowledge, especially of scientific and agricultural matters, that would benefit the new republic of America.

	Jefferson learned much about
EUROPEAN	architecture during his tenure
INFLUENCES	as the minister plenipotentiary
	to Europe under Pres. George

Washington, and later, as Benjamin Franklin's successor in the role of American minister to France. He was thrust into a milieu in which he spent a lot of time with painters and sculptors, and was able to closely examine European architectural styles. Upon his return from the five-year diplomatic mission, Jefferson was appointed secretary of state, a post that he held for four years.

In 1793 he resigned and went home to his Virginia estate, his head filled with plans to modify Monticello's design. "Architecture is my delight," he said, "and putting up, and pulling down, one of my favorite amusements."

During Martha's lifetime the house encompassed 2,500 square feet with eight rooms located on two floors. The central portion of the structure was tall and domeless and the double portico was flanked by two wings. Long balustraded boardwalks extended from either side of the house and led to the North and South pavilions.

Jefferson set about to double the size of his home and to remodel its interior. The house grew from two stories to three, but to all outward appearances it looked to be compressed into a single towering story, the style of the day in Paris. To accomplish this effect, he had the windows in the second-

story bedrooms installed at floor level, making them look like extensions of the tall French windows below when viewed from the East Lawn. The upper portico was removed to allow for a dome similar to one Jefferson had admired in Paris—and it is the crowning feature of Monticello.

This self-taught architect, who is considered to be the greatest American architect of his day, was inspired by the works of Andrea Palladio, the 16th-

century Italian architect. Palladio's influence is evident not only in Monticello, Jefferson's "essay in architecture," but also in the great project that he undertook in his old age, the design for the University of Virginia, which Jefferson could watch slowly rising on its site through a telescope from the top of his mountain.

Jefferson is also called the father of American paleontology and he displayed hundreds of artifacts at Monticello, including several fossils, Native

MULTIPURPOSE FIREPLACE
The mantel in the dining room, above, featured side doors that allowed easy access to the dumbwaiter cleverly hidden behind it. Numerous paintings and engravings adorn the walls.

American artifacts, and mastodon bones presented to him by Meriwether Lewis and William Clark. Guests said his entrance hall was frequently a disorderly jumble of peace pipes, snakeskins, maps, and trophies from hunting expeditions.

A TIME OF RECKONING

Jefferson served as the vice president from 1797 to 1801 and as the nation's president from 1801 to 1809. During his time in office and throughout his retirement, he was consumed by the effort to ward off bankruptcy, for a substantial cloud of debt hung over him. He managed only to postpone the inevitable.

Jefferson's heirs faced debts of $107,000 and were forced to sell his property, books, and paintings at several public auctions following his death in 1826. Monticello became a bargaining chip in a complex estate dispute. Shortly after the Civil War, the home's tenant-overseer was known to be charging visitors 25 cents a tour.

By 1870 visitors reported extensive water damage. Gutters had rotted, the roof and many of its 13 skylights were leaking, windows were shattered, and steps were either broken, rotted, or covered with weeds. Debris littered the interior. Grain was stored in some of the bedrooms, and pigs and cattle may have occupied the parlor in the winter. According to one 1870 tourist, the building had been "criminally neglected."

The house had been purchased in 1836 by Uriah P. Levy, who bequeathed it to the U.S. government if certain conditions were met. After years of litigation, Jefferson M. Levy, Uriah's nephew and a wealthy New York attorney, gained legal title to the property. He acquired the house and 218 acres of the property in 1879 for $10,500. Levy repaired and refurbished the structure and combed the country for Jefferson family heirlooms, which he returned to the house. In 1923 the newly formed Thomas Jefferson Memorial Foundation paid $500,000 to purchase the property, thus ensuring its preservation. Since that time the foundation has continued to renovate, restore, and furnish the house in an attempt to re-create its original appearance. The Garden Club of Virginia was enlisted to restore the gardens and grounds. The entire project

was greatly facilitated by the surviving documents and plans written by Jefferson.

The once-neglected house is orderly today. Its hall displays a replica of a magnificent buffalo hide covered with Native American battle scenes; racks of antlers project from one wall also hung with early American maps; a copy of the Declaration of Independence is on the opposite wall. Two important portraits of Jefferson by Gilbert Stuart and Thomas Sully belong to the collection. Jefferson is reputed to have owned one of the best private collections of paintings and statuary in the country.

COLLECTOR AND TINKERER Along with his penchant for collecting, Jefferson also was an inveterate tinkerer in an age of rapid progress in engineering and scientific innovation. One example of his predisposition for efficiency is the mechanism for the double doors in the parlor: push on one of the doors and a chain hidden beneath the floorboards causes the other to open at the same time. Jefferson designed a large clock that is connected to a Chinese gong on the roof. The timepiece, which hangs above the arched entry doors, was wound once a week on Sundays and powered by twin sets of suspended cannonball weights that were raised on pulleys to near ceiling level. The weights slowly descended all week and then sank through openings in the floor to the cellar, from which they were regularly hoisted for their weekly rewinding. This clock still keeps the accurate day of the week and time of day.

While entertaining guests in his formal dining room, Jefferson preferred as few intrusions by his slave servants as possible. To accomplish this, he installed panel doors on either side of the mantel that gave access to dumbwaiters, which could be loaded with wine from the cellar. On the opposite side of the room, another cabinet door swivels open to reveal a lazy Susan with several shelves. Slaves placed dishes of food on the shelves and rotated them to the butler in the dining room.

Jefferson's office, which he called his cabinet, could be a model for the state-of-the art office of today. It was filled with labor-saving devices such as a revolving book stand, with five rests for holding books, and a revolving tabletop and chair that saved steps and maximized comfort.

Visitors can also take a look at Jefferson's copying machine, a polygraph often mistakenly thought to be of his own design. The device held two sheets of paper and connected pens, allowing the writer to make file copies of all his written documents. Credited with penning some 20,000 letters during his lifetime, Jefferson was enamored of the machine, calling it "the finest invention of the present age."

Jefferson's interest in every detail of the house's decoration—from bed coverings to draperies—caused him to ship 86 crates from France, many of them filled with furniture and art. He placed entablatures at ceiling height above mantels and doors with different designs for each room, most of them modeled after features found in ancient Roman temples. Long triple-sash windows, French doors, and skylights allow natural light to filter into many of the rooms. Frequent use of semioctagonal

DOMED PERFECTION
Light from circular windows is cast on the floor of the dome room, below, located on the third floor of Monticello. The room was used variously as a bedroom and a storage place.

spaces, such as the beautiful bay window in the parlor, gave the house many angles from which its occupants could view the surrounding countryside.

Jefferson entertained his guests in the parlor, which is the most formal room at Monticello and the only one that does not have heart-pine floors. Instead he designed for it what is thought to be the first parquet floor in the nation. The flooring was made of cherry and beech woods and was strong enough to support "delightful recreation" of many kinds. The

parlor also was a music room, furnished with a pianoforte, harpsichord, and guitar. Jefferson would often play his violin while his grandchildren danced around him. Game tables allowed him to indulge a passion for chess as well as other entertainments. The family gathered here to read and the room also served as an art gallery for Jefferson's world-class collection of paintings, which included 35 portraits.

Jefferson, who read in seven languages, once said that he could never live without books, and almost

50

every house or office he occupied is designed to accommodate them. At Monticello, he devoted two rooms and part of a third to his precious volumes—a collection so vast that when he sold it to the government in 1815, it became the nucleus of the Library of Congress. Immediately after Jefferson relinquished his books he began to rebuild his library; a few of those volumes are still at the house.

Introduced to alcove beds in France, Jefferson admired their space-saving qualities and used them in almost every bedroom in his house. His own bedroom contained a unique adaptation: an open-sided space was built into the wall between his bedroom and study so that he could climb into or out of bed on the right side for his study, or the left side for his bedroom.

The author of the Declaration of Independence died in this bed on the 50th anniversary of the document's signing. He had roused himself from unconsciousness repeatedly that day to inquire, "Is it the Fourth?" Assured that the day had arrived, the 83-year-old champion of liberty breathed his last—just hours before his friend John Adams died.

Jefferson left a rich record of his life. His delight in this lofty homestead was a consistent theme. "Our own dear Monticello," he penned, "Where has nature spread so rich a mantle under the eye! Mountains, forests, rocks, rivers! With what majesty do we there ride above the storms!" On another occasion, he declared that his heart's desire had been granted him: "All my wishes end, where I hope my days will end, at Monticello."

*A PLACE OF WORK AND REPOSE
Jefferson's bed, situated in an alcove between his study and bedroom, left, permitted him instant access to either room. A skylight allows natural light to enter the room. The door to the right of the bed leads to a steep staircase that Jefferson used to reach his closet, which is set into the wall above the bed. The oval portholes allow light from the room to illuminate the closet.*

A flower-lined pathway leads to the workers' cottage and garden, below, at Ash Lawn–Highland estate, where James Monroe lived on and off for 24 years.

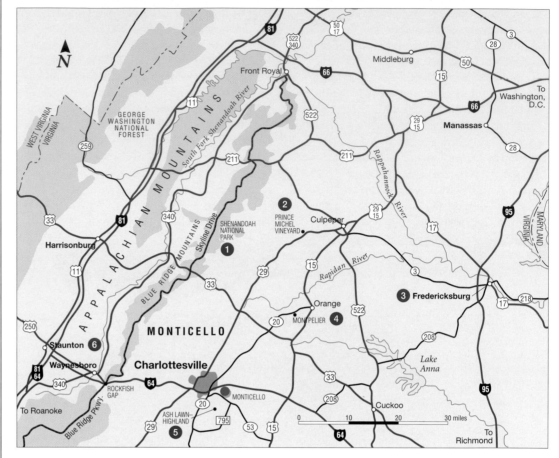

1 SHENANDOAH NATIONAL PARK

This 200,000-acre national park, established in 1935, includes an 80-mile-long swathe of the Blue Ridge Mountains. Shenandoah is an Indian word meaning "Daughter of the Stars," a name that refers to the towering mountain peaks. To the west the land drops sharply to the Shenandoah Valley, and the ridges and wooded hills of the Piedmont dominate the landscape to the east. One of the most popular ways to view the lush terrain is from the 105-mile-long Skyline Drive, which connects Front Royal to Rockfish Gap. Alternatively, visitors can explore the park by taking advantage of its more than 500 miles of hiking and horseback riding trails, including 101 miles of the Appalachian Trail. The flora and fauna here include more than 40 mammal species, 200 bird species, 1,100 species of flowering plants, and 100 tree species. The Harry F. Byrd Visitor Center at Big Meadows and the Dickey Ridge Visitor Center in the North District offer exhibits on the history of the park and the culture of the region. The park's northern entrance is located at Front Royal and the southern entrance at Rockfish Gap.

2 PRINCE MICHEL VINEYARD

This 150-acre vineyard—famous for its chardonnay, Riesling, and merlot wines—offers tours to visitors who want to learn about the history of wine making and about contemporary methods of cultivating grapes to produce wine. Tours take in the vineyard's fermenting tanks and a traditional barrel room, and visitors can examine rare wine bottles and antique wine-making equipment and learn about the history of viticulture through a video presentation. The tour ends with wine tastings of the vineyard's chardonnays and sauvignons. Located 10 miles southwest of Culpeper on Hwy. 29.

3 FREDERICKSBURG

Many of the 18th-century buildings in this historic town are associated with George Washington and his family. The Mary Washington House was given by George Washington to his mother, Mary, in 1770. Washington left from here for his presidential inauguration in New York City in 1789. The Hugh Mercer Apothecary Shop offers demonstrations of medical treatments such as leeching and bleeding, and displays instruments and equipment used by 18th-century American apothecaries. It was opened in 1761 by George Washington's friend Hugh Mercer. Washington often used the shop's sitting room as an office when he was in town visiting his mother. Washington's brother Charles built the Rising Sun Tavern in 1760. It was here that Washington, the Marquis de Lafayette, and Comte de Rochambeau toasted their victory over the British in 1781. Located off Hwy. 95.

④ MONTPELIER

This 2,700-acre estate of rolling pastures and forest was the home of James Madison, fourth president of the United States. He wrote much of the United States Constitution and the Bill of Rights here. The land was bought by Madison's grandparents in 1723, and the family continued to live at the estate for three generations. When James died in 1836, his wife, Dolley, suffered financial woes and was forced to sell much of the family furniture. Montpelier itself was sold in 1844. The estate changed hands six times after that until 1901, when it was purchased by William du Pont. He expanded the mansion and added a number of buildings, including greenhouses, barns, a sawmill, blacksmith's shop, bowling alley, and train station. He also built a two-and-a-half-acre formal garden and a steeplechase course where the Montpelier Hunt Races are held the first Saturday in November. A guided tour of the estate includes the 77-room mansion and a portion of the extensive grounds, which include more than 100 other structures, such as the stables, the bowling alley, and Madison's Temple. Located four miles southwest of Orange on Hwy. 20.

⑤ ASH LAWN–HIGHLAND

James Monroe, the nation's fifth president, bought this 3,500-acre property in order to be close to his friend Thomas Jefferson, whose mountaintop estate, Monticello, is two miles away and visible from Ash Lawn–Highland. Monroe named his estate Highland and a later owner renamed it Ash Lawn. Monroe was about to move to his new property in 1793 when Pres. George Washington sent him to Paris to serve as the American ambassador to France. During Monroe's absence, Jefferson selected a site for Monroe's farmhouse and had

his gardeners plant orchards there. In 1799, two years after Monroe returned from Europe, he took up residence at the house, filling its rooms with French Empire furniture. In 1826, a year after Monroe completed his second term as president, he was forced to sell the estate to pay off his debts. Today Ash Lawn–Highland comprises 535 acres. The house and boxwood gardens are open to the public. A statue of Monroe by Attilio Piccirilli is located on the grounds. During the summer the estate hosts living history programs of 18th- and 19th-century cooking and spinning techniques. Activities that take place during the Summer Festival include concerts and light opera. Candlelight tours and carol singing take place at Christmastime. Located four miles south of Charlottesville off Hwy. 795.

⑥ STAUNTON

First settled by John Lewis in 1732 and laid out in 1749, this village became an important agricultural trading center in the 18th and 19th centuries. Because Staunton was undamaged during the Civil War, much of its historic architecture is preserved. The Trinity Episcopal Church, built in 1846, stands on the site of a building that was once occupied by Gov. Thomas Jefferson and members of the Virginia General Assembly. For 17 days in 1781, while fleeing advancing British soldiers, the members of the general assembly used the building as the territorial capital. The career of the nation's 28th president is described at the Woodrow Wilson Birthplace and Museum. The house has been restored to its 1856 appearance, the year of Wilson's birth. Rooms display family memorabilia, pictures, and furnishings such as chairs and a wood-burning stove. Woodrow Wilson's four-poster bed is on view as is his baby crib. The museum's Princeton Exhibit Gallery re-creates Wilson's study—complete with desk, typewriter, and paintings—from his years as Princeton University president, from 1902 to 1910. A highlight of the museum is the Pierce-Arrow presidential limousine. Located off Hwy. 81.

Betty Washington Lewis, George Washington's only sister, lived at the Kenmore manor house in Fredericksburg. The sitting room, left, displays many fine period features, including the elaborate plasterwork above the mantel.

A rustic split-rail fence, left, borders Montpelier, the estate of Pres. James Madison. Today the 2,700-acre grounds and the house are administered by the National Trust for Historic Preservation.

BILTMORE ESTATE

The Gilded Age finds its ultimate expression in a Vanderbilt castle set in the North Carolina hills.

At 26 years of age, George W. Vanderbilt III decided it was time to build a home. He wasn't interested in a Newport-style mansion like the ones owned by other members of his family. A multimillionaire since the age of 23, Vanderbilt had even bigger ideas and he was willing to spend more than half his $10 million inheritance to see them to fruition. For almost six years, from 1889 to 1895, he devoted his time, energy, and money to the project—creating, in the end, an American castle that boasted 250 rooms, 43 bathrooms, 65 fireplaces, 3 kitchens, a swimming pool, and a bowling alley.

Everything about Biltmore was on a grand scale, from the size of the house, which was measured in acres, to its grounds, which were so vast and mountainous that it took a week on horseback to make a circuit of its 46-mile perimeter. In addition to modern amenities of central heating and electricity, the house also claimed the first elevators in Asheville, several miles of plumbing, and 10 telephones. And Biltmore was

PERFECT ACOUSTICS
The Vanderbilts hosted formal dinners, birthday celebrations, and Christmas parties in the immense Banquet Hall, below. The room's superb acoustics allowed a dinner guest seated at one end of the dining table to converse in normal tones and still be heard at the other.

decorated with more than 70,000 items, including exquisite furniture imported from 13 countries, 23,000 books, 1,600 art prints, and dozens of rare artworks and tapestries.

Such a lavish display of wealth was perhaps to be expected from the grandson of Cornelius Vanderbilt, the person who had founded the family fortune. The son of a Staten Island farmer of Dutch descent, Cornelius had reportedly started his business with a loan of $100, which he invested in a small boat for transporting freight and passengers between Staten Island and New York City. The Commodore, as Cornelius was called, eventually parlayed his one-man ferry into a steamship company numbering more than 100 vessels. During the California Gold Rush, he expanded into ground transportation, offering land and water service from New York to San Francisco via the Isthmus of Panama. After the Civil War Vanderbilt invested in railroads. At his death in 1877, he was worth an estimated $1 billion.

George Vanderbilt's father, William Henry, was the eldest of Cornelius and his wife, Sophia's, 13 children. Having inherited his father's gift for business, William doubled the family fortune. He also initiated the family's taste for grand homes with a 58-room mansion on Fifth Avenue that was billed as the largest private home in Manhattan.

When William Henry died in 1885, he left more than $10 million to his two eldest sons, Cornelius II and William K., and he bequeathed each of his eight children, including his youngest, George Washington, $10 million. George didn't share his brothers' mind for business. Bright, bookish, and quiet, he immersed himself instead in the classics and studied art and architecture. When his parents' Fifth Avenue house was being built, he was still a teenager living at home and was allowed to design his own suite—which included a library for his rapidly growing book collection.

Three years after the death of his father, George and his mother, Maria Louisa Kissam, visited Asheville, North Carolina, a favorite resort for America's elite, and stayed at the city's plush new Battery Park Hotel. As he stood on the hotel porch and looked out on the splendid Blue Ridge vista, George vowed to build his own home within sight of towering Mount Pisgah. Almost immediately he sent real estate agents to acquire land for him, and it wasn't long before George had laid claim to more than 126,000 acres, including the lush 100,000-acre Pisgah Forest.

A DIFFERENT DRUMMER

Vanderbilt called his North Carolina estate Biltmore, a combination of *Bildt*—a town in the Netherlands from which the Vanderbilt name derives—and *more,* an Old English word for high, open countryside. Having been inspired to create something extraordinary, George decided to model his home after the châteaus of the Loire Valley, in particular the 16th-century French castle Château de Blois. He wanted his new acreage to resemble one of the immense European baronies that had so impressed him on his travels. To help make his dream a reality, he retained the services of two influential American artists, architect Richard Morris Hunt and landscape designer Frederick Law Olmsted, both of whom were then in their sixties and at the height of their careers.

Richard Morris Hunt was perhaps the most fashionable architect of his day. In his twenties Hunt had studied in Europe and was the first American to complete his architectural studies at the École des Beaux-Arts in Paris. He had developed a taste

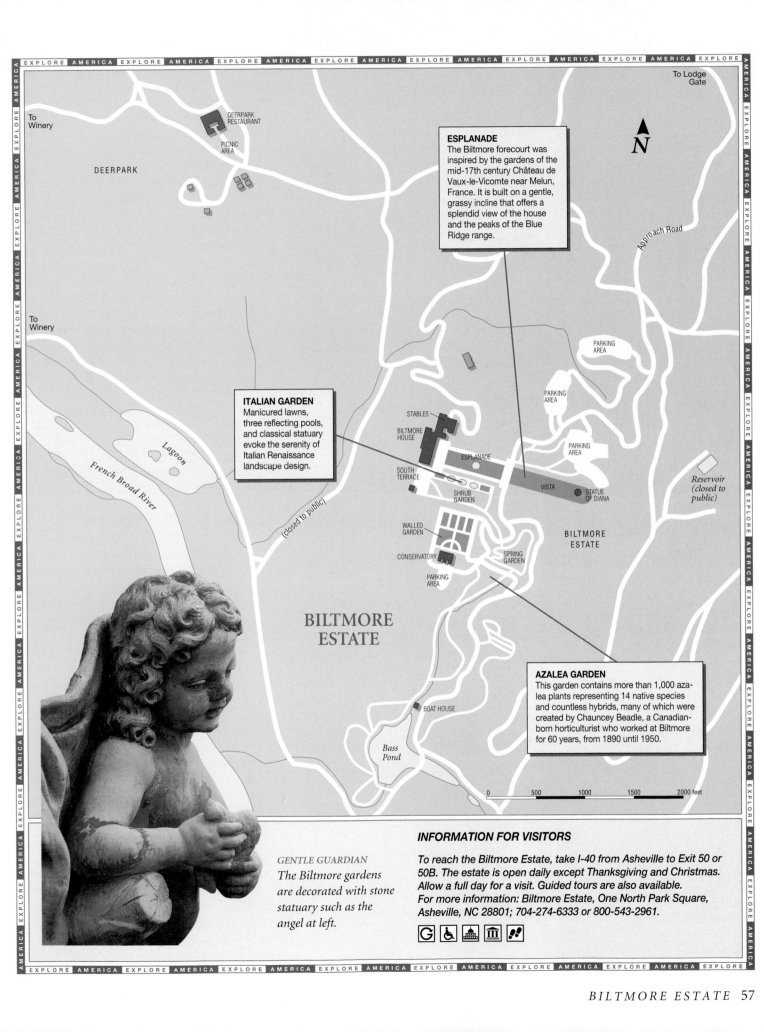

To Lodge
Gate

N

To
Winery

DEERPARK
RESTAURANT

PICNIC
AREA

DEERPARK

To
Winery

Approach Road

ESPLANADE
The Biltmore forecourt was
inspired by the gardens of the
mid-17th century Château de
Vaux-le-Vicomte near Melun,
France. It is built on a gentle,
grassy incline that offers a
splendid view of the house
and the peaks of the Blue
Ridge range.

PARKING
AREA

PARKING
AREA

ITALIAN GARDEN
Manicured lawns,
three reflecting pools,
and classical statuary
evoke the serenity of
Italian Renaissance
landscape design.

STABLES

BILTMORE
HOUSE

ESPLANADE

PARKING
AREA

Lagoon

French Broad River

SOUTH
TERRACE

VISTA

STATUE
OF DIANA

Reservoir
(closed to
public)

SHRUB
GARDEN

(closed to public)

WALLED
GARDEN

BILTMORE
ESTATE

CONSERVATORY

SPRING
GARDEN

PARKING
AREA

BILTMORE
ESTATE

AZALEA GARDEN
This garden contains more than 1,000 azalea plants representing 14 native species
and countless hybrids, many of which were
created by Chauncey Beadle, a Canadian-
born horticulturist who worked at Biltmore
for 60 years, from 1890 until 1950.

BOAT HOUSE

Bass
Pond

0   500   1000   1500   2000 feet

GENTLE GUARDIAN
The Biltmore gardens
are decorated with stone
statuary such as the
angel at left.

INFORMATION FOR VISITORS

To reach the Biltmore Estate, take I-40 from Asheville to Exit 50 or
50B. The estate is open daily except Thanksgiving and Christmas.
Allow a full day for a visit. Guided tours are also available.
For more information: Biltmore Estate, One North Park Square,
Asheville, NC 28801; 704-274-6333 or 800-543-2961.

ROYAL SUITE

The Louis XVI bedroom, above, exemplifies the 18th-century decor named after the last king of France. The style looks back to Greece and Rome and was all the rage after the 1748 excavations at Pompeii, Italy. The second-floor room is one of the Vanderbilts' 32 guest rooms.

SHADY BOWER

A wisteria-draped pergola, right, leads to terraces that look out on the Blue Ridge Mountains.

for French styles and had made his reputation with his châteaulike designs. By the time he began to work for George Vanderbilt, Hunt had numerous American landmarks to his credit, such as the pedestal for the Statue of Liberty and several palatial homes for America's merchant princes, including the New York residence of George's brother William K. Vanderbilt.

Vanderbilt's landscape designer, Frederick Law Olmsted, is considered by some experts to be the founding father of American landscape architecture. Between 1857 and 1861 he had acted as the chief designer of New York's Central Park, and from 1874 to 1891 Olmsted landscaped the grounds of the U.S. Capitol. He also designed many of America's major city parks, Montreal's Mont Royal Park, and the grounds of the World's Columbian Exposition in Chicago. At the Biltmore Estate, he would be responsible for transforming thousands of acres of overcut woodlands and exhausted subsistence farm properties into a planned landscape that would eventually include vast tracts of managed timberland.

Vanderbilt established a collaborative effort with both Hunt and Olmsted that would sustain them through the six long years of construction. In 1889 an estimated 1,000 construction workers and carpenters set to work under Hunt's supervision. Limestone was cut and shipped from Indiana, and marble was imported from Italy. A woodworking factory was constructed on the grounds to provide the lumber needed for flooring and paneling, and an on-site brick-making kiln turned out as many as 32,000 bricks a day—in the end it took more than 11 million bricks to complete the house.

LORD OF THE MANOR The impact of the estate on the surrounding neighborhood quickly became evident. To transport the materials and supplies needed for construction, three miles of railroad track were laid to the nearby village of Best, which Vanderbilt purchased in 1889 and renamed Biltmore Village. He provided generous support for his newfound community, building a school, hospital, church, and cottage-style housing outfitted with plumbing and central heating. Vanderbilt promoted the crafts of local mountain people by starting Biltmore Industries, a school that offered instruction in handicraft skills. He quickly became the region's single largest employer and he paid his staff and workers wages that were considered quite handsome for the day.

Biltmore's scale and modernity must have been staggering to the farmers around Asheville. In the 1890's most residents of North Carolina's Blue Ridge country lived on small farms and carried on

a way of life that was virtually unchanged since the days before the Civil War. A typical mountain farmer had never seen an electric refrigerator and still heated washtub water in a kettle on a woodstove. Most likely he had never even heard of an private swimming pool. Many of the rustic farmhouses continued to be lit by kerosene and heated by wood and coal for almost a half century until the New Deal's Rural Electrification Administration brought electricity to the region. Telephone service would extend to some of the region's mountain communities only in the 1950's, and even in the mid-1960's, many farms still lacked the luxury of indoor plumbing.

AWESOME SPECTACLE Although the Biltmore mansion has become a fixture of the Blue Ridge landscape, first sight of its enormous stone facade, decorated with lions' heads and gargoyles, continues to astound visitors. Some 90 rooms in the house are open to the public.

Visitors cross the threshold to the Entrance Hall, whose polished marble floors and towering limestone arches haven't changed at all since they welcomed Vanderbilt's guests in the 1890's. In Hunt's floor plan most of the first-floor rooms, including the Entrance Hall, the Banquet Hall, and the Bachelor's Wing, are grouped around an airy, glass-roofed indoor garden court known as the Winter Garden, a popular feature among the affluent set in the Victorian era. The indoor garden court provided an elegant spot for receptions and relaxed conversation. Biltmore's Winter Garden features bamboo and rattan furniture arranged around a

Most of the rich woodland, right, on the Biltmore Estate was planted as part of a land management program begun by Olmsted and developed by Gifford Pinchot, America's first professional forester. When Pinchot left Biltmore in 1895 to establish what would become the U.S. Forest Service, Dr. Carl Schenck, a forester from Germany, took over the care of the 100,000-acre timberland. Schenck stayed on until 1909.

PLANT NURSERY
Exotic plants such as desert succulents, bananas, and orchids still grow in the Conservatory, above.

central marble fountain adorned with a bronze sculpture of a boy and two geese by Karl Bitter, a widely admired Viennese sculptor of the period.

Bitter also carved a bas-relief sculpture that is mounted above the cavernous fire pits of the triple fireplace in the Banquet Hall. The Banquet Hall is worthy of a medieval king. Topped by a 70-foot-high ceiling, it stretches 72 feet in length and is 42 feet wide. So cavernous is the room that Hunt had to design custom-made furniture for it. The room's oak dining table seats 64 and is bordered by ornate oversized chairs. The walls are decorated with Flemish tapestries, ancient armor, flags and pennants, and mounted game trophies.

BACHELOR'S WING

During the first few years after the house was built, George lived alone in one of the wings and was attended by a staff of 80 servants. This Bachelor Wing includes a rambling L-shaped hall that leads to an outside entrance, smoking room, gun room, and—an essential retreat in any bachelor's pad—the billiard room. It was here beneath an ornate plasterwork ceiling and surrounded by dark oak-paneled walls decorated with art prints and trophy mounts that Vanderbilt and his male guests would shoot pool and billiards while they talked politics, business, hunting, and prize-fighting—topics that might have bored or shocked the well-bred Victorian lady. The women, for their part, would gather in the Salon, also off the Winter Garden, to talk and read, or perhaps stroll on the balcony and take in the view of the rolling North Carolina hills.

George's favorite room was the Baroque-inspired Library. The ceiling is painted with *The Chariot of Aurora*, a scene showing angels ushering in the dawn. It was produced by the early 18th-century Venetian artist Antonio Giovanni Pellegrini and originally belonged to the ballroom in Venice's Pisani Palace. The ceiling consists of 13 separate canvases and measures about 64 by 32 feet.

Approximately 10,000 volumes of Vanderbilt's beloved book collection are housed in the library today and arranged on two stories of walnut shelves that can be reached by an ornately carved circular staircase. Next to the black marble fireplace is a passageway that leads from the library to the guests' quarters, so that overnight visitors could easily retrieve one of the books for bedtime reading— although author Henry James, a guest in 1905, grumbled that he had to hike "a half mile" from his bedroom to fetch a book.

George ended his bachelorhood three years after Biltmore was completed. In June 1898 he married an affluent socialite named Edith Stuyvesant Dresser, a descendant of the governor of New

Amsterdam, Peter Stuyvesant. The newlyweds enjoyed an extended honeymoon in Europe, and then returned to Biltmore to live. Two years later, Edith gave birth to their only child, Cornelia, whose son William Cecil now maintains Biltmore as a self-sustaining private estate.

UPSTAIRS, DOWNSTAIRS

Biltmore's upper three stories were reached via the magnificent 102-step Grand Staircase; alternatively, visitors could take an Otis elevator Vanderbilt had installed. A 1,700-pound wrought-iron chandelier illuminates the stairwell. The stair tower that houses the Grand Staircase was modeled after one at the Château de Blois, although Biltmore's has been modified so that the stairs spiral upward in a different direction according to Hunt's own specifications.

The bedroom suites on the second and third floors—which bear such descriptive names as the Sheraton Room, Chippendale Room, and North Tower Room—encircled central sitting rooms where guests of both sexes could mingle freely without breaking the strict rules of etiquette that governed Victorian society. As was the fashion among their set, the Vanderbilts occupied separate bedrooms in living quarters on the second floor. They shared the Oak Sitting Room, modeled after the oak-paneled Jacobean design of the Great Hall at Hatfield House, a 17th-century English estate seen by Vanderbilt and Hunt in 1889.

George's bedroom is distinctly masculine in tone, featuring heavily carved and turned walnut furniture, deep ceiling moldings, and gold-glazed wall coverings. The room's southwest-facing windows look out on Mount Pisgah. Visitors especially like the round paw-footed bathtub in the adjoining bathroom, where a turn of the tap once produced water warmed by two coke-fired water heaters.

Edith Vanderbilt's oval-shaped bedroom, a light, feminine counterpart to George's, is preserved today just as it looked when she arrived at Biltmore after the honeymoon. Decorated in the French Louis XV style popular with wealthy Americans of the Victorian era, it features cut-velvet draperies, a marble fireplace, exquisitely decorated mirrors, and silk wall coverings. Edith's lilac-painted bathroom has no sink because it was customary for the maid to bring the lady of the house a basin of warm water, along with fresh towels, whenever she called

WINTER GARDEN
Cornelia Vanderbilt and John Cecil celebrated their wedding breakfast in the Winter Garden room, below. A marble fountain, adorned with a bronze figure of a boy with two geese, is surrounded with a profusion of exotic plants. The rattan and bamboo furniture was purchased by Mr. Vanderbilt in France.

BOOKISH GEORGE
The walnut-lined library, left, was looked after by George Vanderbilt's personal librarian, who was kept busy cataloging and maintaining its collection of 23,000 volumes. Vanderbilt could speak and read in eight languages, and his books reflect his wide range of interests in architecture, agriculture, art, science, and the classics.

for them. The bathtub does have the unusual feature of a shower, however, and visitors can still read the directions inscribed on its enameled faucet: "2 turns cold, 4 turns mixed, and 6 turns hot."

Some maids, including Edith's, slept on the second floor to be near their employers, while other maids and servants were housed in fourth-floor rooms. The rest of the staff lived in the basement, in rooms organized along separate corridors, according to the occupant's sex and stature in the rigidly observed servant hierarchy. On display here is a variety of servants' liveries, including the pink uniforms with white trim that maids were expected to wear during the day, and their evening attire, black uniforms with white collars and cuffs.

The Vanderbilt household went through an enormous quantity of food on a daily basis. A typical day's order included enough fresh fish from New York to feed 50 people, with the same amount of lobster shipped in twice a week. Perishables were stored in two walk-in refrigerators, which were cooled by a solution of chilled brine that circulated through pipes. Non-perishable food was stocked in pantries, which now are supplied with an array of authentic reproductions of popular canned goods of the time. Nearby are the Pastry Kitchen, the Rotisserie Kitchen, and the Main Kitchen, where the staff prepared 20-course dinners for the Vanderbilts and their guests. The meals were either

carried upstairs or sent in one of the two dumbwaiters that connected the kitchen pantry to the dining room. One dumbwaiter was operated manually, and the other was electric and could lift up to 250 pounds at 100 feet a minute.

As well as the staff and service rooms, the downstairs level holds Biltmore's recreational rooms, including a bowling alley; a 53-foot-long, 70,000-gallon swimming pool; and a gymnasium with parallel bars, a rowing machine, fencing set, Indian clubs, and medicine balls. Originally used as a storage area, the Halloween Room, whose walls were imaginatively painted by guests at a party in 1924, now serves to display exhibits on the history and collections of Biltmore.

DAZZLING PARKLAND

If anything can compete with Biltmore mansion, it is the surrounding estate, Olmsted's last project and his favorite. Vanderbilt had set aside some 250 acres for a pleasure park and gardens, including a shrub garden, walled garden, and azalea garden. To satisfy Hunt's taste for European grandeur, Olmsted designed formal French and Italian gardens in the vicinity of the house. But farther from the mansion the gardens become less formal until they are finally graded into natural woodland areas and pastures. Olmsted set up a commercial dairy and an ample

Vanderbilt's vision of turning Biltmore into a self-sustaining property was realized in his lifetime, and it has been carefully maintained by his heirs. During the Great Depression, Asheville city officials persuaded Cornelia and John Cecil to open Biltmore to the public, and since the 1970's, the estate has undergone extensive renovations under the direction of Cornelia's son William Vanderbilt. He has opened several more refurbished rooms to the public and has had the grounds upgraded. Every year, more than 800,000 visitors tour the halls and gardens of the Biltmore Estate—fascinated by this grand creation of the Gilded Age.

riverside nursery, which eventually held no fewer than 5 million plants. He oversaw the creation of extensive fruit and vegetable gardens along the bottomland of the adjacent French Broad and Swannanoa rivers, and perhaps his single greatest achievement was to persuade Vanderbilt to turn the estate's sprawling forest into a viable European-style commercial timberland. Once the depleted forest was replanted it yielded more than 3,000 cords of firewood a year and a vast harvest of lumber that was processed at an on-site sawmill. An institute called the Biltmore School of Forestry was established to train foresters for the estate. The school operated from 1898 to 1913 and had the distinction of developing America's first generation of conservationists and foresters.

LEGACY OF A DREAMER
George Vanderbilt's dream of a baronial estate ended on March 6, 1914, when he died of complications arising from an emergency appendectomy while in Washington, D.C. Edith continued to reside at Biltmore for 11 more years, but during that time she reduced the size of the estate by deeding 87,000 acres of woodland to the federal government for the Pisgah National Forest. She also divested some estate industries and sold Biltmore Village. In 1925 Edith married U.S. senator Peter Gerry of Rhode Island. Her daughter, Cornelia, married an Englishman, the Honorable John Cecil, a direct descendant of William Cecil, Lord Burghley, the lord high treasurer to Queen Elizabeth I.

NEARBY SITES & ATTRACTIONS

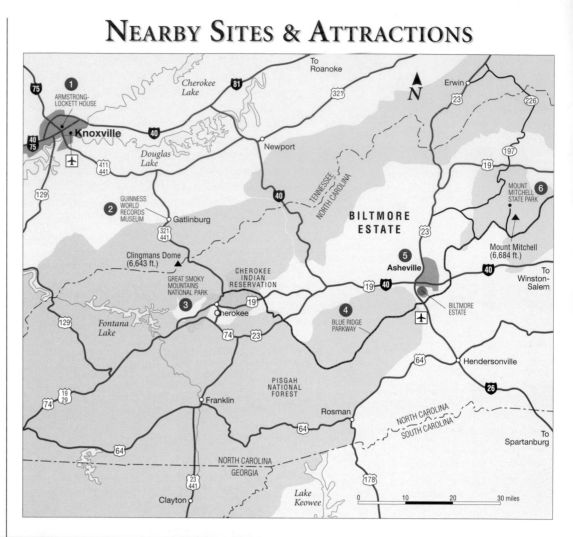

A thick fog engulfs the veranda at the Moses Cone Mansion, below, off the Blue Ridge Parkway. The 3,516-acre estate includes a craft center and 25 miles of carriage roads used by hikers in the summer and skiers in the winter.

1 ARMSTRONG-LOCKETT HOUSE, TENNESSEE

Built in 1834 by Drury Paine Armstrong, this house is one of the oldest continuously occupied residences in the region. Today the historic building features items from the Toms Collection of 18th-century American and European furniture and contains a wealth of decorative arts of the same period. The real showstopper of the restored home is an outstanding collection of English silverware dating from 1640 to 1820, including a massive 489-ounce silver candelabrum made in 1820 by London silversmith Paul Storr. Visitors to the Silver Room can also examine works by female silversmiths of the 18th and 19th centuries. Outside are terraced gardens with fountains. Located at 2728 Kingston Pike in Knoxville.

2 GUINNESS WORLD RECORDS MUSEUM, TENNESSEE

Featuring exhibits that range from the slightly odd to the truly bizarre, this museum is a showroom for the heaviest, lightest, fastest, slowest, tallest, and shortest humans and animals on earth. Ten galleries illustrate record-breaking events from under the sea to outer space and give visitors a glimpse of the protagonists behind the remarkable feats. One of the most fascinating exhibits pertains to the infamous water torture chamber from which Harry Houdini made so many escapes. The museum also contains a large collection of memorabilia, including authentic Beatles souvenirs and the original 1960's Batmobile. Located at 631 Parkway in Gatlinburg.

3 GREAT SMOKY MOUNTAINS NATIONAL PARK, NORTH CAROLINA/TENNESSEE

Almost equally divided between North Carolina and Tennessee, this park preserves one of the world's most extensive temperate deciduous forests. In all, almost 95 percent of the 800-square-mile park is covered by thick vegetation similar to that faced by the region's first pioneers, including 1,500 types of flowering plants, 2,000 varieties of fungi, and 230 types of lichens. Named for the mist-enshrouded Smoky Mountains that roll through the area, the park's forest cover changes according to elevation. At lower levels, stands of hemlock predominate, giving way at 4,500 feet to American beech and yellow birch. The ridge crest above 6,000 feet is the realm of spruce, fir and other conifer trees. Visitors can follow any of more than 800 hiking and horseback-riding trails across this lush wilderness, including a section of the Appalachian Trail that climbs to the top of 6,643-foot Clingmans Dome—the range's highest peak. A scenic road from Newfound Gap also leads to the top of the mountain. Although green is the park's primary color, spring wildflowers and autumn-tinged leaves add spectacular seasonal flourishes. The park is situated toward the southern end of the Blue Ridge Parkway, with entrances on Hwys. 441 and 321.

4 BLUE RIDGE PARKWAY, NORTH CAROLINA/ VIRGINIA

A 470-mile treasure of scenic splendor, the highway takes travelers along the crest of the Blue Ridge Mountains. On the way, the road dips and climbs between elevations of 600 and more than 6,000 feet, affording travelers spectacular vistas of rolling hills, fertile valleys, and rocky outcrops. Throughout spring and summer, splashes of colorful wildflowers brighten the roadside, enticing travelers to leave their cars for hikes through the many trails along the route. The highway has two terminuses: one in Cherokee near the border of Great Smoky Mountains National Park, North Carolina, and one in Rockfish Gap, Virginia.

5 ASHEVILLE, NORTH CAROLINA

The summer resort town of Asheville attracted the likes of Thomas Edison, George Vanderbilt, Henry Ford, and Theodore Roosevelt. The town preserves and features historical architecture that dates to the early 20th century. Asheville's City Hall is an Art Deco masterpiece in pink marble, brick, and terra-cotta, completed in 1928. The Queen Anne–style Thomas Wolfe House, where the novelist grew up, contains numerous family furnishings and memorabilia. Wolfe's first novel, *Look Homeward, Angel,* is said to reflect his hometown experiences. Located on Hwys. 40 and 26.

6 MOUNT MITCHELL STATE PARK, NORTH CAROLINA

North Carolina's first state park, established in 1915, is dominated by 6,684-foot-tall Mount Mitchell, the highest peak in the country east of the Mississippi River. Mount Mitchell's slopes are covered with thick stands of red spruce and Fraser fir. The 1,677-acre park is home to black bears, deer, and peregrine falcons. There are six hiking trails in the park, one of which climbs less than a half mile from the parking lot to the summit of Mount Mitchell and its stone observation tower. Beside the tower is the tomb of the reverend Elisha Mitchell, who, in 1847, was the first person to accurately measure the mountain's height. A small museum chronicles Mitchell's adventures. In 1857 a dispute between Mitchell and Thomas Clingman over the mountain's height inspired Mitchell to climb and measure the mountain a second time. On this attempt he fell to his death. The state named the mountain, and later the park, in his honor. Mount Mitchell State Park offers summer programs that include informative ranger-led walks. Located 33 miles northeast of Asheville via the Blue Ridge Parkway.

Spruce and fir trees compete for space atop Mount Mitchell, above, in Mount Mitchell State Park. A park observation tower provides views of the rugged Black Mountains.

The Methodist Church, below, nestles amid the autumn splendor around Cades Cove, in Great Smoky Mountains National Park.

SAN FRANCISCO PLANTATION

Restored to its 1850's splendor, this mansion displays a unique blend of Creole and Victorian styles.

Louise Von Seybold Marmillion got the first glimpse of her new Louisiana plantation home from the deck of a Mississippi riverboat in 1856. Rising three stories above the flat sugarcane-growing bottomland, where oaks spread their branches as if to welcome her, the newly constructed French Creole–style mansion was ablaze with light. The yellow glow of lard-oil lanterns spilled out across the beginnings of an ornamental garden that stretched down to the river. On each side of the house, dual cisterns—water towers of wood and stone topped by copper Oriental spires—were cast in soft silhouette.

The sight took Louise's breath away, tour guides tell visitors to the spectacular 140-year-old dwelling. "Oh, Valsin, what a wonderful way for your family to greet me," she is said to have uttered to her husband of only a few months.

Antoine Valsin Marmillion's father, Edmond, had been a highly successful sugarcane planter

whose great-grandfather had emigrated to the area from France in 1709, and Edmond had worked for more than three years on the construction of the estate that glowed in the subtropical night. San Francisco Plantation House was almost completed when Valsin arrived with his 20-year-old bride.

As the newlyweds disembarked from the boat that had brought them 40 miles upriver from New Orleans, they were invigorated by the song of insects and the pungent fragrance of the river, the fields, and blossoms. But their happiness was fleeting. The lanterns had been lit not as beacons for their arrival, but for the departure of Valsin's father, who had died only days before. In many ways the moment foreshadowed the tragedy and the joy that would be visited on the House of Marmillion.

The Marmillion family faced a series of setbacks in the coming years. Valsin's brother Charles, who fought for the Confederacy in the Civil War, was taken prisoner twice and then returned home in such poor health that he never quite mended. Only three of Louise's five children survived to adulthood. The mercurial Mississippi gnawed away at the grounds of the estate, shifted course, and sliced off the front garden. The plantation, which relied on the family-owned slaves to keep house and sugarcane business running smoothly and profitably, never recovered from the abolition of slavery at the end of the Civil War.

Valsin died suddenly in 1871 at the age of 42, and four years later, his brother Charles followed him to the grave at age 35. With little left to keep her in Louisiana, Louise sold the house and returned with her three daughters in 1879 to her native Germany.

TIME OF PROSPERITY

Before the Civil War, San Francisco Plantation House enjoyed a spectacular, if brief, period of prosperity. As the new master of the estate, Valsin remodeled and decorated it with flair—influenced in large measure by his wife. The ceilings in five rooms were painted in fresco fashion with intricate arrangements of roses and cherubs, and wood trim and fireplace mantels were painted to look as if they were fine-grained or marbled. Taffeta hangings, European carpets, and fine rosewood furniture bestowed the feel of luxury.

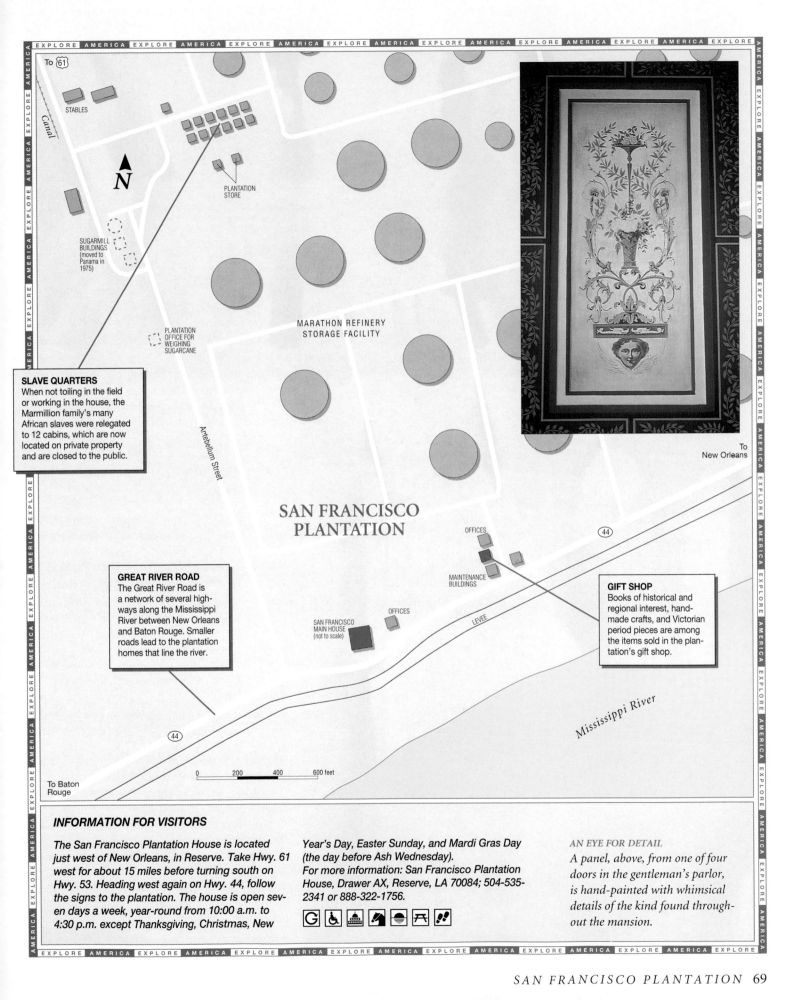

To (61)

STABLES

Canal

N

SUGARMILL
BUILDINGS
(moved to
Panama in
1975)

PLANTATION
STORE

PLANTATION
OFFICE FOR
WEIGHING
SUGARCANE

MARATHON REFINERY
STORAGE FACILITY

SLAVE QUARTERS
When not toiling in the field
or working in the house, the
Marmillion family's many
African slaves were relegated
to 12 cabins, which are now
located on private property
and are closed to the public.

To
New Orleans

Antebellum Street

**SAN FRANCISCO
PLANTATION**

OFFICES

(44)

GREAT RIVER ROAD
The Great River Road is
a network of several high-
ways along the Mississippi
River between New Orleans
and Baton Rouge. Smaller
roads lead to the plantation
homes that line the river.

MAINTENANCE
BUILDINGS

OFFICES

GIFT SHOP
Books of historical and
regional interest, hand-
made crafts, and Victorian
period pieces are among
the items sold in the plantation's gift shop.

SAN FRANCISCO
MAIN HOUSE
(not to scale)

LEVEE

Mississippi River

(44)

0   200   400   600 feet

To Baton
Rouge

INFORMATION FOR VISITORS

*The San Francisco Plantation House is located
just west of New Orleans, in Reserve. Take Hwy. 61
west for about 15 miles before turning south on
Hwy. 53. Heading west again on Hwy. 44, follow
the signs to the plantation. The house is open sev-
en days a week, year-round from 10:00 a.m. to
4:30 p.m. except Thanksgiving, Christmas, New*

*Year's Day, Easter Sunday, and Mardi Gras Day
(the day before Ash Wednesday).
For more information: San Francisco Plantation
House, Drawer AX, Reserve, LA 70084; 504-535-
2341 or 888-322-1756.*

AN EYE FOR DETAIL
A panel, above, from one of four
doors in the gentleman's parlor,
is hand-painted with whimsical
details of the kind found throughout the mansion.

EXPLORE AMERICA EXPLORE AMERICA EXPLORE AMERICA EXPLORE AMERICA EXPLORE AMERICA EXPLORE AMERICA EXPLORE AMERICA EXPLORE AMERICA EXPLORE

SAN FRANCISCO PLANTATION 69

LOUISIANA-STYLE OPULENCE
Few homes in the nation are as visually striking as San Francisco. The Empire-style ceiling, right, in the gentleman's parlor is ringed by fanciful hand-painted pictures of deer and heads crowned with flowery wreaths. Numerous layers of paint were removed during the mansion's restoration in the 1970's to get down to the original woodwork. The bedroom of a Marmillion daughter, below, has been restored to its mid-1800's appearance, complete with mosquito netting over the bed and baby's crib.

It was this spurt of redecorating activity that gave the plantation its name. Valsin is said to have told friends that that he had spent so much money on the house, he was *sans fruscins*—"without a penny to my name," in the contemporary Acadian French slang. Crop reports of 1860 list the plantation as St. Frusquin and by 1891, the documents identified it as San Francisco.

HEIGHT OF CREOLE STYLE

Even in a region that is rich with historic plantations, San Francisco stands out. There are other estates that are bigger (nearby Nottoway is the largest plantation in the South) or that have more elaborate landscaping (Oak Alley sits at the end of a majestic corridor of 28 live oaks). Some of these estates possess a more familiar history—for example, the Laura plantation, where folk tales told by Senegalese slaves became the *Br'er Rabbit* children's stories. But San Francisco is unique in that it offers a meticulously restored remnant of the Creole culture that flourished in the area during the century before the Louisiana Purchase of 1803.

Edmond Bozonier Marmillion acquired the plantation in 1830 from Elisée Rillieux, a free man of color who had patched together the property from smaller parcels of land. It is believed that one of the Mississippi River's frequent floods destroyed the first home, perhaps the flood of 1852. This was also the year that the eldest of the three Marmillion sons, Pierre, died at the age of 26, leaving his two unmarried brothers, Valsin and Charles, to tend the plantation. The next year Edmond Marmillion, his coffers enriched by a bumper crop of sugarcane, began building the unique mansion that would be his enduring legacy.

By 1853 Creole architectural decoration had fallen out of style, but Marmillion embraced it anyway. For example, he did not build corridors between rooms, preferring a layout that allowed rooms to open en suite to create larger rooms. He installed old-style 15-foot-high ceilings of tongue-and-groove cypress wood, rather than plaster, and fireplace mantels. The main rooms, including the foyer, parlors, bedrooms, and boudoirs, are all situated on the second level, and other rooms, such as the dining room, larder, and wine cellar, are on the ground floor—a typical Creole configuration. The attic was used for storage, but it served primarily as a ventilation chamber to draw cooling air into the house. The cisterns, each with a more than 8,500-gallon capacity, collected rainwater from the roof and returned it to the house through a system of lead pipes.

Edmond Marmillion deviated from Creole tradition in one notable respect. Commonly, homes in that style were constructed with the bedrooms situated at the front of the house. Guests entered the home through a bedroom, giving their reception a quality of genteel intimacy. At the San Francisco Plantation House, a grand entry room faced the front gallery. Parlors on either side, one for men and one for women, have massive doors that can be swung open to allow the three rooms to combine into one large ballroom for entertaining.

| ORNATE DECORATION |

Marmillion's design for San Francisco's exterior sharply deviates from the traditional Creole facade of trim, clean lines. Instead, he combined the ornate architectural touches common to Victorian tastes, such as the Corinthian-columned gallery that extends across the front and halfway down both sides of the second floor; the Bavarian-style blue louvered blinds that encircle the attic level; Gothic Revival dormers; and painted latticework and inlays.

The color scheme and imaginative blending of the styles give decorative expression to Louisiana's melding of cultures, and to the eccentric personal tastes of Edmond Marmillion. The exterior of the house presents a dazzling palette of peach-tinted walls, lime green columns and banisters, cerulean shutters, and yellow exterior star ornaments.

Some features of the house remind visitors that, while plantation life afforded many comforts, it also was not without its inconveniences. The gauze-like curtains that hang from the bed canopies and the glass flycatchers on the dining room table were weapons in the residents' never-ending war against insects before the advent of chemical repellents. Toilet facilities were out back, away from the house, and the elegantly attired ladies who attended galas

at the mansion had to be escorted to them by slaves when the need arose. The kitchen was also housed in a separate building to keep odors away from diners, lessen the chances of a fire spreading to the house, and minimize heat.

Visitors who tour the San Francisco Plantation House or pause to rest beneath the leafy canopy formed by the moss-covered live oaks and water oaks on the exterior grounds may not realize how close this magnificent home came to meeting its fate beneath the wrecking ball.

Louise Von Seybold Marmillion kept the plantation going for eight years after her husband's

THE GREEN ROOM
The gentleman's parlor, above, is named for its green curtains and mantel. The walls are painted a tobacco color. The room was one of the most difficult to restore because thick layers of paint had obliterated so much of the original stenciling.

site for their new refinery and, when they sold it to the Marathon Oil Company three years later, most of the land was set aside for the processing and storage of petroleum products.

HISTORIC DEBATE

The mansion and its shaded grounds were spared the ravages of industrialization, however, and in the mid-1970's the house was deeded to the San Francisco Plantation Foundation, which funded a painstaking restoration. Extensive research preceded the actual work. Numerous layers of paint were scraped away to the original colors, and the decorative ceilings, long since painted over, were scanned with a powerful light to detect the underlying designs so that an accurate replication could be made.

One of the two staircases leading to the second level was rebuilt. Many modern additions—such as an indoor kitchen and bathrooms—were removed, and heating and air-conditioning systems were reinstalled out of sight. Carpets, window hangings, and lanterns were replaced with ones that carefully matched the originals.

DESIGNED FOR ENTERTAINING
Typical of Creole floor plans, there are no hallways in the San Francisco Plantation House. Most of the rooms, such as the foyer, above, are separated by common doors, which could be removed to create a large ballroom for dancing.

death in 1871. According to the on-site historians, she had never intended to stay in Louisiana when she married Valsin. After he died, the burdens of running a large plantation by herself weighed more heavily each day and in 1879 Louise sold the property to Achille D. Bougère.

Bougère kept the plantation until 1905, when he sold it to the Ory family. When Bougère and his family moved, they took with them all the original furniture, including numerous rosewood pieces made in the style of the celebrated New York cabinetmaker John Henry Belter. Tragically, the furniture was destroyed by fire a few years later.

The Ory family owned San Francisco Plantation until 1973, but from 1952 on they rented it to Mrs. Clark Thompson, who was instrumental in restoring the house and opening it to the public. In 1973 the Energy Corporation of Louisiana bought the

The bottle racks and a drying table are all that remain of the original wine cellar. Other rooms in the house have been furnished with donated period pieces. A sleigh bed, invalid's recliner chair, wardrobe, and Beau Brummel washstand lend authenticity to Charles' bedroom. A rosewood bedroom suite was purchased for Valsin and Louise's sleeping quarters; a daybed, reading stand, and chaise lounge for the adjoining boudoir; a replica of an 1855 French Pleyel piano for the children's room; and an antique bronze and ormolu chandelier for the gentleman's parlor. An antique snooker table similar to one listed in old family inventories now sits in the rear room on the ground floor.

By the time the restoration was completed, the Marmillions would have felt right at home in San Francisco. Although the front garden is gone, as are most of the 2,500 acres of sugarcane, the mill, and the bathhouse, the house is little changed since

their day. Live oaks older than the plantation itself cast their shadows on the grounds. Large cast-iron cauldrons that were once used to boil sugarcane into syrup sit among the young cypresses, azaleas, sago palms, and magnolias.

This was the state of the San Francisco Plantation House that the descendants of Louise and Valsin were excited to find when they first visited Louisiana in 1981. The group held a family reunion in 1983 at a nearby plantation. Louise and Valsin's granddaughter, Gertrude, as well as her daughter, Yohanna, brought documents that had been found in their attic in Munich. Among the papers was Louise's passport for her return to Germany, which is on display in the 130-volume library and sitting room.

These few yellowed and tattered papers and photographs lend a face to the house of Marmillion and commemorate the times—at once glorious and wretched—of the family who created it.

DELICATE MAIDEN
A terra-cotta Grecian statue, left, perched on a marble pedestal, graces the mansion's entrance hall.

GRACIOUS LIVING
Louise Marmillion was especially fond of the light purple walls and hand-painted frieze in the upriver drawing room, left. The wooden fireplace mantel is painted to look as if it were made of blue marble.

NEARBY SITES & ATTRACTIONS

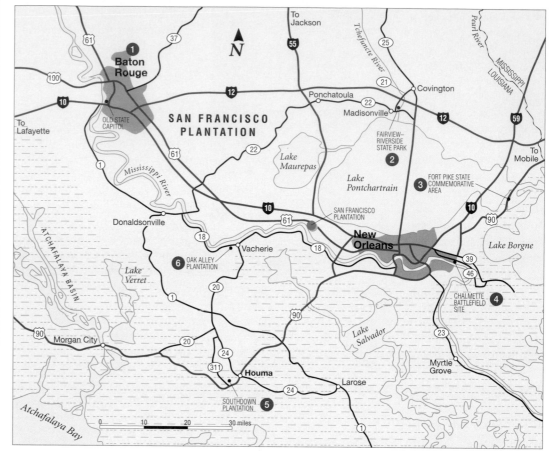

Light filters through the stained-glass dome of the Old State Capitol, below, in Baton Rouge. The building was designed by James Dakin, a New Orleans architect, and was completed in 1850. It was destroyed by fire 12 years later and rebuilt between 1880 and 1882.

1 BATON ROUGE

Seventeenth-century French mapmakers called this area Baton Rouge, or "Red Stick," after the pole that was smeared with animal blood and set in the ground to separate the hunting grounds of the native Houma and Bayougoula peoples. A busy port city, Baton Rouge has been the state capital of Louisiana since 1846. Among the many interesting sights here are the 1806 Beauregard Town, with its early 19th-century residences; and the Old Governor's Mansion, which was built during Huey Long's administration and is now furnished to reflect the life and times of the nine governors who occupied it. The Louisiana Arts and Science Center Riverside Museum features an art gallery, children's gallery, and Egyptian tomb exhibit. The crenellated exterior of the Old State Capitol is an excellent example of Gothic architecture. The building housed the state legislature until 1932, when the state capitol was constructed. There is an observation deck on the 27th floor that offers a panoramic view of Baton Rouge and the Mississippi River. Located on Interstates 12 and 10.

2 FAIRVIEW–RIVERSIDE STATE PARK

This 98-acre park runs parallel to the Tchefuncte River, which empties into Lake Pontchartrain. The park property once belonged to Frank Otis, a Louisiana lumber baron who bought the land in 1930 to be his summer residence. The estate was donated to the state in 1961. Tall moss-draped live oak trees line the river, which is stocked with channel catfish, bass, white perch, bream, bluegill, and speckled trout. Lake Pontchartrain is a popular spot for crabbing. The park offers picnic tables and barbecue pits by the riverside and 85 camping sites. Located one mile east of Madisonville off Hwy. 22.

3 FORT PIKE STATE COMMEMORATIVE AREA

Fort Pike is one of six masonry forts built in Louisiana during the 19th century as part of a coastal defense system designed to protect the United States from attacks by land and sea. Constructed between 1819 and 1826, the fort never had to fire its cannons in defense. Instead, it served as a staging area in the 1830's for troops setting off for Florida to fight in the Seminole Wars, and in the 1840's for soldiers en route to Texas and Mexico during the Mexican War. Confederate troops torched the fort when they withdrew in 1862 and it was burned a second time in 1887 during a fire that was started by natural causes. The wooden structure was destroyed, leaving behind the present brick shell. The fort was decommissioned three years later. Uniforms, maps, and cannons are on display in the fort museum, and visitors can tour the carefully restored soldiers' barracks. Located 19 miles north of New Orleans on Hwy. 90.

4 CHALMETTE BATTLEFIELD SITE

This historic park, a unit of the Jean Lafitte National Historical Park and Preserve, is the site of the last battle of the War of 1812, in which American forces led by Gen. Andrew Jackson delivered a crushing defeat to the British army. The objective of the British force of approximately 9,000 men, led by Gen. Edward Pakenham, was to capture the port city of New Orleans and cut off the Mississippi River supply route. Andrew Jackson was at the head of an army of some 5,400 men. The two forces first met south of New Orleans in early December 1814. After an inconclusive nighttime skirmish, the Americans withdrew to Chalmette Plantation, where they set up a strong defensive position. Twice the British attempted to dislodge the Americans from their positions and twice they failed. Finally, on January 8, 1815, Pakenham threw 5,900 troops against General Jackson's ranks. The British were mowed down in less than two hours at the cost of more than 1,200 lives. The Americans suffered 71 casualties. Visitors to the battlefield usually begin their tour at the park's visitor center, located near the Chalmette Monument. The center contains exhibits on the Battle of New Orleans and a small bookstore, and it presents a 30-minute video on the Battle of New Orleans. A nearby tower, called the Chalmette Monument, commemorates the battle. Its cornerstone was laid in 1840 on the 25th anniversary of the battle, but the monument was completed only in 1908. The British infantry positions were turned into the Chalmette Cemetery in 1864. Only one soldier who fought at Chalmette National Battlefield is buried here, the final resting place for many of the Union soldiers who died in Louisiana during the Civil War. The cemetery also contains the graves of soldiers who died in battles during the Spanish-American War, the two world wars, and the Vietnamese War. Located six miles southeast of New Orleans off Hwy. 46.

5 SOUTHDOWN PLANTATION

This Greek Revival plantation home was built for William Minor and completed in 1859. Minor's son, Henry Minor, added a second floor in 1893, transforming the house into a 21-room Queen Anne–style mansion. A plaque in the central hall lists the names and dates of all the descendants of William Minor who lived on the sugarcane plantation. Stained-glass windows depicting sugarcane, magnolias, and palmettos frame the main doorway. The Minor Room contains original bedroom furniture, including an antique shaving stand, an armoire, and a day-bed. The Ellender room is a re-creation of the Washington, D.C., office of Allen J. Ellender, who served the area as U.S. senator for 36 years. The room contains Ellender's office furniture, framed autographed photographs, and memorabilia. Located two miles west of Houma on Museum Dr. at the intersection of Hwy. 322 and St. Charles St.

6 OAK ALLEY PLANTATION

When Jacques Telesphore Roman built the Oak Alley Plantation home for his wife in the late 1830's, there were 28 mature oak trees that formed a quarter-mile alley from the site of the house north to the edge of the Mississippi River. The trees had been planted by a French settler more than 100 years earlier. Now the trees form a lovely natural canopy over the main walkway up to the Greek Revival house and are one of the primary attractions for the nearly 215,000 people who visit this plantation each year. The plantation was spared the torch during the Civil War and sold at auction in 1866. Then it passed through a succession of owners until 1925, when Josephine and Andrew Stewart rescued it from an advanced state of deterioration. The house has been restored to its antebellum appearance and is operated by a foundation set up by Mrs. Stewart before her death in 1972. The living room features mahogany chairs and a sofa upholstered in blue velvet arranged around an 1830's hand-stitched wool rug in the living room. The doors in several rooms have been treated with a process called faux-bois to simulate a mahogany wood grain. Hanging over the table in the dining room is a punkah, or "shoofly" fan, used to keep guests cool and chase away flies. An upstairs bedroom is set up to look as it might have on a typical morning in 1837, with a breakfast tray and clothing laid out on the hand-carved pineapple bed. Located one mile west of Vacherie on Hwy. 18.

Oak Alley Plantation, below, now a National Historic Landmark, was the first of the Great River Road plantations to be restored.

THE MOSS MANSION

This lovely Montana home evokes the spirit of a family that made its fortune on the frontier.

At "half after eight" on July 17, 1903, Mattie Moss welcomed 325 friends and neighbors to celebrate the completion of her palatial new home in Billings, Montana. It was the society event of the season. She greeted her guests in the Louis XVI French parlor, a resplendent room with rose silk damask wall coverings and white pine woodwork finished in ivory enamel. Every detail was done to perfection, and Mrs. Moss was dressed to the nines. According to the *Billings Gazette*, she wore a "lace robe of rich cluny and renaissance, combined over cream duchess satin, with a handsome chiffon drapery. The gown was decollette with elbow sleeves; and lace mits of the same material as the robe completed this exquisite toilette." As a final touch, she carried "a bouquet of pink carnations."

Mattie's sense of style is exhibited throughout this grand 35-room house, which was designed by Henry Janeway Hardenbergh of New York, one of the premier architects of early 20th-century America. A pioneer hotel builder, Hardenbergh

TURN-OF-THE CENTURY DOMICILE
The Billings Preservation Society has maintained the Moss Mansion, above, in its original turn-of-the-century state. At Christmas the society hosts a tree-decorating contest, and in May a country fair is set up on the grounds.

18TH-CENTURY GRANDEUR
Overleaf: The Louis XVI French parlor in the Moss Mansion was used for formal occasions only. The fireplace, which is fashioned of Algerian onyx, employs ruby-colored glass lit by electric bulbs to suggest a coal fire.

had designed the original Waldorf-Astoria Hotel in New York City and Washington, D.C.'s Willard Hotel by the time he was hired by Preston Boyd Moss, Mattie's husband, for their home.

Hailed as one of the finest homes ever built in the state, and certainly the most opulent Billings has to offer, the Moss Mansion stands as a reminder of the city's boomtown past. Billings was founded in 1882, the year the Northern Pacific Railroad was completed. The initial mainstays of the community were cattle and sheep ranching, but the town's site in the Yellowstone River valley soon drew homesteaders to farm the rich bottomlands. Some of the settlers were Russian-Germans who saw potential in the region's soil and climate for growing sugar beets. Before long, sugar beet farms began to spring up from Sidney to Laurel, 285 miles away, and now Montana is one of the nation's major sugar beet producing states. In the early 1900's, when Moss was on the lookout for promising business ventures, he too saw the value of sugar beets for the future of the community and he invested $650,000 in a $1 million sugar factory, which currently injects some $50 million each year into the Billings economy.

AMERICAN DREAMER

Moss was always actively seeking a variety of good business opportunities—that was what had attracted him to Billings in the first place. Preston Boyd, known as P.B., was born in Paris, Missouri, to a prosperous middle-class family. He attended Harvard briefly and stud-

ied business at a college in upstate New York before returning to Paris, where he worked first with his father at the local bank, and then in his own lumber business. Moss was an ambitious man with a strong imaginative bent. In 1892 he caught wind of various opportunities opening up in the Montana frontier town of Billings, and wasted little time moving Mattie and their son, Woodson, and daughter, Kula, to the bustling community of some 2,000 inhabitants. The 29-year-old entrepreneur soon bought into the First National Bank and over the next 30 years or so invested in other local businesses, started a newspaper, and built the Northern Hotel, which still offers lodging today. One of Moss' greatest ambitions was to build a model city about 10 miles from Billings, which he dubbed Mossmain. The city's site—at the junction of three railroads— was selected in the hope that it would become the greatest shipping center in all of the Northwest. Moss went so far as to hire city planner Walter Burley Griffin for the job. Griffin, who had studied with Frank Lloyd Wright, would begin designing Australia's federal capital, Canberra, in 1912. The railroad junction never materialized, and P.B.'s dream town was not built.

Moss did oversee the completion of his dream house, however, a project that took two years and $105,000 to build and was finished in 1903. This was a great deal of money at a time when, according to the *Ladies Home Journal* of that year, the average home cost about $3,000.

By hiring a nationally recognized architect to design the mansion, P.B. was getting the best that money could buy. The innovative Hardenbergh drew inspiration from disparate styles and eras. For the Moss Mansion, Hardenbergh incorporated architectural features and motifs from different periods and places that ranged from the ancient Near East and pre–Revolutionary France to contemporary Art Nouveau. The imposing exterior of the house was built of massive red blocks of Lake Superior sandstone that were shipped to Montana by rail, and the mansard roof was shingled with red clay Conosera tiles from New York State. A reporter for the *Billings Gazette* described the effect as one of "stern simplicity," adding "it combines classic purity of outline with reticent refinement." The severity of the exterior is offset by the rich colors and luxurious fabrics of the interior.

Visitors enter the house through a vestibule with a marble mosaic floor and mahogany-stained wainscoting that create a somewhat somber ambience. But the mood changes as they walk into the entrance hall under the exotic Arabic-style arches that are carved and painted with flowers, leaves, and vines. Similar Moorish patterns decorate the doors off the hall. Kelim runners have been used

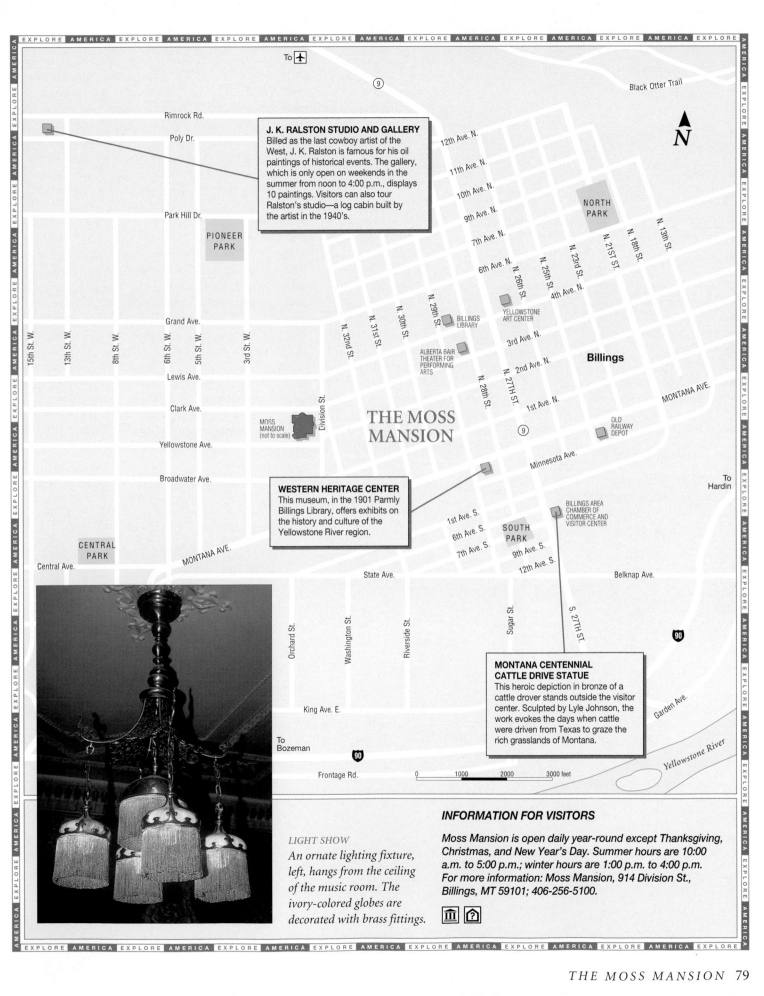

J. K. RALSTON STUDIO AND GALLERY
Billed as the last cowboy artist of the West, J. K. Ralston is famous for his oil paintings of historical events. The gallery, which is only open on weekends in the summer from noon to 4:00 p.m., displays 10 paintings. Visitors can also tour Ralston's studio—a log cabin built by the artist in the 1940's.

WESTERN HERITAGE CENTER
This museum, in the 1901 Parmly Billings Library, offers exhibits on the history and culture of the Yellowstone River region.

MONTANA CENTENNIAL CATTLE DRIVE STATUE
This heroic depiction in bronze of a cattle drover stands outside the visitor center. Sculpted by Lyle Johnson, the work evokes the days when cattle were driven from Texas to graze the rich grasslands of Montana.

THE MOSS MANSION

Billings

LIGHT SHOW
An ornate lighting fixture, left, hangs from the ceiling of the music room. The ivory-colored globes are decorated with brass fittings.

INFORMATION FOR VISITORS

Moss Mansion is open daily year-round except Thanksgiving, Christmas, and New Year's Day. Summer hours are 10:00 a.m. to 5:00 p.m.; winter hours are 1:00 p.m. to 4:00 p.m. For more information: Moss Mansion, 914 Division St., Billings, MT 59101; 406-256-5100.

as draperies, and the ceiling's plasterwork creates a domelike effect. The light fixture also is Moorish in design, featuring a ruby red glass globe inside a wrought-iron cage from which hangs a crescent moon. One feature of the entrance hall is definitely more Montana than Moorish: ever the gracious host, P.B. had the closets heated by hot-water pipes so that his wintertime guests would exit to the cold outdoors in warmed coats.

LOUIS XVI REVIVAL STYLE

The Moorish theme is abandoned in favor of late 18th-century France in the house's most formal room, the French parlor. The large 33-foot-long room is divided by two Corinthian columns and furnished with several Louis XVI Revival–style pieces, including a settee and a couple of armchairs upholstered in Gobelin tapestry. Gold leaf highlights the mirror frame, as well as wall moldings, wainscoting, columns, and the arms and legs of the furniture. Bowknots and laurel wreaths—symbols of the ill-fated Louis and his queen, Marie Antoinette—decorate portieres, light fixtures, and furniture, as well as the Aubusson carpets, which were custom-made in France at a cost of $32 a yard.

The carpets were secured to the floor with snaps to prevent anyone from tripping or slipping on them. The drapes, also custom designed in France, are made of ivory-colored Ottoman silk and velvet panels and display a rose motif.

The furnishings benefited considerably from Mattie's keen artistic sense and training. She had received a college education—an uncommon advantage for a woman at that time—and had also studied art and music in St. Louis, Missouri, before marrying P.B. at the age of 25. Several of her still lifes and landscapes, painted in oils, are exhibited on the walls of her home today.

Mattie was involved at every stage of the work done by the W. P. Nelson Company, an upscale interior design firm from Chicago. In the months leading up to her housewarming, she searched far and wide for furnishings, often traveling East for particular items. On one of her trips, Mattie wrote to P.B. that she had bought "the swellest dresser in all of Chicago." The mahogany piece now stands in the master bedroom. The year 1903 was a busy one for Mrs. Moss. Besides furnishing her house, the 39-year-old mother of five gave birth to her sixth child, Virginia, on Valentine's Day, and joined the Christian Science Church in June.

GRAND ENTRANCE
The elaborate Moorish entrance-way, below, was inspired by a design in the Alhambra, the 14th-century royal palace in Granada, Spain. Beyond the arches is the main hall, which also served as a music room. The room is carpeted with Serebent rugs from southeastern Persia. The stairs lead to a landing with a window seat that was used by musicians when they played for parties. The Moss children sometimes assembled here to watch the downstairs festivities.

The endeavors of Mattie and the W. P. Nelson Company were written about in the *Architects' and Builders' Magazine* in June 1904, which stated, "the interior has been handled with the utmost care that an exquisite taste would suggest, and no efforts or money have been spared to make its artistic development all that could be demanded." Preston Boyd himself was so pleased with the results that he hired a photographer to take pictures of each room. These photographs, displayed throughout the house, show how faithful the interior renovation is to the original 1903 decor.

A MUSEUM OPENS ITS DOORS

In 1986 the historic house was taken over by the Billings Preservation Society—two years after the death of Melville Moss, the third of Mattie and P.B.'s six children. Melville was the last member of the family to live in the house and photographs exhibited there show how much she resembled her mother. Both Mattie and Melville were musical, as was Kula, and the two girls often played piano and harp together in the music room. The ceiling in this room is decorated with Islamic designs and the floor is covered with a rare Garovan rug from northern Persia. Blue silk velour wall coverings appear above red birch wainscoting, which has been stained to resemble a rich mahogany color. Volunteer performers sometimes play period music on a 1909 Steinway piano during tours of the house.

Music would often filter from here into the library, P. B. Moss' favorite room in the house. The library's bookcases run the full length of the room's back wall behind the large desk. Leaded-glass doors open to shelves lined with the family's collection of volumes—novels by Sir Walter Scott and Victor Hugo, as well as reference sets, including the *Twentieth Century Cyclopedia and Dictionary*. Three windows decorated with stained glass line the wall behind the bookcase and let in natural light; a likeness of William Shakespeare is painted on the middle window; the other two windows display the fleur-de-lis motif. The room's curly birch wainscoting and a beamed ceiling create a somewhat sober Victorian atmosphere. Paintings by Mrs. Moss, of Yellowstone Falls and of Hagar and Ishmael in the wilderness, adorn the walls. Giving the room a personal touch is Mattie's collection of Salish Indian baskets, which is displayed along the top of the bookcases.

GREENERY INSIDE AND OUT
No prosperous turn-of-the-century home was considered complete without a greenhouse filled with both exotic and native plants. The Moss family's small glass-enclosed conservatory, left, was an indoor oasis of greenery.

THE PINK ROOM
Melville and Kula's bedroom, below, located on the second floor, is decorated with hand-painted canvas-covered walls and a wallpaper border of pink roses.

The Moss Mansion was built at the western end of Billings, right, which was the fashionable part of town at the turn of the century.

A DESK FOR TWO

The library's leather-topped, partners desk, below, is equipped with drawers on both sides and enough surface space for two to work facing each other and still have ample knee and elbow room.

ART NOUVEAU

A gift shop operated by the Billings Preservation Society now occupies the family sitting room, which is located just off the music room. The birch woodwork in this south-facing room has a light, natural finish. Art Nouveau–style plant designs stenciled in gold paint decorate the burnt orange walls and a floral pattern is embroidered on the portieres. On the wall hangs a portrait of P. B. Moss, painted when he was 78 years old. The portraitist, LeRoy Greene, is well known locally for depicting the founding fathers of Billings.

The house's hot-water heating was supplemented during Montana's bitterly cold winters by warmth from five fireplaces in the house. A sixth fireplace in the French parlor was for decorative purposes only. A handsome molded fireplace with a bronze firebox and green-gray oxidized luster tiles adorns the sitting room. The room opens onto a spacious veranda and a conservatory with a glass dome at one end of it. The conservatory is filled with geraniums and ferns, and Mattie spent many pleasurable hours here. The sitting room was wired for a wall telephone, and a series of electric call buttons were used to summon the Swedish housekeeper and cook from their quarters on the third floor and the groundskeeper from his room in the carriage house, situated behind the main house.

The Mosses dined nightly in the oak-paneled dining room, which bears a marked resemblance to the Oak Room in New York's Plaza Hotel, also designed by Hardenbergh and completed four years after the Moss Mansion. An elaborate Second Empire lamp, topped by a lion holding a shield decorated with the fleur-de-lis, is suspended from the ceiling, a massive built-in sideboard and china cabinet runs along the back wall, and woven tapestries hang on the other walls, giving the room the look of an English manor. Within the formal setting, however, the Moss family dined as they liked, sometimes ordering their cook to prepare their favorite treat—baking powder biscuits—for all three meals of the day!

While work on the dining room and the other first floor rooms was still progressing in 1902, the Mosses moved onto the second floor. The floor's six bedrooms and large family bathroom are organized around a sizable central hall, called the billiard room, although a billiard table was never set up here. Its ceiling is decorated with a Moorish design of interwoven flowers and leaves, a motif that mimics the entrance hall theme. Attractive tile work in the family bathroom shows off the area's most interesting feature—a circular shower, the very latest in early 20th-century bathing amenities. It is equipped with faucets and temperature controls.

Moss once recollected that he was 30 years old before he enjoyed the luxury of drawing water from a faucet, and 35 before he ever saw a bathtub.

Each of the six bedrooms has its own dressing room equipped with a marble-topped sink and an electric warmer for the curling irons of the day. Mattie and P.B.'s three boys slept in a blue bedroom, and Kula and Melville shared a bedroom decorated entirely in pink, right down to the tile work on the fireplace. The nursery, which is connected to the master bedroom through a curtained doorway, once belonged to Virginia, who died of diphtheria at the age of five.

THREE-GENERATION HOUSE

Mattie's parents, "Captain" George and Iantha Woodson, slept in the large sunny bedroom across the hall. Captain Woodson was the master of the covered wagon train that took the Woodsons from Paris, Missouri, to Amity, Oregon, in 1865 when Mattie was about 18 months old. After Mattie's marriage to P.B., the Woodsons moved in with the newlyweds and lived in the house until their deaths. A delicate frieze of wisteria blossoms decorates their cheerful room.

Moss once said, "I belong to the horse and buggy age, spring and lumber wagons and two-wheel horse carts." While he was the second person in Billings to buy a car—the dealer was the first—he never quite got the hang of it. On one occasion P.B. ran the vehicle through the garage door; another time he rammed into a lamppost, trying to brake. On the other hand, Mattie—who was nicknamed "Fun" by her children—became the first woman in Billings ever to drive an automobile and reportedly she got to be quite good at it.

The Mosses, who lived into their eighties, were devoted to each other. Both born in 1863, two years before the end of the Civil War, they witnessed two world wars and the Great Depression. No doubt they dreamed that their fabulous house would be home to generations of Mosses—but that was not to be. One by one their sons grew up and left home. Kula was married in the French parlor and moved away. Melville, who never married, lived alone in the mansion after her parents' death, teaching music and treating herself to an occasional boat cruise. She loved her childhood home and took great care of it. As visitors tour the house today they gain the sense of security and well-being felt by the Moss family in boomtown Billings.

THE OAK ROOM
A carved oak fireplace with ruby-finished tiles heats the dining room, above. A built-in sideboard and china cabinet topped by ferns, dominate the west wall, and the windows look into the conservatory.

NEARBY SITES & ATTRACTIONS

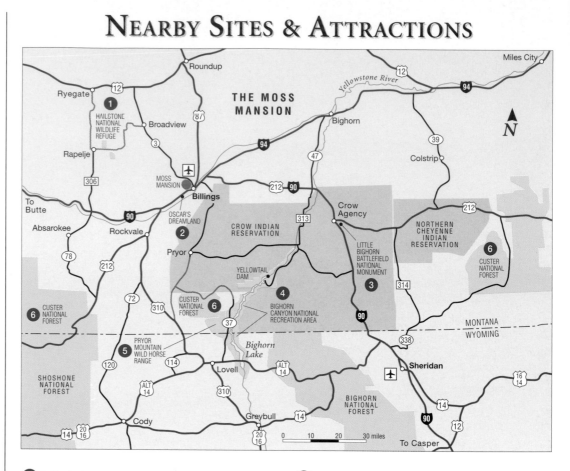

An antique steam tractor stands guard over the grave of Oscar Oliver Cooke, below, who founded Oscar's Dreamland in 1968. The site has exhibits ranging from a windmill to the world's largest rotating clock, which has two faces. The clock is 64 feet in height and weighs 17 tons.

1 HAILSTONE NATIONAL WILDLIFE REFUGE, MONTANA

This 1,988-acre wetland refuge was established in 1942 as a breeding ground for migratory birds, including eared grebes, American avocets, and wigeons. A nearby prairie dog colony also attracts raptors, which are often seen circling overhead, scanning the area for a meal. Hailstone Basin is also famous as the site of an 1885 gun battle fought by area ranchers and Crow warriors against some Piegan warriors who had stolen their horses. Located five miles east of Rapelje off Hwy. 306.

2 OSCAR'S DREAMLAND, MONTANA

This assemblage of antique farm machinery—which includes more than 500 steam and gasoline tractors, plus cars and horse-drawn vehicles—also exhibits turn-of-the-century buildings rescued from various parts of Montana. The museum was founded in 1968 as the culmination of the lifelong dream of Oscar Cooke, an avid collector, pilot, businessman, and farmer who wanted to pay tribute to the lives of early American farmers. A highlight of the museum is the 1906 Best steam engine, which is more than 18 feet tall. It was once used to help extract silver and nickel from mines in the mountains of Utah. The museum also displays a steam-powered saw, a wooden oil-well rig, covered wagons, more than 100 threshers, and a Corlis steam engine that weighs 120 tons. The restored early 1900's town includes a barber shop, railroad station, and a jail. Located three miles southwest of Billings on Hwy. 90.

3 LITTLE BIGHORN BATTLEFIELD NATIONAL MONUMENT, MONTANA

This park preserves the site where Lt. Col. George Armstrong Custer's U.S. 7th Cavalry was wiped out by Lakota and Cheyenne warriors on June 25, 1876. The battle, known as Custer's Last Stand, was one of the largest setbacks suffered by the U.S. Army in the Indian Wars. In an effort to punish a large band of Lakota and Cheyenne for refusing to report to the Great Sioux Reservation, Custer and some 600 men attacked a massive Indian village that included several thousand warriors. The Indians surrounded

Rain clouds cast dark shadows over the rolling hills and towering pines in Bighorn Canyon National Recreation Area, left. The park was established in 1966 to protect the area's unique wildlife and topography.

Custer's detachment and killed 210 U.S. Army soldiers, including Custer himself. The park's visitor center tells the story of the battle through documentary films, dioramas, photographs, maps, and battlefield artifacts. There are exhibits on Plains Indian culture, and a buckskin suit once owned by the flamboyant Custer is on display. A simple stone monument at the summit of Custer Hill lists the names of all the soldiers who died that day and white tombstones scattered over the hillside mark the spots where each man fell. Located one mile south of Crow Agency off Hwy. 90.

4 BIGHORN CANYON NATIONAL RECREATION AREA, MONTANA/WYOMING

The centerpiece of this 120,000-acre recreation area is 71-mile-long Bighorn Lake, created in 1966 when the Yellowtail Dam tamed the surging Bighorn River. Before the 525-foot-high dam was built, the river was considered unnavigable. Today the lake attracts swimmers, boaters, water-skiers, anglers, and scuba divers. Ancient footpaths once used by the Crow, Lakota, and Cheyenne run along the edge of the canyons that flank the lower section of Bighorn Lake. The Bad Pass Trail takes visitors to archeological finds that date back 10,000 years. The 1883 Mason-Lovell Ranch is open to the public. The restored structures on this successful open-range operation include a bunkhouse, a blacksmith's shop, and a cabin used as quarters for married couples. The recreation area is also home to a variety of animals, including coyotes, bighorn sheep, mountain lions, wild horses, deer, and black bears, as well as more than 200 species of birds. During the spring and summer months, visitors to the region can enjoy the sight of some 200 varieties of wildflowers in bloom. Located on Hwys. 37 and 313.

5 PRYOR MOUNTAIN WILD HORSE RANGE, MONTANA

Given free reign over some 38,000 acres of East Pryor Mountain's south slope, several bands of wild horses have enjoyed the protection of this range since it was officially designated in 1968. The rugged slopes, steep-walled canyons, and grassy plateaus overlooking Bighorn Basin make an ideal environment for these sturdy animals—whose numbers are maintained at around 120 to preserve an ecological balance. No one is sure how the horses got here: some experts believe they are descended from horses brought to North America by Spanish explorers; others say their ancestors were released by destitute Depression-era ranchers. The horses usually travel in herds of 4 or 5, but sometimes number as many as 10. In the spring visitors may be lucky enough to watch as foals are born or see young stallions challenging each other for herd dominance. Located 30 miles north of Lovell off Hwy. 37.

6 CUSTER NATIONAL FOREST, MONTANA/ SOUTH DAKOTA

The scenery in this forest of more than 1 million acres ranges from the grasslands of North and South Dakota to the towering peaks of the Absaroka-Beartooth Wilderness in Montana. The forest encompasses waterfalls, glaciers, and some 300 alpine lakes. Among its notable natural features are the mile-long Grasshopper Glacier, named for the millions of grasshoppers frozen inside of it; Montana's highest point, the 12,799-foot-tall Granite Peak; and the pink snow, which gets its color from microscopic plant life on the surface. Sections of the scenic Beartooth Highway have been carved through these mountains. Located on Hwys. 212 and 89.

Red limestone formations, below, add a warm hue to the dry south slope of Pryor Mountain. Wild horses share this landscape with bears, elk, and bighorn sheep.

TALIESIN WEST

Architect Frank Lloyd Wright's home and apprentice studio in Arizona embodies his genius.

The road to Taliesin West crawls up a hill studded with low shrubs and cacti. Wooden roof beams that slice across the brilliant blue sky give the first hint that a man-made structure lies at the top. Canted rock walls appear to grow out of the ground, and a low-slung profile in stone, wood, and glass blends in perfectly with the desert surroundings. The understated exterior of the main house masks its true proportions. But visitors who explore the winter home and apprentice workshop built by American architect Frank Lloyd Wright will discover a variety of details and features that awaken the senses and engage the intellect—again and again. As one guide at Taliesin West puts it, "You interact with a Frank Lloyd Wright home whether you want to or not."

Taliesin West, set in the rocky, arid foothills of Arizona's McDowell Mountains, comprises 45,000 square feet of buildings, walkways, terraces, and courtyards, surrounded by nearly 600 acres of desert. Once the residence of Frank Lloyd Wright, his third wife, Olgivanna, and his coterie of

A carved wooden panel, right, adorns the inside of the main door to the Cabaret Theater. The theater houses a collection of artworks from Asia. The door also has elaborate brass handles.

HARMONIOUS INTENT

Overleaf: Taliesin West's stone masonry walls, reflected in the triangular pool, resemble out-croppings of the foothills of the McDowell Mountains, which rise behind them.

DESERT MASONRY

At the core of Taliesin West lies an enormous drafting studio for apprentices, right, which, like most of the other buildings on the site, was built with rock-and-concrete masonry. The 96-by-30-foot struc-ture was the first building erected here. The studio is used today by students at the Frank Lloyd Wright School of Architecture. Wright found the large boulders covered with petroglyphs (at the left side of the picture) in the desert and had them moved onto the terraces and courts of the compound.

apprentices, the compound is now occupied by architects and students who follow the basic principles of the master architect.

Frank Lloyd Wright did not begin to build his home in the Sonoran Desert until 1937, when he was 70 years old. He had been to Arizona a decade earlier to consult on the design of the ele-gant Arizona Biltmore Hotel, and he returned in 1928 to design San Marcos in the Desert, a hotel that was never built. On that excur-sion, Wright, who was always hard-pressed for funds, decided to save money on hotel bills by setting up a tent camp in the desert. He named the camp Ocatilla, after the ocotillo, an eye-catching native plant. The Arizona desert captivated Wright, taking second place in his heart only to the green forests of his native Wisconsin. He wrote of this arid land: "We have met the desert, loved it and lived with it, and the desert is ours."

ARIZONA CURE

Eight years later, when he was suffering from a bout of pneu-monia, Wright returned to the desert in the hope that its dry air might help speed his recovery. Olgivanna Hinzenberg, whom he had married in 1928, went with him, and they purchased a plot of land on Maricopa Mesa in the McDowell Mountains, more than 20 miles outside the then small city of Phoenix.

It was on this rocky piece of real estate that the master architect would endeavor to construct Taliesin West.

Taliesin, which is pronounced tally ehssen, means "Shining Brow" in Welsh. Wright first gave the name to his home in Spring Green, Wisconsin, which he began constructing in 1911 on the side, or brow, of a hill. The house, now called Taliesin East, was intended to be a sanc-tuary for Wright and his mis-tress, Mamah Cheney, for whom he left his first wife, Catherine. Mamah Cheney and Wright set-tled at Taliesin East, but, tragically, while Wright was on a trip to Chicago in 1914, a deranged ser-vant murdered Mamah, her two children, and four guests, and set fire to the house. The murders dev-astated the 47-year-old Wright.

It took years for Wright to recover from his per-sonal trauma, and only his work, he later claimed, allowed him to survive. In the last decades of his life, Wright went on to design some of his greatest struc-tures, among them Fallingwater, a private residence in Pennsylvania that is cantilevered over a waterfall; numerous low-cost homes scattered all over the United States that Wright called his Usonian hous-es; and Taliesin West.

Like the earlier Ocatilla, Taliesin West began life as an open-air desert tent camp. Having decided in 1937 that the Sonoran Desert was the ideal place

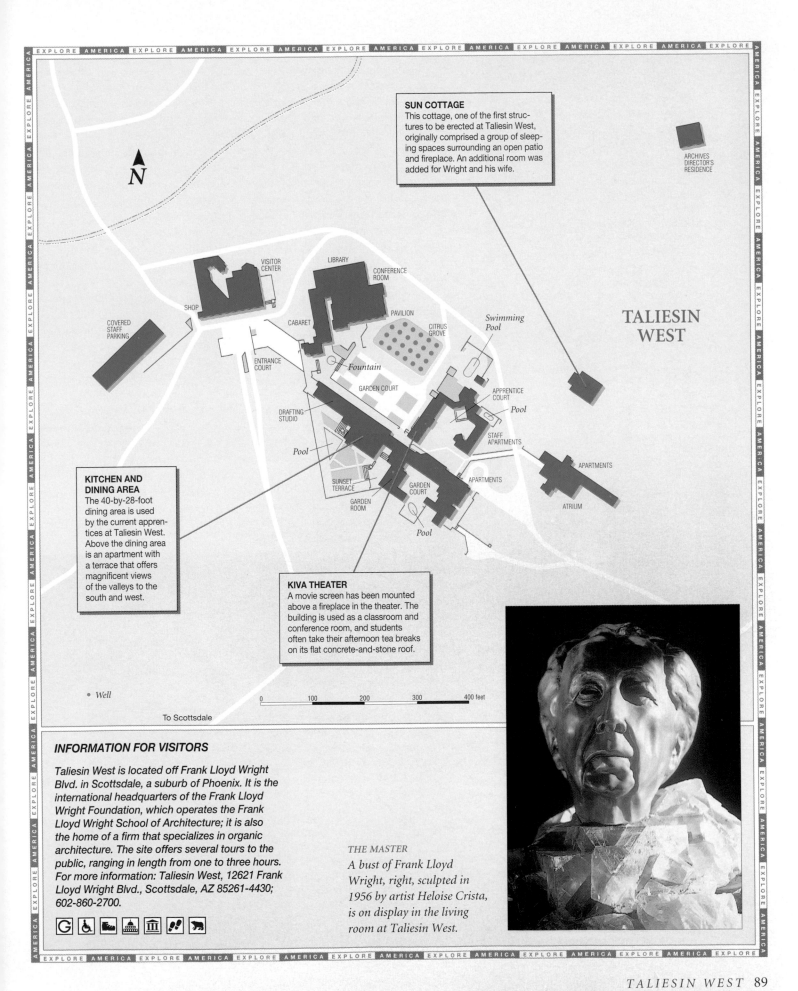

SUN COTTAGE
This cottage, one of the first structures to be erected at Taliesin West, originally comprised a group of sleeping spaces surrounding an open patio and fireplace. An additional room was added for Wright and his wife.

ARCHIVES DIRECTOR'S RESIDENCE

TALIESIN WEST

N

VISITOR CENTER

LIBRARY

CONFERENCE ROOM

SHOP

PAVILION

COVERED STAFF PARKING

CABARET

CITRUS GROVE

Swimming Pool

ENTRANCE COURT

Fountain

GARDEN COURT

APPRENTICE COURT

Pool

DRAFTING STUDIO

Pool

STAFF APARTMENTS

APARTMENTS

SUNSET TERRACE

GARDEN COURT

APARTMENTS

ATRIUM

GARDEN ROOM

Pool

KITCHEN AND DINING AREA
The 40-by-28-foot dining area is used by the current apprentices at Taliesin West. Above the dining area is an apartment with a terrace that offers magnificent views of the valleys to the south and west.

KIVA THEATER
A movie screen has been mounted above a fireplace in the theater. The building is used as a classroom and conference room, and students often take their afternoon tea breaks on its flat concrete-and-stone roof.

• Well

0   100   200   300   400 feet

To Scottsdale

INFORMATION FOR VISITORS

Taliesin West is located off Frank Lloyd Wright Blvd. in Scottsdale, a suburb of Phoenix. It is the international headquarters of the Frank Lloyd Wright Foundation, which operates the Frank Lloyd Wright School of Architecture; it is also the home of a firm that specializes in organic architecture. The site offers several tours to the public, ranging in length from one to three hours. For more information: Taliesin West, 12621 Frank Lloyd Wright Blvd., Scottsdale, AZ 85261-4430; 602-860-2700.

THE MASTER
A bust of Frank Lloyd Wright, right, sculpted in 1956 by artist Heloise Crista, is on display in the living room at Taliesin West.

to escape the frigid Wisconsin winters, the Wright family began making yearly treks to Arizona in car caravans and visiting for three months. Later they extended their stay from Thanksgiving to Easter. They were always accompanied by a gaggle of apprentices from the Taliesin Fellowship, Wright's training program for architects and artists, which he established in 1932. The program continues to this day as the Frank Lloyd Wright School of Architecture.

While Wright worked on his designs, the apprentices got ample hands-on experience, laboring long days to build Taliesin West. Once a plan was set in motion, Wright would often leave it up to the apprentices to complete. When Olgivanna reminded him of some unfinished detail, he replied, "Anybody can finish it—I must sketch out new ones."

One of the first things visitors to Taliesin West notice about the compound is that it seems almost to grow out of the dry landscape. Wright believed that buildings should be "of" and not "on" a site. His philosophy, which he referred to as organic architecture, aimed at creating structures that were appropriate to "time, place, and man." Taliesin West seems in harmony with the desert—that

REACH FOR THE SKY
A rough-hewn monolith, above, thrusts upward from the grounds of the visitor center, at the entrance to Taliesin West.

PERSONAL FAVORITE
The Taliesin 1 lamp, right, originally designed by Wright for his personal use, grew to be so popular among his clients that they requested their own. The shape of the lamp shade was inspired by the sloping roof of a pagoda. Its base is made of cherry wood.

is, with the essence of the desert as much as its physical aspects. To achieve this Wright built walls out of gold- and umber-colored rocks gathered from the desert and he had the roof beams angled so as to echo the slope of the mountains beyond.

OUT OF THE DESERT

The desert was a source of endless inspiration for Wright. "With its rim of arid mountains," he wrote about the area in 1949, "spotted like the leopard's skin or tattooed with amazing patterns of creation, [it] is a grand garden the like of which in sheer beauty of reach, space, and pattern does not exist, I think, in the world." The textures and shapes of the desert, from the woody skeletons of saguaro cacti to the beaded skin of the Gila monster, are reflected throughout the house. "At every turn, Nature—with a capital N—greets you," one of Taliesin West's guides tells visitors during a tour of the site.

Even the orientation of the house is a response to the desert conditions. Wright skewed Taliesin West just off the cardinal directions, rather than in a traditional north-south orientation, which would subject it to the full brunt of the hot southern sun and the cool northern temperatures.

Wright sought to integrate the exterior and interior of the structure. Expansive rooms lead into intimate courtyards, and doorways open to promenades and terraces. Inside various parts of the buildings, multiple levels are divided by only a few steps and flow one into another with apparent abandon. His aim was to destroy "the box," the sense of confinement imposed by the rigid layouts of traditional architecture.

Wright used low-cost native building materials, including mortar, redwood, canvas, and rock. He left the wood unpainted or had it lightly stained to bring out its true nature. He also devised a clever way to construct interior and exterior walls that was carried out by the Taliesin apprentices. They placed uncut, irregular rocks from the site in wooden forms that were then filled with concrete, rubble, and sand from nearby washes. After this desert masonry set, it was removed from the wooden forms and the wood was recycled.

Massive stone fireplaces are a Wright trademark. The architect believed that hearths drew people together. In keeping with this, he had an imposing fireplace installed in the living room at Taliesin

West, where he and Olgivanna spent many an evening entertaining friends and apprentices.

Wright experimented with the play of light and shadow and the juxtaposition of opaque and transparent materials. He enjoyed the effect of soft light filtering into a room, so at Taliesin West he used off-white canvas flaps to cover window openings and canvas stretched on a framework of redwood for roofing material. Wright also liked the cloth because it provided the house with natural air conditioning, not to mention a tent effect reminiscent of his desert camp days. However, as the house was occupied for longer periods of time, the canvas roofing began to wear out and had to be replaced, so Wright relented and replaced the canvas wall flaps with glass and the roof with more durable acrylic, which still admitted a diffused light.

BEHIND THE RED DOOR
The door to Taliesin West's Cabaret Theater was painted in Wright's favorite color, Cherokee, or Taliesin, red. The elaborate brass door handles exhibit a Chinese dragon motif that is repeated in the statue of the dragon above the door.

DESERT LIGHT
The 56-by-34-foot living room, below, which Wright called the Garden Room, is dominated by a stone fireplace. Clerestory windows look east toward the garden and let in the sparkling light of early morning; others face south and let in the golden light of late afternoon.

LIVING LABORATORY

For Wright, Taliesin West was an architectural laboratory, a work in progress that was generated by his artistic ideas. The architectural critic Robert Campbell once wrote: "Wright's best work always seems to be in process, as alive as a forest, open to change and growth."

Famous for continually redesigning his buildings as he went along, if Wright decided he didn't like a wall once it was up, he would, with an imperious wave of his cane, simply direct his apprentices to "take the wall down."

EYE FOR BEAUTY

As visitors stroll through the rooms and grounds of Taliesin West, they come face-to-face with Wright's keen appreciation of beauty in all its manifestations. Porcelain tablets showing traditional Chinese theater scenes adorn the rugged masonry walls; huge boulders, etched with petroglyphs by Native American artists, have been set on the terraces; a flowering tree has been planted to shade some stone steps; pools and a fountain shimmer under the blazing Arizona sun; and splashes of Wright's favorite color, Cherokee red, brighten doorways and other features.

Wright's love of other art forms is evident at Taliesin West as well. He had the Cabaret Theater and the Music and Dance Pavilion added to the site in the 1950's, and visitors can see where Olgivanna and the apprentices staged dance and musical performances. There was always ample seating in high-back chairs designed by Wright,

ARTISTIC GATHERING
Statues by Heloise Crista, right, are displayed on the terrace by the Music and Dance Pavilion. A dancer as well as an artist, Crista was an apprentice of Frank Lloyd Wright's in the 1950's and continues to live at Taliesin West as a resident artist and instructor. The bronze sculpture in the foreground, called Thought Waves, *shows a woman, who from one view appears to be pregnant and from the opposite view appears not to be.*

which, despite their angular and awkward appearance, are actually quite comfortable.

"Architecture is life," wrote Wright in 1939, "that great living creative spirit which, from generation to generation, from age to age, proceeds, persists, creates, according to the nature of man, and his circumstances as they change." Wright's ability to breathe life into his man-made creations has inspired generations of architects.

Vernon Swaback of Scottsdale served as an apprentice at Taliesin West, and for him his teacher's genius as an architect was revealed in an encounter he had with Wright on the first day of his apprentice-

ship in 1957. Swaback was seated at a drafting table and had just laid out a line of colored pencils in preparation for work when Wright walked by and paused. "Doesn't that just make you want to draw?" asked Wright, looking at the pencils. Swaback was astounded: after designing over 1,000 works, his 89-year-old teacher still felt passionate about the basic tools of architecture. "At that moment, I understood something I couldn't have learned from a textbook. I experienced the gift of having a master." Swaback is not alone in his appreciation of Frank Lloyd Wright and of Taliesin West—one of the architect's most outstanding works.

FOUNTAINHEAD

Wright used the lid from a storage tank as the centerpiece for the terrace pool fountain, above. He cut holes in the lid to hold fishbowls, which, when splashed by water, produced a bell-like sound. In time, the bowls had to be removed because they kept breaking.

MADE IN CHINA

A porcelain theater tablet from China, left, embedded in a wall at Taliesin West, is one of a dozen pieces of Chinese tourist art at Taliesin West. These replicas of ancient Chinese art were made for amateur collectors in America. Wright obtained them at a reduced price because they had been damaged en route.

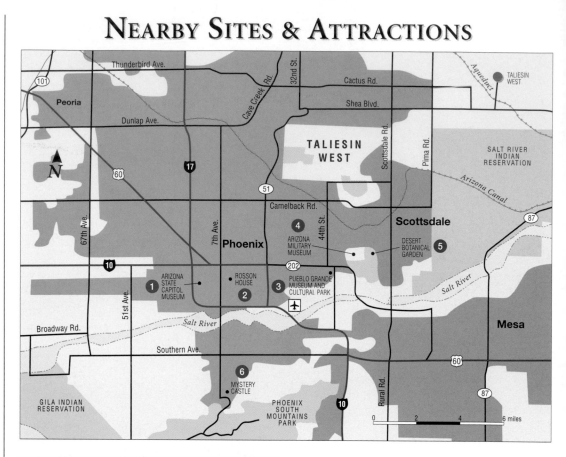

The 1895 Rosson House, right, is one of eight structures in Phoenix's Heritage Square, which preserves the only surviving residential buildings of the original town site.

1 ARIZONA STATE CAPITOL MUSEUM

The building that served as the territorial capitol from 1900 to 1912 and the state capitol from 1912 to 1960 now houses a museum dedicated to Arizona's political history. The restored Executive Branch offices on the second floor include those of the mine inspector, the secretary of state, and the governor. A life-size wax statue of George Hunt, Arizona's first governor, shows him seated at his desk. The

third floor of the museum originally included the Senate and the House of Representatives chambers. Extensively restored, these rooms are furnished with reproductions of the original carpets, furniture, and lamps. The fourth floor contains rooms that were used as the public galleries of the Senate and House of Representatives. Documents and memorabilia are displayed on the walls in the hallways between the offices and the chambers. Restoration of the tufa-and-granite building began in 1976 when the state's copper industry earmarked 15 tons of copper to refurbish the capitol's dome. Located at 1700 East Washington St. in Phoenix.

2 ROSSON HOUSE

Constructed in 1895, this mansion in the Victorian Eastlake style—named after the architect Charles Eastlake—is noted for its elaborately carved ornamentation, expansive latticed veranda, and elegant octagonal turret. The building was designed by the Phoenix architect A. P. Petit for Dr. Roland Lee Rosson. During his long public career, Rosson served as the Maricopa County coroner, treasurer, and public administrator. He was also the mayor of Phoenix from 1895 to 1896. The house's 10 rooms are furnished in late 19th-century style, and the parquet floors are inlaid with mahogany, walnut, and oak. When the house was restored in 1976, care was taken to duplicate the wallpaper patterns, and samples of the house's paint and varnish were analyzed to find an exact match. Located at 139 North 6th St. in Phoenix.

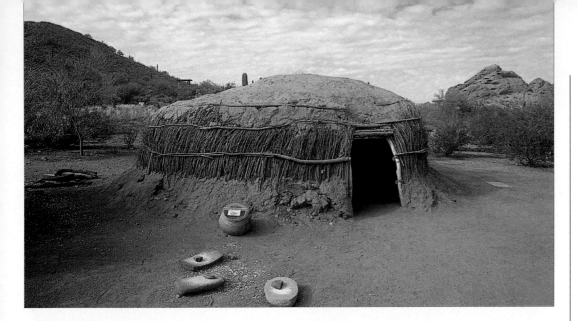

The Plants and People of the Sonoran Desert Trail at the Desert Botanical Garden takes visitors past some grinding stones and a Pima roundhouse constructed of desert plants, left.

③ PUEBLO GRANDE MUSEUM AND CULTURAL PARK

Designated a National Historic Landmark in 1964, the museum preserves the ruins of a Hohokam Indian village that thrived here from A.D. 1150 to 1450, when the civilization collapsed. The park has grown from a little over 3 acres, when it was established in 1929, to 100 acres, and includes the ruins of a platform mound, a ballcourt, a village, and irrigation canals. The museum houses permanent exhibits that describe the life of the Hohokam, with separate displays on the discipline of archeology. Changing exhibits highlight prehistoric and modern Native American culture. Located at 4619 East Washington St. in Phoenix.

④ ARIZONA MILITARY MUSEUM

The more than 8,000 items on display in this museum chronicle Arizona's military history from the time of the Spanish conquistadors to the Persian Gulf War. The exhibits housed in the adobe building include maps, weapons, uniforms, and photographs. Artillery on display outside the museum ranges from a Huey gunship helicopter to armaments captured from the Iraqi army in 1991. During World War II, the building was a maintenance shop where captured German submariners repaired motors. Located at 52nd St. and East McDowell Rd. in Phoenix.

⑤ DESERT BOTANICAL GARDEN

Established in 1939 by the Arizona Cactus and Native Flora Society and devoted exclusively to floras that thrive in arid climates, this outdoor museum encompasses more than 145 acres. Nature trails wind through the grounds, providing visitors with a close-up view of 20,000 desert plants—including many cactus species, as well as yuccas, century plants, and other desert succulents. The Sonoran Desert Nature Trail focuses on the ecological relationships between the plants, insects, birds, and reptiles of the region. Interpretive plaques along the Plants and People of the Sonoran Desert Trail demonstrate how desert plants have been, and continue to be, used as food and construction material: for example, mesquite beans can be ground into flour, and the fibers of yucca plants can be twisted together to make rope. Located at 1201 North Galvin Pkwy. in Phoenix.

⑥ MYSTERY CASTLE

In 1930 free-spirited Boyce Luther Gulley left his wife and daughter in Washington and set out on a journey that led him to the South Mountains of Phoenix. Here he constructed his personal version of a life-size sand castle, made of native stone and found objects that he incorporated into an unusual design. It was an ongoing project that lasted from 1930 to 1945. By studying Native architecture, Gulley learned how to make building materials by mixing native caliche stone and goat's milk. Gulley also used the sides of boxcars and old railroad ties in the construction of the house. Today the 18-room, 8,000-square-foot Pueblo-style house includes such unusual elements as a room that is built around the upright skeleton of a saguaro cactus killed by lightning; the windows in the kitchen and chapel that were recycled from an old Santa Fe Railroad depot; a small bar in the living room that was built with tequila bottles; and an oven that employs an inverted bathtub as an air vent. Much of the house is adorned with Native American rugs and baskets, and 13 fireplaces provide the house with central heating. Located at the end of South 7th St. in Phoenix.

The image of a lively group of dancers, below, originally appeared on Hohokam pottery and was adapted for the wall of the Pueblo Grande Museum. The site preserves a Hohokam settlement that thrived until the 15th century.

HEARST CASTLE

The full scope of W. R. Hearst's passion for art and architecture is on display at his California estate.

William Randolph Hearst always loved a grand entrance, and in his palatial home at San Simeon he got what he wanted. To reach the estate his guests had to travel along a foggy stretch of California's coast to the village of San Simeon, and then follow a private road for five miles into the hills. Beyond the first gates of the estate, a sign proclaimed "Animals Have The Right Of Way At All Times"—warning that kangaroos, zebras, pronghorn antelopes, and even a group of emus might amble across the road at any time. Near the top of the hill, visitors drove through a fragrant grove of citrus trees. Suddenly the towers of the main house loomed out of the evening mist, dramatically illuminated by dozens of floodlights, and appearing like nothing less than the turrets of a fairy-tale castle. Once inside, the bedazzled guests would be shown to luxuriously appointed quarters, each decorated with a veritable trove of artistic treasures. San Simeon was W. R. Hearst's stage, where he played one of the monarchs of old entertaining visitors to his court.

Overleaf: The sea horse and mermaid mosaics in the Roman Pool at the Hearst San Simeon State Historical Monument are set aglow by the soft light of hidden skylights and alabaster globes on marble lamp standards.

HILLTOP RETREAT

A bird's-eye view captures the vast dimensions of the Hearst estate, below, with its 127 acres of gardens. Tons of rich topsoil were hauled up the rocky hill for the thousands of native and exotic plants that still thrive on the grounds. Today hundreds of Barbary sheep and about a dozen zebras roam an area inhabited by other wild animals. The turquoise basin of the Neptune Pool and its colonnades can be seen on the left side of the picture.

Today Hearst Castle is a California State Historical Monument. Visitors come by the millions from all over the world to tour the fabulous estate and learn about its owner. Gazing out at the Pacific from the mansion's sunny promenade, they relive a time in the fantastic era that produced newspaper magnates, Hollywood starlets—and one of America's most flamboyant homes.

THE MASTER OF SAN SIMEON

La Cuesta Encantada, or "The Enchanted Hill" as Hearst called his home, represents the full range of its owner's complex personality. While ruthless and possessive, Hearst could also be sensitive and generous. He was shy and refined, yet his name became synonymous with tabloid journalism. Although intensely private, Hearst was one of the most famous Americans in an age of celebrity worship that he helped to shape.

William Randolph Hearst was born into wealth in 1863. His father, George Hearst, had built the family's fortune in the silver mines of Nevada, and the gold and copper mines of North and South America before he turned to public service and become a California senator. His mother, Phoebe, a patron of education and the arts, doted on "Willie." When he was 10, Hearst toured Europe and gained exposure to the masterpieces of Western art. The stamps, coins, and beer steins he carted home were the seeds of a collection that would one day fill seven castles and several warehouses.

Yet for all his love of the finest things, Hearst was no snob. He enjoyed vaudeville shows and had a mischievous streak that got him expelled from Harvard University. Possessed of tremendous energy, he took over his father's struggling *San Francisco Examiner* while still a young man and gradually built a media conglomerate that included 28 newspapers, 13 magazines, 8 radio stations, plus wire services, movie studios, paper mills, and other related holdings. As an editor and tycoon, Hearst contributed to a brand of yellow journalism that attracted millions of Americans readers. In his newspapers, Hearst incited his readers to call for war and for peace, he exposed corruption and crusaded for social justice, and he campaigned for political office.

Hearst brought this same aggressive spirit to the building of his mansion at San Simeon. He had inherited the ranch, as his family called this favorite retreat, from his mother after her death in 1919, when he was 56 years old. A rustic homestead, it sprawled for thousands of acres across the spectacular coastal hills of southern Big Sur. Hearst decided he wanted a stylish residence that would also serve as a showcase for his collection of artworks. In addition, he began building because he needed to replace the tents on Camp Hill that had served as his first abode. Hearst did not originally have in mind to create such a large estate; its grandeur and sheer size developed through nearly three decades of construction. When this married father of five sons fell in love with a Ziegfeld Follies dancer, Marion Davies, he was determined to make her a movie star, and that meant living near influential figures in the film industry. His new house—midway between his hometown, San Francisco, and Hollywood—was the perfect solution.

Hearst hired as his architect Julia Morgan, whose impressive work was grounded in the classical European tradition and yet resonated with a love for the California landscape. Like Hearst, Morgan never balked at a challenge—even one that called not for a house, but for an imperial compound reminiscent of the Renaissance Italian hill villas Hearst had so admired in his youth.

A scouting trip in April 1919 convinced Morgan that construction of Hearst's castle was not going to be easy. The chosen site was perched atop a 1,600-foot hill at the end of a 5-mile-long dirt trail that turned into a river of mud in the rainy winter season. The nearest railhead lay 42 miles away by hazardous coastal roads and there were no local laborers or durable building materials.

But Morgan rose to the occasion. For the next 28 years she spent nearly every weekend at San Simeon supervising construction of the compound from her makeshift shack and communicating with

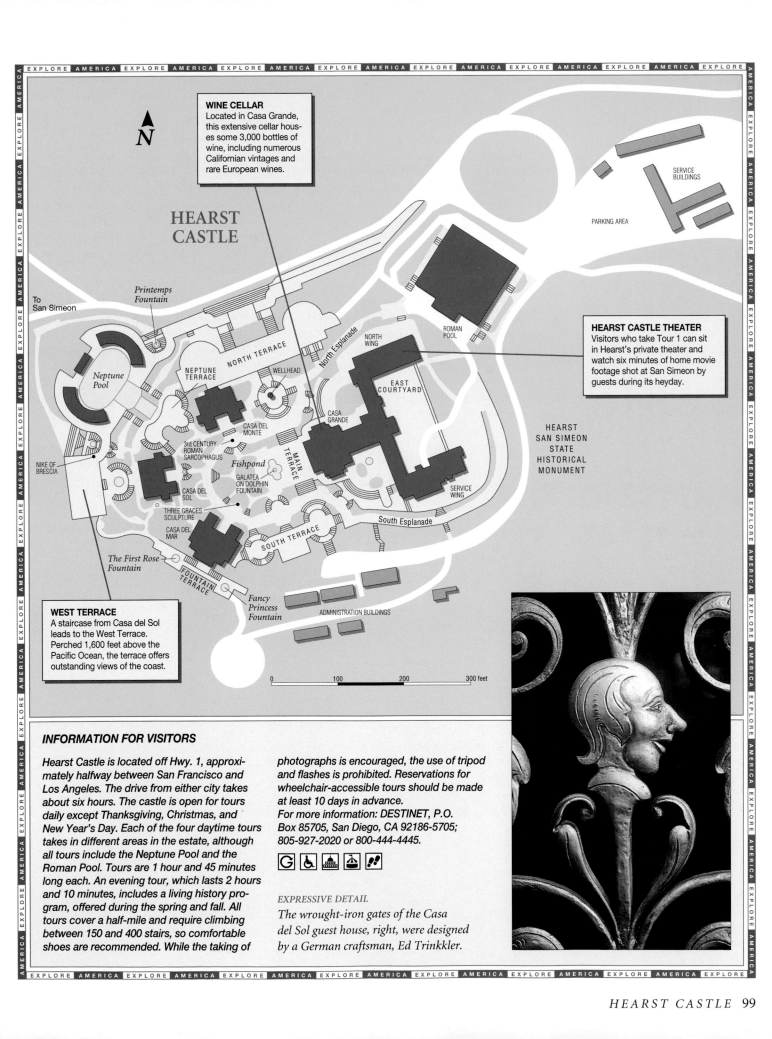

N

WINE CELLAR
Located in Casa Grande, this extensive cellar houses some 3,000 bottles of wine, including numerous Californian vintages and rare European wines.

HEARST CASTLE

To San Simeon

Printemps Fountain

NORTH TERRACE

North Esplanade

SERVICE BUILDINGS

PARKING AREA

ROMAN POOL

HEARST CASTLE THEATER
Visitors who take Tour 1 can sit in Hearst's private theater and watch six minutes of home movie footage shot at San Simeon by guests during its heyday.

NORTH WING

NEPTUNE TERRACE

WELLHEAD

Neptune Pool

EAST COURTYARD

CASA DEL MONTE

CASA GRANDE

3rd CENTURY ROMAN SARCOPHAGUS

Fishpond

MAIN TERRACE

HEARST SAN SIMEON STATE HISTORICAL MONUMENT

NIKE OF BRESCIA

GALATEA ON DOLPHIN FOUNTAIN

CASA DEL SOL

SERVICE WING

THREE GRACES SCULPTURE

CASA DEL MAR

South Esplanade

The First Rose Fountain

FOUNTAIN TERRACE

SOUTH TERRACE

WEST TERRACE
A staircase from Casa del Sol leads to the West Terrace. Perched 1,600 feet above the Pacific Ocean, the terrace offers outstanding views of the coast.

Fancy Princess Fountain

ADMINISTRATION BUILDINGS

0   100   200   300 feet

INFORMATION FOR VISITORS

Hearst Castle is located off Hwy. 1, approximately halfway between San Francisco and Los Angeles. The drive from either city takes about six hours. The castle is open for tours daily except Thanksgiving, Christmas, and New Year's Day. Each of the four daytime tours takes in different areas in the estate, although all tours include the Neptune Pool and the Roman Pool. Tours are 1 hour and 45 minutes long each. An evening tour, which lasts 2 hours and 10 minutes, includes a living history program, offered during the spring and fall. All tours cover a half-mile and require climbing between 150 and 400 stairs, so comfortable shoes are recommended. While the taking of

photographs is encouraged, the use of tripod and flashes is prohibited. Reservations for wheelchair-accessible tours should be made at least 10 days in advance.
For more information: DESTINET, P.O. Box 85705, San Diego, CA 92186-5705; 805-927-2020 or 800-444-4445.

EXPRESSIVE DETAIL
The wrought-iron gates of the Casa del Sol guest house, right, were designed by a German craftsman, Ed Trinkkler.

EXPLORE AMERICA EXPLORE AMERICA EXPLORE AMERICA EXPLORE AMERICA EXPLORE AMERICA EXPLORE AMERICA EXPLORE AMERICA EXPLORE AMERICA EXPLORE

HEARST CASTLE 99

WINGED VICTORY

A striking bronze statue, below, called the Nike of Brescia, *stands on the West Terrace near the Neptune Pool. It is a replica of a Roman statue of the winged victory goddess, the original of which is in Brescia, Italy.*

TWIN TOWERS

The facade of the cathedral-like Casa Grande, right, is dominated by its imposing towers. Housed in each tower are 18 cast-iron bells, which were made in Tournai, Belgium. Each of the carillon bells is operated by its own electric motor and played by a keyboard. Three different octaves can be played at the same time. The pool in front was once stocked with fish.

Hearst by letter and telegram. She built warehouses for Hearst's art treasures, a pier on the ocean to receive and store supplies, homes for the staff, and workshops for the craftsmen. And she conquered a force more capricious than nature—W. R. Hearst.

At their employer's whim, Morgan's crews transplanted 100 year-old-plus oaks, relocated massive stone fireplaces, and made structural alterations to the main house—after construction on the buildings was well under way. When the work was halted in 1947, Morgan and Hearst had transformed a rocky crag into an architectural gem.

WEEKENDS AT THE CASTLE On weekends, the guests at San Simeon might find themselves sipping cocktails with playwright George Bernard Shaw, playing a game of billiards with Charlie Chaplin, or sunning themselves at poolside with Greta Garbo. Business moguls, financiers, politicians, and Miss Davies' movie-star friends mingled freely amid the estate's gardens and classical statuary.

Weekend guests generally arrived on Friday evening and retired immediately to their quarters in the main house or to one of the three fabled guest cottages: Casa del Mar, Casa del Sol, and Casa del Monte. These first permanent structures erected on the hill were situated to take full advantage of the breathtaking views. The rooms of Casa del Mar enjoyed a stunning panorama of the coast, while Casa del Sol was oriented for spectacular views of the sunset, and Casa del Monte opened up to vistas of the Santa Lucia mountains. The cottages were modeled after the Spanish and Italian Renaissance style, with white stucco walls, red-tile roofs, and large arched windows. The scent of roses, fuchsias, and camellias trailed through the guest houses year-round, the result of Hearst's insistence that his Enchanted Hill stay continually in bloom.

Mornings at San Simeon were for lounging or exploring and a time when many guests went to Hearst's private zoo, which counted more than 600 animals, including bisons and bears. Strolls along the main promenade might bring guests up close

to extraordinary art treasures. The Sekhmet fountain, for instance, is an amalgam that includes four Egyptian statues of a lion-headed war goddess dating from approximately 1350 B.C. The pieces were obtained, like most of the art at San Simeon, through New York City auction houses.

CASA
GRANDE

The main house, called Casa Grande, rises above a series of terraced promenades, fountains, and gardens. The building's towers were inspired by the cathedral in Ronda, Spain. The simple grandeur of Casa Grande contrasts with its elaborately carved portal. Stone balconies encircle the building, and the third story features a teak cornice intricately carved with the figures of wild animals. Most of the wood was found by Morgan in a San Francisco warehouse, and had been originally intended for the construction of a ship. The rooms of the Celestial Suite, which are concealed behind ornamental grilles

within the building's two bell towers, are linked by a balcony faced with colorful tiles. The building is a work of solid engineering: one of Morgan's trademarks was her use of reinforced concrete, which she employed to help stabilize the structure to withstand the earthquakes and wildfires that frequently plagued the region.

Around 7:00 p.m. Hearst and Davies would descend from their chambers in Casa Grande to receive weekend guests in the cavernous Assembly Room. The enormous 82-by-30-foot space was filled top to bottom with Hearst's collection. Fragments of antique ceilings, columns, and fittings were incorporated in the room, and where necessary, Morgan's wood-carvers, masons, and metalworkers replaced missing parts, blending the disparate pieces perfectly. Here, as elsewhere, Morgan integrated an array of architectural elements to create a harmonious overall design. Dark walnut choir stalls of the 15th and 16th centuries ring the room and immense 400-year-old tapestries,

The Doge's Suite, above, in Casa Grande, consists of a central sitting room flanked by two bedrooms. It is decorated with oil paintings and opulent furnishings, including blue brocade wall coverings with gold trim, an ornately designed ceiling, and a marble fireplace. A balcony off the suite was inspired by the doge's palace in Venice.

woven with scenes of Roman battles, hang from the walls below a coffered ceiling. When sunlight streams in, the gilded Baroque doorway is set aglow. On chilly evenings, the room was warmed by a two-story fireplace made of marble. Overstuffed parlor chairs and a Steinway reproduction player piano suggest the room was meant for having fun too. Over the years the Assembly Room served as the setting for everything from costume parties to ballroom dancing.

After the official welcome, the revelers repaired to the Gothic-style Refectory for a lively dinner. Here, Morgan raised the ceiling to accommodate a 14-foot-high stone fireplace with a modern extension; a bank of high windows allowed the sun to pour in. Brightly colored banners from Siena, Italy, hung from the walls. According to historians, Hearst and Miss Davies would sit in the middle of a massive table upon which Hearst would set bottles of ketchup and mustard in an effort to make the occasion less intimidating.

During the day guests were offered the choice of many outdoor activities. Hearst loved organized picnics and horseback riding, but his guests were also free to walk through the pergola, a mile-long arbor covered in vines and lined with apple trees. During rainy weather, guests might seek refuge in the second-floor library, where, seated amid ancient Greek vases, they could take a look at reading materials as varied as a Persian medical textbook from 1609 to an autographed edition of Washington Irving's *Works*. The shelves of the library now hold more than 4,000 volumes, a fraction of the original collection of books and letters, which Hearst was forced to auction off in 1937 and 1941 to minimize the financial constraints of the Depression.

After cocktails and dinner in the Refectory, guests might adjourn to the Billiard Room, which was decorated with an early 16th-century Franco-Flemish millefleurs tapestry of wool-and-silk depicting a royal stag hunt. The rare tapestry, one of few surviving examples of the period, gets its name from the *mille fleurs*, or "thousand flowers" that are woven into the background of the scene.

NEPTUNE POOL
Twin Ionic colonnades stand at both ends of the pool, below. They bracket a Greco-Roman temple on the left that is an assemblage of authentic granite columns, marble pediment fragments, and sculptures from parts of Hearst's collection.

SACRED AND SECULAR
The facade of Casa Grande, right, incorporates a reproduction of a 16th-century statue of the duke of Burgundy on his steed and an original 13th-century statue of the Madonna and Child.

HEROIC FOUNT
A magnificent fountain, below, of Verona limestone and marble, topped by a bronze copy of Donatello's 1432 masterpiece, David, *is the centerpiece of the Casa del Sol guest house terrace. The fountain was inspired by one in Granada, Spain, that Hearst saw pictured in a book.*

Sometimes Hearst's guests strolled down to the Neptune Pool for a dip or to drink tea and watch the sun sink into the glassy sea. Like the main house, the Neptune Pool is a heroic blend of artistic grandeur and engineering prowess. It began as an ornamental pool in a projected sculpture garden. Twelve years and two renditions later, Morgan put the finishing touches on a 104-foot-long, 345,000-gallon pool. The Neptune Terrace cups the water like an amphitheater. Balustrades trail down the hill, around the water, and along the tops of the Ionic colonnades at each end. As always for Hearst, function was never far from fancy: the Terrace is equipped with 17 dressing rooms, and a Greco-Roman temple facade built on one side of the pool is fully fitted with electric lighting.

One invitation no guest dared refuse was Hearst's evening summons to preview some of the latest Hollywood film releases in his private theater. Completed in 1930, the silk-draped theater seats 50 in plush chairs upholstered in red damask. Ten gilded ornamental plaster of paris caryatids, created in Morgan's workshops, hold lights in the form of blossoms that illuminate the room. The screen sinks into the floor with the push of a button to make way for live stage performances. Beside Hearst's front-row seat there was a telephone to the projection booth by which he could—and did on occasion—ask for better movies to be screened.

It has been said that Cary Grant considered the indoor Roman Pool to be the most romantic spot on the hillside. Marble lamps with alabaster shades cast their light on flecks of hammered 22-carat gold leaf fused in the room's millions of glass tiles. The tiles were made on the island of Murano, in Venice, Italy. After a show or a swim, guests retired to their rooms in the main house or in the three cottages. With 38 guest bedrooms in the main house, there was rarely a shortage of sleeping quarters. The four duplexes—which featured spiral staircases leading to cozy sleeping lofts—were likely coveted.

WORKING MILLIONAIRE

When his guests went to bed, Hearst went to work. San Simeon may have been a pleasure palace for friends, but for Hearst it was also an office. Phones were never far away, and business calls kept operators busy around the clock. The center of all this activity was Hearst's Gothic Study, a vaulted chamber on the third floor where he would spread out on the table and floor the pages of that day's papers and absorb their contents. Only when he had put the proofs of his East and West Coast dailies to bed did Hearst himself retire. In the middle of these opulent surroundings, Hearst's master bedroom is a surprisingly simple affair. The room features a 14th-century Spanish ceiling and displays a Madonna and Child by a follower of the Sienese master Duccio di Buoninsegna. Sharing wall space with this masterpiece are simple photographs of Hearst's parents and grandparents that bring the figure of Hearst poignantly into focus as a man.

During its heyday, Hearst Castle was in a permanent state of construction. Hearst was always changing his mind about what had already been built or dreaming up other additions, perhaps an aviary, or an art gallery. Today the grand halls, elaborate rooms, and sparkling grounds are maintained by the California State Parks. As they walk wide-eyed through this magnificent historical monument, visitors see constant reminders of the orders Hearst issued to his staff of buyers as they set out to comb the globe for treasures to add to the collection on his estate: "Don't spare the costs."

SUITE DREAMS
Sunlight filters into the Celestial Suite, below, through the exquisitely designed grillwork. Located in one of the Moorish bell towers of Casa Grande, this guest room was probably sought after by Hearst's visitors because of its 360-degree view of the surrounding landscape.

NEARBY SITES & ATTRACTIONS

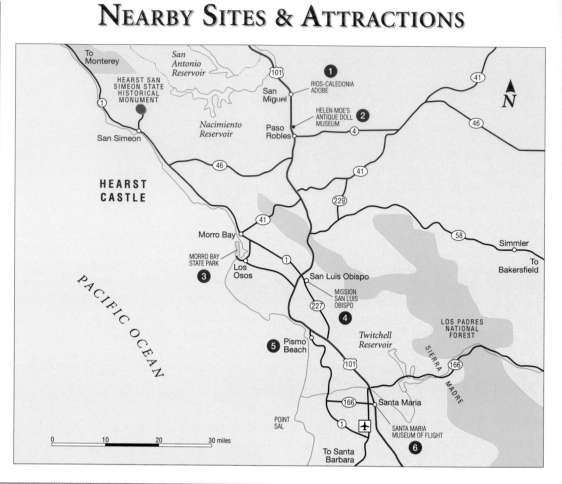

Morro Rock, below, looms impressively in front of a couple feeding seagulls. Once an important port for local cattle ranchers, Morro Bay now maintains a large commercial fishing fleet.

1 RIOS-CALEDONIA ADOBE

Commissioned by the Mexican government in 1835 to serve as the residence of the administrator of the nearby Mission San Miguel Archangel, this two-story adobe building with its tiled gable roof was constructed using bricks salvaged from the ruined outer walls of the mission itself. Under the supervision of Petronilo Rios, a sergeant of artillery in the Mexican army, the building was completed in early 1836. In July of that year a government official named Ygnacio Coronel and his family moved into the house—which served as both home and office. From 1868 to 1890 the house was used as a stagecoach stop and inn. The building was later owned by several families before it was purchased by the county of San Luis Obispo in 1964; the adobe structure was opened to the public in 1971. Inside, visitors can tour spacious rooms, furnished with 19th-century pieces. Of special note are some architectural details such as the small window on the west wall that was once used to pass food from the kitchen to the dining room. Located at 700 Mission St. in San Miguel.

2 HELEN MOE'S ANTIQUE DOLL MUSEUM

With more than 800 antique and foreign dolls on display, this museum rekindles memories of an era when dolls were not just children's toys, but also conversation pieces and examples of fine craftsmanship. The museum exhibits dolls in a variety of settings that have been faithfully made so that they are scaled to the height of each doll. Some of the sets, enclosed in glass display cases, include an old schoolhouse, a circus, an attic, and a Christmas scene. The oldest doll in the collection is made of wood and once belonged to Edward VI, the son of England's King Henry VIII. A collector's paradise, the museum's gift shop sells everything from music boxes and German teddy bears to doll clothing and reference books. Located three miles north of Paso Robles off Hwy. 101.

③ MORRO BAY STATE PARK

Located on California's Central Coast, this park is noted for its demanding hiking trails, spectacular vistas, 18-hole golf course, boat marina, and natural-history museum. Trails to 135 campsites take hikers past a salt marsh and a heron rookery. One of the most impressive sights is Morro Rock, a volcanic rock just offshore that rises 578 feet above sea level. The exhibits at Morro Bay State Park's Museum of Natural History focus on the geology and wildlife of the area, and the region's first inhabitants, the Chumash Indians. The museum's art gallery offers rotating exhibitions of coastal landscape paintings done by local artists. Located south of Morro Bay off Hwy. 1.

④ MISSION SAN LUIS OBISPO

Founded in 1772 and constructed between 1792 and 1794, this was the fifth mission built by the Spanish in California. The first Franciscans found the local Chumash Indians friendly and eager to convert. The Chumash quickly turned the mission into a small industrious colony that produced wines, fruits, vegetables, and olive oil. On three different occasions the enemies of the Chumash set fire to the mission's thatch roof with flaming arrows and caused heavy damage to the structure. Following one such attack, an experimental red-tile roof was installed that proved to be both waterproof and fireproof. The roof of San Luis soon became the standard for all area missions, and for California architecture in general. The mission fell into disrepair in the late 19th century, but in 1934 restoration work began that continues today. Among the features of the mission that have been restored are a large, impressive colonnade as well as the belfry. A museum exhibits Chumash artifacts along with pioneer memorabilia, and visitors can walk through the tranquil gardens. Located at Monterey and Chorro streets in San Luis Obispo.

⑤ PISMO BEACH

This California Central Coast community is noted for both its wide sandy beaches, rocky shoreline, world-famous clams, and the thousands of monarch butterflies that congregate here each winter. Chumash Indians settled in the region some 9,000 years ago; the first European arrived in 1840 when rancher Jose Ortega bought more than 8,000 acres of land. In the early 1900's Pismo Beach was known for its saloons and brothels. The area's popularity skyrocketed following World War II, when many veterans who had trained here before going overseas returned to its sunny climes. Today vacationers sail, kayak, swim, surf, or sunbathe at more than 23 miles of pristine beaches. The rockier northern section of Pismo Beach offers adventurers the opportunity to explore secluded caves and coves populated by sea otters and sea lions. Anglers fish for red snapper and ling-cod off Pismo Pier, and clam-diggers search the sand for clams; conservation efforts limit the number and size of clams that are allowed to be taken from the beach. Perhaps the most beautiful attraction in the area is the annual arrival of thousands of monarch butterflies in November; they congregate in a grove of eucalyptus and pine trees in Pismo Beach State Park and stay until March. Located on Hwy. 1.

⑥ SANTA MARIA MUSEUM OF FLIGHT

During World War II, this was a training center for pilots of the P-38 Lightning, a fighter-bomber used extensively in the Pacific Theater. Today two of its hangars display aircraft and miniature models from the turn of the century to the present. The Early Aviation Hangar contains aircraft, models, photos, and memorabilia from the time of the Wright brothers to World War II. The highlight of this hangar's collection is a restored 1929 Fleet Model 2. The second hangar focuses on the postwar period up to today. Located at 3015 Airpark Dr. in Santa Maria.

A pair of monarch butterflies, above, at Pismo Beach feed on milkweed. The plant's poisonous sap makes the butterflies taste bitter, protecting them from hungry birds.

Mission San Luis Obispo, left, was named for Saint Louis, Bishop of Toulouse. Its belfry houses bells that were made in Peru in 1818 and then recast in 1878.

IOLANI PALACE

A royal residence in downtown Honolulu keeps alive the last years of Hawaii's monarchy.

Raising the gold, jewel-encrusted crown over his head with the dignity and self-assurance suited to a descendant of an ancient line of chiefs in Hawaii, David Laamea Kalakaua confirmed his royal status before God, his people, and representatives of the governments of the United States, Europe, and Asia. The coronation ceremony, which took place nine years after Kalakaua's election to the throne, was carefully timed to coincide with the completion of a new palace adjacent to the domed gazebo where the king was crowned in mid-February 1883.

The palace was called Iolani—"Heavenly Hawk" in Hawaiian. It took its name from a more modest royal residence that had occupied the same site for some 30 years until termites had infested it so badly that it was torn down in 1874. The new palace was started in 1879 at a projected cost of no more than $50,000. However, by the time the king returned from a tour of the world in 1881, the price tag had already climbed to almost double—with major work still pending.

SEAT OF POWER
Overleaf: At only 140 by 100 feet, Iolani Palace is relatively small by royal standards, but the palace exhibits a regal exterior. Two architects worked on the drawings for the palace before Charles J. Wall of San Francisco produced the final renderings in 1880.

GATEWAY TO THE KINGDOM
The coat of arms of the Hawaiian Kingdom, above, is displayed on the four gates of Iolani Palace. The motto translates as "The life of the land is preserved in righteousness."

ROYAL CELEBRATIONS
The Coronation Pavilion, right, was the setting for the coronation of King Kalakaua in 1883. In the early 1900's a concrete basement was added to the pavilion, and it served as a bomb shelter during World War II.

In the end the palace took more than three years to complete and the cost of the interior detailing, woodwork, and custom-designed furnishings alone exceeded the original estimate. The final price tag, which was paid for by the Hawaiian people, was approximately $350,000.

The palace speaks volumes about the impact that European civilization has had on the island kingdom. The grandeur of the royal residence and the magnificent coronation ceremony in 1883 were designed to affirm Kalakaua's status as an equal to the mighty rulers of Europe, worthy therefore of their full respect and support. However, the cost overruns exacerbated a political crisis that had pitted the king against a legislature dominated by resident Americans who controlled Hawaii's economy. The Americans' ethnocentric prejudices caused them to show little regard for Kalakaua. During his reign these men sought to reduce the king's political power and advocated that Hawaii join the United States. Iolani Palace figured prominently in the events that led to that outcome.

THOROUGHLY MODERN During its heyday in the last quarter of the 19th century, King Kalakaua's new official residence was one of the most modern buildings in the world. The palace was a model of innovation in everything from its architectural use of concrete and cast iron to its cutting-edge technologies. It had indoor plumbing even before Buckingham Palace or the White House did. The telephone system that linked the king's and queen's suites and the office of the Royal Chamberlain was one of the world's first, the telephone having only been invented in 1876. Electric lights glowed from the palace's verandas for Kalakaua's 50th birthday jubilee in 1886, and the following year—less than eight years after Thomas Edison invented the incandescent lamp—electric lighting was installed in Iolani's main rooms.

Iolani Palace displays a mix of late Victorian and British Colonial architectural design. Long verandas dominate its four sides, each embellished with cast-iron columns, made in San Francisco, and wrought-iron rails, which were manufactured by the Honolulu Iron Works. A half-dozen slate-roofed towers give the palace its distinctive silhouette.

The building's decor exhibits the intriguing combination of European and Asian influences that characterized the tastes of the upper class in 19th-century Hawaii. More than 250 furnishings by the American manufacturer A. H. Davenport & Co. of Boston, Massachusetts, add Victorian flourishes to the overall design. But references to Hawaiian history are found in important details throughout: a coat of arms bearing feather-caped Hawaiian warriors graces the ceiling of the veranda; portraits of Hawaii's kings and queens hang in the Grand Hall; native woods, such as lightly hued kamani and koa, replace the dark woods favored in most Victorian homes; and the gilded thrones in the first-floor Throne Room take visitors back more than 100 years to the golden age of Hawaiian royalty.

The proportions of Iolani Palace are modest by imperial European standards. It comes closer in size to the mansions of rich entrepreneurs built on San Francisco's Nob Hill and New York's Fifth Avenue. Yet even from a distance, Iolani Palace is strikingly regal. An elegant iron fence surrounds the 11 acres of landscaped grounds, which once were accessible only by way of four gates bearing glazed metal renderings of the royal coat of arms.

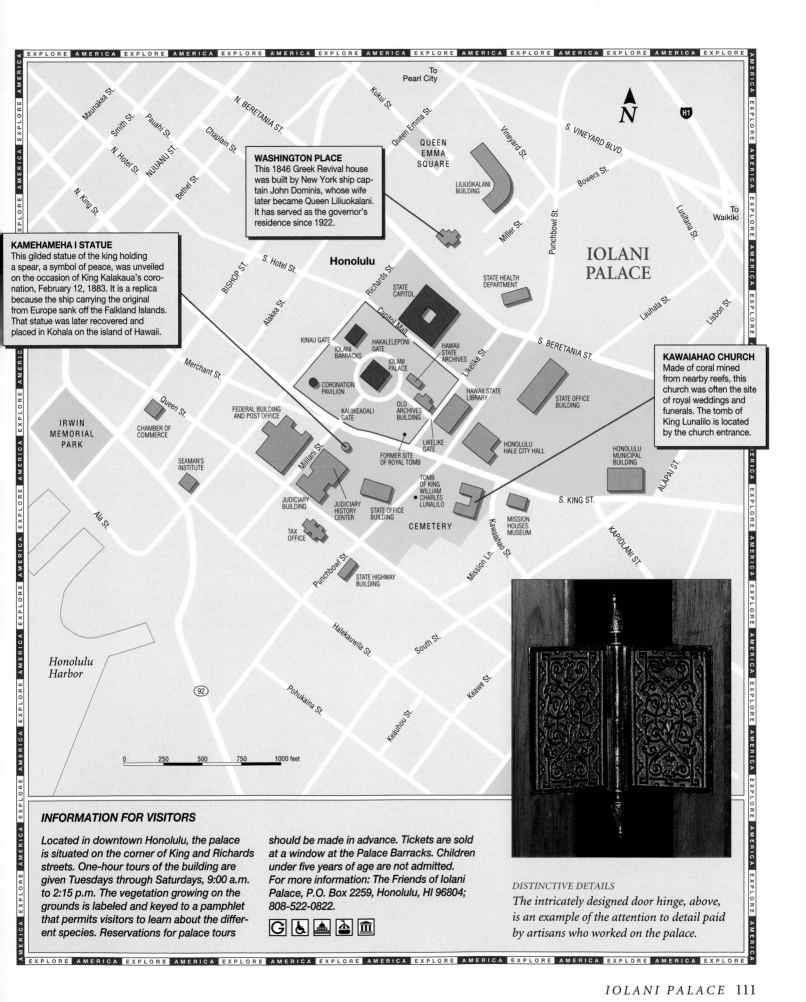

WASHINGTON PLACE
This 1846 Greek Revival house was built by New York ship captain John Dominis, whose wife later became Queen Liliuokalani. It has served as the governor's residence since 1922.

KAMEHAMEHA I STATUE
This gilded statue of the king holding a spear, a symbol of peace, was unveiled on the occasion of King Kalakaua's coronation, February 12, 1883. It is a replica because the ship carrying the original from Europe sank off the Falkland Islands. That statue was later recovered and placed in Kohala on the island of Hawaii.

KAWAIAHAO CHURCH
Made of coral mined from nearby reefs, this church was often the site of royal weddings and funerals. The tomb of King Lunalilo is located by the church entrance.

Map labels

To Pearl City
To Waikiki
Honolulu
IOLANI PALACE
Honolulu Harbor

QUEEN EMMA SQUARE
LILIUOKALANI BUILDING

N. BERETANIA ST.
Maunakea St.
Smith St.
Pauahi St.
N. Hotel St.
NUUANU ST.
Chaplain St.
Bethel St.
N. King St.
Kukui St.
Queen Emma St.
Vineyard St.
S. VINEYARD BLVD.
Bowers St.
Miller St.
Punchbowl St.
Lusitana St.
Lauhala St.
Lisbon St.

BISHOP ST.
S. Hotel St.
Alakea St.
Richards St.
STATE CAPITOL
Capitol Mall
STATE HEALTH DEPARTMENT
S. BERETANIA ST.

Merchant St.
KINAU GATE
IOLANI BARRACKS
HAKALELEPONI GATE
IOLANI PALACE
HAWAII STATE ARCHIVES
Likelike St.
HAWAII STATE LIBRARY
STATE OFFICE BUILDING

Queen St.
IRWIN MEMORIAL PARK
CHAMBER OF COMMERCE
FEDERAL BUILDING AND POST OFFICE
CORONATION PAVILION
KAUIKEAOALI GATE
OLD ARCHIVES BUILDING
HONOLULU HALE CITY HALL
HONOLULU MUNICIPAL BUILDING
ALAPAI ST.

SEAMAN'S INSTITUTE
Mililani St.
LIKELIKE GATE
FORMER SITE OF ROYAL TOMB
S. KING ST.

Ala St.
JUDICIARY BUILDING
JUDICIARY HISTORY CENTER
STATE OFFICE BUILDING
TOMB OF KING WILLIAM CHARLES LUNALILO
CEMETERY
Kawaiahao St.
MISSION HOUSES MUSEUM
KAPIOLANI ST.

TAX OFFICE
Punchbowl St.
STATE HIGHWAY BUILDING
Mission Ln.
S. King St.

Halekauwila St.
South St.
Keawe St.

92
Pohukaina St.
Keauhou St.

0 250 500 750 1000 feet

DISTINCTIVE DETAILS

The intricately designed door hinge, above, is an example of the attention to detail paid by artisans who worked on the palace.

INFORMATION FOR VISITORS

Located in downtown Honolulu, the palace is situated on the corner of King and Richards streets. One-hour tours of the building are given Tuesdays through Saturdays, 9:00 a.m. to 2:15 p.m. The vegetation growing on the grounds is labeled and keyed to a pamphlet that permits visitors to learn about the different species. Reservations for palace tours should be made in advance. Tickets are sold at a window at the Palace Barracks. Children under five years of age are not admitted. For more information: The Friends of Iolani Palace, P.O. Box 2259, Honolulu, HI 96804; 808-522-0822.

EXPLORE AMERICA EXPLORE AMERICA EXPLORE AMERICA EXPLORE AMERICA EXPLORE AMERICA EXPLORE AMERICA EXPLORE AMERICA EXPLORE AMERICA EXPLORE

IOLANI PALACE 111

GRAND ENTRY HALL

The magnificent Grand Hall, below, leads to the main staircase, which is made primarily of koa wood with kamani and walnut trim. The koa stair treads and some of the balustrades are all that remain of the original staircase; many of the balustrades were destroyed by termites and had to be replaced during the restoration.

GATES TO
THE PALACE

The Kauikeaouli Gate faces south, toward the harbor, and was dedicated to Kamehameha III. It served as a ceremonial entryway for the king and foreign dignitaries when they entered the palace. Looking out at the Koolau Mountains to the north, the Hakaleleponi Gate, in honor of Queen Kalama, was the palace staff's entrance. Just outside this gate stood the crenellated Iolani Barracks, built in 1870 from plans drawn by Hawaii's first professional architect, Theodore C. Heuck, who had also designed the Royal Mausoleum in Nuuanu Valley. The barracks housed the Royal Guard and were later moved inside the palace compound.

The east gate is named after Likelike, one of Kalakaua's sisters, and was used by the royal family when they wanted to leave the compound unnoticed. The western gate, named Kinau, honors the daughter of the first King Kamehameha, who was also the mother of Kamehameha IV and V, the last two kings in the dynastic line. The gate was used by workmen and as a delivery entrance.

The site of the original Iolani Palace had been chosen by Mataio Kekuanaoa, Kinau's husband and the governor of Oahu, who built a residence for his daughter there. In 1845, when King Kamehameha III chose Honolulu as the first permanent capital of Hawaii, the governor suggested that the king use the palace. Accepting the offer,

the monarch moved the royal court from the port of Lahaina, on Maui, to Iolani Palace. For the next 30 years or so, the palace served as the official residence of Kamehameha III, IV, V, and William Charles Lunalilo, until Kalakaua decided to go ahead with construction of a more stately building. This new edifice, he hoped, would bestow on Hawaii a landmark of outstanding architectural merit, historic significance, and great beauty. A visit to the palace quickly confirms his success.

Upon entering the building, visitors are struck by the majesty of the Grand Hall. At midday bright sunlight streams through the trees on the grounds and is filtered by the frosted glass on three imposing front doors, casting pools of light on the hall's

polished wood floors. Ten portraits of Hawaiian kings and queens line the walls, and niches shelter bronze statuary and delicate, hand-painted ceramic vases given to the king by the emperor of Japan during Kalakaua's circumnavigation of the globe—the first made by any monarch. Other objets d'art on display were also gifts to Kalakaua, among them, statuettes from France, brass from India, and porcelain vases from England.

| | Eight tall, polished koa doors |
| THE BLUE ROOM | open to rooms off the Grand Hall. One of them, the Blue Room, was the site of intimate |

receptions. It is decorated in blue with luxurious satin draperies and antique furniture and used to contain a grand piano that was often played during evening musicals. Portraits of King Kalakaua and his sister, Queen Liliuokalani, hang alongside a picture of King Louis Philippe of France, shipped to Kamehameha III in 1848.

HUB OF ACTIVITY
King Kalakaua conducted much of his royal business in the library, above. The massive koa wood desk, some nine feet long and five feet wide, was custom-made in Hawaii. The restoration of the room to its appearance in 1883, when King Kalakaua moved into the palace, was made possible through grants from the General Telephone and Electronics Foundation and the Hawaiian Telephone Company.

ROYAL SLUMBERS
Queen Kapiolani, wife of King Kalakaua, occupied a separate suite that included a spacious bedroom, above, an anteroom, dressing room, toilet, and bath. The rooms are decorated with a number of the queen's personal mementoes, and her monogram is sewn onto the Chinese silk bedspread and pillow shams.

Large wooden sliding doors separate the Blue Room from the State Dining Room, which accommodated up to 60 honored guests for elaborate eight-course dinners accompanied by fine wines drawn from the well-stocked cellar. The Gothic Revival chairs, tables, and sideboards were all made by A. H. Davenport & Co. Meals were delivered by dumbwaiter from the kitchen in the basement, where the offices for the Royal Chamberlain and other palace staff were also located. When the royal couple dined alone or with family and friends, their meals were frequently taken upstairs to the second-floor central hall outside of the royal suites. Extending along the walls of this hall are massive curio cabinets that once held Kalakaua's collection of Hawaiian artifacts.

King Kalakaua loved music and dancing, and, during his reign, Iolani Palace was the scene of many lively entertainments. On special occasions, such as visits by European diplomats, a glittering, late-night ball might be held in the Throne Room. Tall windows line two of the Throne Room walls, their wooden louvers tightly drawn; lighting is provided by crystal chandeliers that are suspended from the room's 16-foot-high ceiling. Other than the twin thrones positioned on a raised dais at one end, the room is sparsely furnished with only a dozen or so gilded, straight-backed chairs set against the walls and a large red silk–upholstered circular settee in the center. In preparation for a ball, the richly woven red carpet would be rolled up to uncover the highly polished wood floor. The Royal Hawaiian Band would take their place outside on the veranda, waiting for the signal to begin playing waltzes and polkas for the royal residents and their guests. Many of these parties lasted into the early hours of the morning.

PIVOTAL EVENTS

The palace also was the setting of more serious events. In 1889 partisans of native Hawaiian rule attempted a palace coup aimed at restoring executive powers to the king that were being assumed by the legislature. In 1893, two years after she took the throne and moved into the palace, Queen Liliuokalani was forced to surrender to armed vigilantes who were supported by U.S. troops. A provisional government was formed under the leadership of American Sanford Dole, a former associate justice of Hawaii's supreme court. In 1895 Liliuokalani was accused of "misprision of treason" against the newly formed Republic of Hawaii. Originally sentenced to five years hard labor, her sentence was commuted to eight months imprisonment in Iolani Palace, where she lived in confinement in a second-floor suite.

By the time the queen was released later that same year, the palace had been converted to executive and legislative use. Hawaii's royal building served as the capitol of the provisional government (1893), of the republic (1894–98), and of the territory of Hawaii (1898–1959). From 1959 to 1969, during Hawaii's first decade of statehood, official business was carried out within its storied walls until a new state capitol was completed on the former site of the barracks.

In the early 1960's a movement to preserve the historic building culminated in the formation of the Friends of Iolani Palace, established in 1966.

Under Liliuokalani Kawananakoa Morris, a descendant of Queen Kapiolani's sister, and Morris' daughter, Abigail Kinoiki Kekaulike Kawananakoa, the organization began to undo the almost fatal damage inflicted by years of overuse and neglect.

Restoration called for major structural rebuilding and extensive repairs on the termite-damaged interior, and the arduous task of locating, reclaiming, and cataloging long-dispersed furnishings and objects that adorned the palace during the royal years. More than 3,000 pieces have been donated to or bought for the palace, and are on display. Their pedigree and placement are confirmed by photographs taken during the last years of the monarchy. The hunt continues, with costly renovations, meticulous research, and limited budgets making the process a time-consuming one. For the Friends of Iolani Palace, now guardians of this central monument to Hawaii's royal past, the ongoing commitment to preservation and restoration is a labor of love.

The sight of Iolani Palace bathed in the warm light of the afternoon sun proves the worth of the group's efforts. The palace is a tribute to the Friends' dedication, the skill of local artisans—and the enduring legacy of a kingdom.

CRYSTAL MAIDEN
The etched crystal paneling, left, underwent an epic journey before it was installed in the palace's front door. The glass was made in England, designed and etched in San Francisco, and then shipped to Hawaii in the early 1880's.

DINING ROOM FIT FOR A KING
Custom-made flatware, china, and stemware imported from the United States and Europe are set out on the Davenport table in the State Dining Room, left, re-creating the days when the king and queen entertained foreign dignitaries here. This and other rooms in the palace are adorned with portraits of some of the great European monarchs, as well as political and military men.

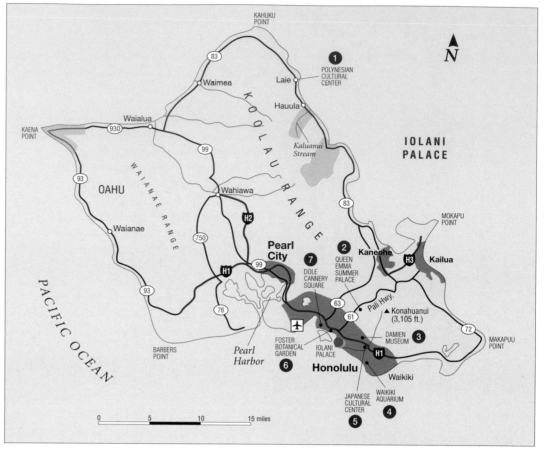

A cannonball tree blossom, above, in the Foster Botanical Garden displays its radiant crimson and yellow coloring.

1 POLYNESIAN CULTURAL CENTER

The cultural history of the Polynesian people is brought to life on a walking and canoeing tour of seven model villages, representing the people of Hawaii, Samoa, Fiji, Tonga, New Zealand, the Marquesas, and Tahiti. The center offers demonstrations of coconut husking, taro pounding, and palm-leaf weaving, and a theater presents two IMAX films on Polynesia. Live performances of traditional dances and songs of Polynesia are performed as well. Located in Laie on Hwy. 83.

2 QUEEN EMMA SUMMER PALACE

The summer home of Queen Emma and King Kamehameha IV, who ruled the Hawaiian Islands from 1854 to 1863, is a prefabricated New England–style house that was shipped from Boston in 1847 for Emma's uncle, John Young II. Emma inherited the small, intimate home when her uncle died and it served as a retreat for the royal family from the heat of Honolulu. The house displays portraits of Hawaii's great royal families, and the rooms are filled with gifts from other monarchs. A cape worn by King Kamehameha IV made from the plumage of the extinct o'o bird is on display in one room. The tall, feathered standards of Hawaiian royalty stand in every room and one of the two bedrooms contains the canoe-shaped cradle of Emma's only child, Prince Albert, who died at the age of four.

The baby's ornate engraved silver christening cup, sent by his godmother, Queen Victoria, arrived in Hawaii just hours after his death. Devastated by Albert's death, Kamehameha IV shut himself in this house for more than a year. In the accounts by the Daughters of Hawaii docents he died "of a broken heart." Located at 2913 Pali Hwy.

3 DAMIEN MUSEUM

This museum features photographs, mementoes, and the personal papers of Father Damien, the altruistic priest who spent the last 16 years of his life with a leper colony on Molokai's Kalaupapa peninsula. Born in Tremeloo, Belgium, Father Damien arrived in Hawaii in 1873, where he helped build churches, hospitals, and orphanages. Tragically, he contracted leprosy himself and died in 1889, earning him the nickname "the Martyr of Molokai." Located at 130 Ohua Ave. in Honolulu.

4 WAIKIKI AQUARIUM

Specializing in Hawaiian and tropical Pacific sea life, this is the only aquarium built on a live coral reef and the first to breed coral. More than 350 species of plants and animals thrive in its exhibits. The South Seas Marine Life gallery houses sharks, giant 100-pound clams, sea horses, turtles, and eels found in the Pacific. The aquarium also has 3 male Hawaiian monk seals out of just 1,500 worldwide. Located at 2777 Kalakaua Ave. in Honolulu.

⑤ JAPANESE CULTURAL CENTER

This 4,500-square-foot gallery contains permanent and changing exhibits detailing the history of the Japanese presence in Hawaii from 1868 to the present. Photographs, maps, furniture, tools, and charts are on permanent display, and the center features a Japanese teahouse and garden and a school for the martial arts. Located at 2454 South Beretania St. in Honolulu.

⑥ FOSTER BOTANICAL GARDEN

Hawaii's oldest botanical garden encompasses 15 acres of the former estate of William Hillebrand, a German botanist and physician to the Hawaiian royal court. Hillebrand established the garden in 1855 using specimens of plants, trees, and flowers that he had collected on trips to India. One of the garden's original kapok trees—a species whose seedpods produce the waterproof fibers used in the manufacture of life preservers—now rises 161 feet and has a 20-foot-wide trunk. Other commercially viable trees include cinnamon, allspice, nutmeg, vanilla, chocolate, and sapodilla, a South American tree whose sap is the primary ingredient in chewing gum. The garden also supports rare trees such as the loulu palm, 1 of 20 species of palm trees found only in Hawaii. Other protected trees include the bo, a tree sacred to Buddhists that was grown from a sprig of the world's oldest known bo tree in Sri Lanka. The mother tree dates from 288 B.C. and is said to be a descendant of the tree under which Buddha sat and gained enlightenment. Also on display is a Caribbean royal palm, which produces palm hearts, and a wax palm, used to make Carauba wax. One of the most interesting plants is the Hong Kong orchid, a hybrid discovered in Hong Kong in 1908 that must be grafted to regenerate because it does not produce seeds. Located at 50 North Vineyard Blvd. in Honolulu.

A pile of stones props up a traditional tiki pole, left, at the Polynesian Cultural Center. The center was established in 1963 to promote the history and culture of the Polynesians.

⑦ DOLE CANNERY SQUARE

The Dole pineapple factory has been refurbished and reopened as the Dole Cannery Square, which includes the old cannery and a mini-mall with shops and a cafeteria. The Palm Galleria, a central atrium, is decorated with reproductions of Dole pineapple can labels. A tour of the cannery grounds begins with an audiovisual display chronicling the history of the pineapple industry in Hawaii. Vintage photographs and memorabilia related to the industry are also on display. Self-guided tours of the busy factory provide visitors with opportunities to see how the fruit is processed, including the use of the Ginaca machine. Invented in 1913, the processor can peel, core, cut, and slice 100 pineapples per minute; it takes only 20 minutes to prepare a can of fruit for the supermarket shelf. Located at 650 Iwilei Rd. in Honolulu.

The serene exterior of the Queen Emma Summer Palace, left, belies the tragedy that was visited on the royal family here—the deaths of both the queen's son and husband. Afterward, the grieving Emma auctioned off most of the furnishings to raise money for a hospital. When the house was scheduled to be razed in 1913, the Daughters of Hawaii stepped in to rescue it. They eventually retrieved most of the building's original furnishings.

GAZETTEER: *Traveler's Guide to Great American Homes*

Saint-Gaudens National Historic Site, New Hampshire.

ALABAMA
Gaineswood   119

CALIFORNIA
Larkin House   120

CONNECTICUT
Gillette Castle   121

FLORIDA
Vizcaya   122

ILLINOIS
Glessner House   123

IOWA
Brucemore   124

LOUISIANA
1850 House, Lower Pontalba
Building   125

MASSACHUSETTS
Naumkeag   126
The Mount   127

MICHIGAN
Meadow Brook Hall   128

NEW HAMPSHIRE
Saint-Gaudens Home   129

NEW MEXICO
Kit Carson Historic Museums   130

NEW YORK
Olana   131

OHIO
Stan Hywet Hall and Gardens   132

OKLAHOMA
Marland Mansion and Estate   133

PENNSYLVANIA
Fallingwater   134

RHODE ISLAND
The Breakers   135

SOUTH CAROLINA
Drayton Hall   136

TENNESSEE
Hunt-Phelan Home   137

TEXAS
The Bishop's Palace   138
McFaddin-Ward House   139

UTAH
Beehive House   140

VIRGINIA
Pope-Leighey House   141

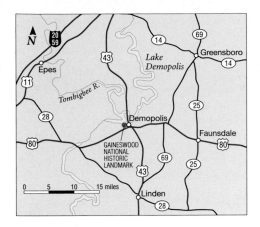

In an 1856 letter to his cousin Rachel, General Whitfield wrote that the large drawing room, above, was finally complete, "and I think is the most splendid room in Alabama."

Gaineswood was once the centerpiece of a huge plantation in Alabama's Black Belt, a region named for its dark, fertile soil. One of the few Southern houses that still contains its original furnishings, the Greek Revival mansion evokes the height of elegance in the antebellum era.

In 1843 Gen. Nathan Bryan Whitfield, a wealthy cotton planter, gifted inventor, musician, and architect, purchased a 480-acre property near present-day Demopolis from Indian agent George Gaines. The general gradually transformed the two-room log cabin that stood on the grounds into an imposing villa.

The erudite general spent almost two decades directing the work and refining the 20-room house. Whitfield lacked formal training as an architect; nevertheless, he sketched floor plans, deliberated over

proportions, supervised workmen, and pored over the pattern books of the popular New York architect Minard Lafever. The general designed lathes, routers, and other precision machinery to speed the fashioning of cornices, moldings, and pilasters. The former cabin evolved into a mansion that by 1860, had grown to become the social center of the region.

Although Gaineswood was spared the destruction that befell so many plantation homes during the Civil War, its glory days ended with the war. The general went bankrupt and was forced to sell Gaineswood, which was eventually abandoned. Goats took up residence in the drawing room and a mulberry tree put down roots in the dining room. The state of Alabama acquired the estate in 1968. The villa's subsequent rebirth lends truth to a sign on the grounds, written in Latin, which translates as: "Still Here Are the Things of Yesterday."

ELEGANT SURROUNDINGS

The beige house with white trim contains 20 rooms embellished with friezes and medallions of wood and plaster. Family portraits, many painted by the general himself, hang on some of the walls.

A portrait of Edith Winifred Whitfield, one of the general's 13 children, hangs above a Grand Square Chickering piano, left.

Flanking the main hallway are two reception rooms, one for ladies and one for gentlemen, which lead into a magnificent drawing room. Corinthian columns line the room and elaborate plasterwork adorns the ceiling. Thirteen full-length vis-à-vis mirrors reflect multiple images, creating an illusion of greater space. Original Chippendale rosewood furniture, Italian marble statuary, jib windows, and Venetian glass in this room make it the epitome of splendor and charm.

The dining room is topped by a domed skylight and features pocket doors. A rosewood case against one wall was designed to hold the silver ornamental stand that graces the table in the dining room.

The master bedroom features Ionic columns and an original custom-made bed carved with a pineapple motif, the symbol of hospitality. The family bedroom down the hall is decorated with columns patterned after the Tower of Winds in Athens, Greece. It is said that the ghost of a former housekeeper's sister wanders about the mansion singing her favorite melodies.

FOR MORE INFORMATION:
Gaineswood National Historic Landmark, 805 South Cedar Ave., Demopolis, AL 36732; 334-289-4846.

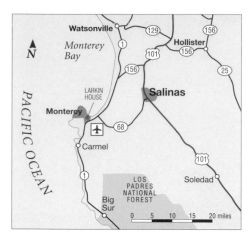

Cooper. Three years later Larkin set up his own business, trading in lumber, hides, flour, potatoes, and cattle. His work took him as far afield as the Hawaiian Islands and made him a wealthy man.

Larkin set up his enterprises in a house built on a plot of land that he had bought in 1835 for $12.40. The house featured adobe and redwood construction. Adobe is a Spanish word derived from Arabic that refers to a sun-dried brick of clay and straw. It also had wrap-around verandas and a walled garden. The ceilings in the first-floor rooms were made of wide hand-hewn planks. The house sports many New

who added a balcony, several windows, and a door to the back upper story in 1891. Leese also laid a coat of colored cement over the adobe walls and built a separate two-story frame house next door. Robert F. Johnson, the one time mayor of Monterey, bought the house in 1902. Johnson tore down Leese's new house, removed the exterior stairwell, and installed a fireplace and benches. His daughter Juanita later married J. B. Cooper, who was the grandson of Larkin's half-brother.

FAMILY HERITAGE

In 1922 one of Larkin's granddaughters, Alice Larkin Toulmin, who had been raised in New Hampshire, decided to go to California to live in her grandfather's house—a home that was a vivid part of the family lore and that she had visited on previous visits to Monterey. She paid $10,000 for the building and moved in with her husband, Henry Wroughton Toulmin, who was the baronet of Childwick, St. Alban's, Herfordshire. Over the next 35 years, Alice Toulmin devoted much of her energy to enhancing the adobe structure.

With the help of the interior designer Frances Adler Elkins, Toulmin decorated the house and made several structural changes, such as adding servants' quarters to the kitchen and a powder room on the first floor. In 1938 brick was used to replace the first-floor porches, originally constructed of packed earth. Toulmin had the exterior walls plastered and painted and central heating installed as well.

Larkin House is decorated with antiques, some of which belonged to Thomas Larkin, and others are 18th- and 19th-century French and English pieces collected by Mrs. Toulmin during her extensive world travels. Her bedroom features an ornately carved opium bed bought in China in 1920, and the dining room contains Mrs. Toulmin's cherished splendid Hepplewhite breakfront dating from around 1795. When her husband died in 1957, she is reported to have said, "Well, now no floozy will get my breakfront."

Alice Larkin Toulmin died in 1963 and her legacy, Larkin House, is now a unit of the Monterey State Historic Park. It serves as a tangible reminder of that early chapter in California's history.

The unpretentious Larkin House, above, has a balcony that provides access to the second-floor family rooms. Thomas Larkin operated his general store on the first floor of the house.

Thomas Oliver Larkin built a house in Monterey, California, that set the standard for a style known as Monterey Colonial, which is characterized by the use of adobe and glass in a symmetrical two-story floor plan. Larkin was born in 1802 in the small town of Charlestown, near Boston. Orphaned at age 16, he lived and worked for a time in the Carolinas before sailing from Boston in 1831 on a tough seven-month voyage around Cape Horn that would deliver him to a new life in California, then a Mexican territory. It was during this sea voyage that Larkin met Rachel Hobson Home, a Boston sea captain's widow. He later married her and together they had six children.

In Monterey, Larkin worked for his half-brother, John Rogers Cooper, a sea captain turned merchant. Cooper had settled there nine years earlier, become a Mexican citizen, and changed his name to Juan Bautista

England features, including a floor plan that radiates from a central hall, a symmetrical two-story construction, multipaned glass windows, an interior staircase (possibly added later), and a neat, compact shape.

Thomas Larkin's status as a prominent public figure was affirmed by his appointment as the United States Consul to Mexico in 1842—the first and only one. He held that post for four years, playing a vital role in the transferral of California from Mexican to American control. Dedicated to a peaceful annexation, Larkin was distressed by the outbreak of war between the United States and Mexico in 1846 and the subsequent hostile annexation of California.

In 1850, the same year that California entered the Union, Larkin moved with his family to New York City. He returned to California a few years later and settled in San Francisco, where he died in 1858. Larkin House was sold to Jacob P. Leese,

FOR MORE INFORMATION:

Larkin House, Monterey State Historic Park, 20 Custom House Plaza, Monterey, CA 93940; 408-649-7118.

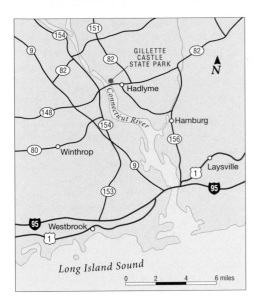

A wooden door in Gillette Castle, left, displays one of the intricate latches that were fashioned by William Gillette himself.

A bizarre Rhinelike castle overlooking the Connecticut River is the legacy of William Gillette (1853–1937), the celebrated actor and playwright. Gillette designed the quirky mansion himself, and spent about $1 million to have it built. The money was only a portion of the ample earnings he made by portraying Sherlock Holmes on the stage.

The castle expresses the eccentric personality of its creator. Among its unusual features are a table mounted on tracks and 47 doors locked with ingenious latches designed by Gillette. He also installed mirrors in his bedroom that were angled so that he could see who was downstairs.

Gillette introduced the Sherlock Holmes trademark accessories to the stage—the deerstalker cap, Inverness cape, and curved pipe. He played the eccentric sleuth more than 1,300 times and wrote and staged his own dramatizations of Sherlock Holmes' adventures. Gillette also penned two Civil War tales called *Held by the Enemy* and *Secret Service.*

Gillette married in 1882, but six years later his wife died of a ruptured appendix. Widowed and childless, Gillette turned his attention and considerable wealth to building a dream house. In 1913, while cruising in his riverboat, the *Aunt Polly,* he found the ideal site: 122 acres on a peak known as the Seventh Sister, the last in a row of hills along the Connecticut River.

Gillette designed a castle with walls three to four feet thick at the base, tapering to

The exterior of the castle, right, is made of native fieldstone. The unusual crenellated structure befitted a man who was described by a friend as someone "who loved the unexpected."

roughly two feet at the top. He hired a team of 26 men, who labored for five years to construct a steel framework covered over with native fieldstone.

Shortly after the castle's completion in 1919, Gillette built a reduced-scale, three-mile-long railroad with a locomotive on the grounds. Manning the throttle himself, he took his guests on tours of the gardens.

The home's doorways and cabinets were made of hand-carved southern white oak. Gillette covered the walls with Javanese raffia matting to absorb humidity and lit the rooms with Tiffany lamps and wall sconces decorated with bits of colored glass bottles he had solicited from his friends.

Visitors can tour the uniquely furnished rooms, including nine bedrooms, seven bathrooms, a kitchen and pantry, a third-floor suite, a library, and a 1,500-square-foot living room. To protect the finish on the house's hardwood floors, the dining room table was set on metal tracks and moved with the pull of a drawstring.

SHERLOCK HOLMES ROOM

The third floor, constructed between 1923 and 1926, is finished in pine and cedar instead of the white oak that predominates at the lower levels. An art gallery on the third floor displays pastoral landscapes and seascapes by Amelia Watson, John Whorf, Maxfield Parrish, Paul Marny, and William Richards. In the Sherlock Holmes Room, a collection of furniture, stage props, and artifacts is arranged to re-create the detective's quarters at 221B Baker Street.

Gillette spent the last 17 years of his life at his castle and he died in 1937 at the age of 83. He was very fond of his fanciful creation and stipulated in his will that the estate not be sold to some "blithering idiot" after his death. In 1943 the state purchased the property and reopened it as Gillette Castle State Park.

FOR MORE INFORMATION:

Gillette Castle State Park, 67 River Rd., East Haddam, CT 06423; 860-526-2336.

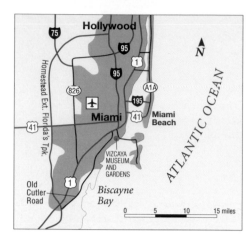

Vizcaya's Tea Room, left, features impressive trompe-l'oeil scenes painted on canvas panels and a central floor medallion made up of a geometric pattern of marble. The doors were moved from a hotel in Paris.

International Harvester magnate James Deering constructed this Renaissance-style villa at the edge of Biscayne Bay in 1916 as a winter retreat. He named it Vizcaya, a Basque word meaning "Elevated Place." Accompanied by designer Paul Chalfin, a graduate of the École des Beaux-Arts in Paris, Deering scoured the great French and Italian houses of Europe to acquire the finest antique furnishings for his estate. Resplendent in Old World elegance, Vizcaya's 34 decorated rooms are filled with gilded furnishings, rich tapestries, carved wood paneling, and sculptures representing four centuries of European decorative arts.

Architect F. Burrall Hoffman designed the mansion around a central courtyard that was later enclosed by glass to protect its valuable contents from the weather. Constructed of native limestone, the villa took 1,000 laborers two years and a reported $15 million to complete. Colombian-born landscape architect Diego Suarez planned the gardens and the great stone barge, an unusual breakwater filled with flowering shrubs and statues of mythological figures associated with the sea.

INSIDE THE MANSION

Deering's bedroom suite in the Napoleonic Empire style includes a marble-walled bathroom decorated with Sheffield silver plaques, a sitting room paneled in woven silk and Italian carved wood with gold leafing, and a bedroom containing gilded mahogany furniture and an Aubusson rug with a sea horse motif—Deering's symbol for Vizcaya. The sea horse reappears on the stained-glass windows in the Tea Room, whose canvas panels are elaborately painted with fantasy cityscapes. The gardens were designed to be moved through as though they were one vast, outdoor room.

The Reception Room is modeled after an 18th-century rococo salon, complete with wall coverings of painted silk and a plaster ceiling that were transferred from a Venice palazzo. A 17th-century altar screen in the Renaissance Hall stands behind a large pipe organ. The hall's priceless antiques include a 2,000-year-old Roman marble tripod and a Hispano-Moresque rug, one of the few remaining 15th-century Spanish heraldic carpets in the world. In 1987 the room was the meeting place for Pope John Paul II and Pres. Ronald Reagan.

Trained in Florence, Italy, Suarez adapted the garden designs of the Renaissance and Baroque eras to Florida's climate and terrain. Orange jasmine trees were pruned and shaped in the Italian topiary style and Suarez created America's first parterres, hedges trimmed in curves. Arranged in a fan-shaped design, the gardens feature an elegant array of fountains, pools, and cascades, and shaded walkways complemented by sculptures, balustrades, and decorative urns.

The Fountain Garden, a Baroque-inspired masterpiece, is surrounded by waterways that lead to smaller fountains, and the Water Stairway is built as a series of basins that collect water tumbling from a fountain made in the 16th century. The clipped hedges in the Maze Garden offered a puzzle-solving diversion for guests staying at the mansion, while the walled Secret Garden invited contemplation and privacy. The Casino, a miniature house, was a perfect place for visitors to sip tea and enjoy the expansive views of the villa and gardens.

FOR MORE INFORMATION:
Vizcaya Museum and Gardens, 3251 South Miami Ave., Miami, FL 33129; 305-250-9133.

The Secret Garden, left, was a private sanctuary where family members went when they tired of the formality of the villa. An arched doorway leads from here to Biscayne Bay.

Bright's disease at age 47, three weeks after he made the last changes to the interior designs. Richardson's pragmatic approach to his work served as a model for the Chicago school of architecture. Flourishing in the 1880's and 1890's, the Chicago school influenced John Wellborn Root, Louis Sullivan, and Frank Lloyd Wright.

John and Frances Glessner, prominent Chicago business and society leaders, engaged Richardson after they had consulted with other architectural firms of the day, including the prestigious McKim, Mead &

architectural concept, and his firm fashioned the dining room furniture and the library desk. On Richardson's advice, the Glessners sought furniture made by practitioners of the English Arts and Crafts movement, which favored craftsmanship as a reaction to the industrial revolution's mass-produced goods.

The longer wing of the L-shaped house includes a dining room, a kitchen, and a parlor where the Glessners displayed their collection of early Dutch engravings. Forming the cornerstone of the house, the library features a beamed ceiling and a huge partners desk that could be used by two people at once. The shorter wing of the house contains the master bedroom suite, which is decorated with wallpaper and fabrics designed William Morris, the foremost proponent of the Arts and Crafts style in England. The room's bed, armoire, and small bookcase are examples of the Reform Gothic style of American designer Isaac Scott, a Glessner family friend whose works grace various rooms in the house.

The living hall, which is located upstairs, contains two more prized Isaac Scott pieces. The second-floor Courtyard Guest Room features fireplace tiles designed by William De Morgan. The servants occupied rooms above the kitchen, now used as office space, and the attic served as a butler's apartment, sewing room, and storage area.

To cut down on noise, Richardson had a layer of wooden soundproofing strips inserted under the oak floors. He also designed a spiral stairway that extended from the basement to the attic and connected the family bedrooms. Because the Glessners' son suffered from severe hay fever, Richardson created a large cross-ventilated room for him on the basement level, where the boy received his home schooling.

The mansion changed hands several times after John Glessner's death in 1936. When it was put up for sale in 1966, a group of local citizens established the Chicago School of Architecture Foundation to purchase the mansion and halt plans for its demolition. Many of the Glessners' possessions have since been returned to the house by their descendants. Today Richardson's architectural masterpiece and much of its original furniture are on display for the enjoyment of the public.

The library, above, is located on the main floor of Glessner House. It resembles the study in the Brookline home of H. H. Richardson, the architect who designed the house.

Presenting a severe granite exterior to Chicago's exclusive Prairie Avenue, the John J. and Frances M. Glessner House marked a radical departure from other Gilded Age mansions in the area. The massive walls, limited number of windows, and innovative floor plan of the 1887 structure were conceived by Boston architect Henry Hobson Richardson, whose imaginative designs helped spur the progress of early modern architecture.

The two-story mansion is characterized by stark lines, a red-tiled gabled roof, and a rusticated Braggville granite facade. Unadorned except for Richardson's trademark arched doorways, the house bears few references to styles favored by Victorians.

Glessner Mansion was the last house designed by Richardson, who died of

White team. The architect asked the Glessners if they would be willing to let him build a house with few windows facing onto the street, an unconventional design. After the couple agreed to the idea, Richardson accepted the commission.

RICHARDSON'S DESIGN
Prairie Avenue neighbors denounced the completed mansion's forbidding exterior, but the Glessners welcomed the privacy lent by Richardson's design. From the street, the mansion looks dark; in fact, the main rooms are flooded with sunlight through bay windows that overlook an interior courtyard surrounded by pink brick walls and picturesque towers.

Richardson regarded furnishings and interior design as part of the overall

FOR MORE INFORMATION:
Prairie Avenue House Museums,
1800 South Prairie Ave., Chicago, IL 60616;
312-326-1480.

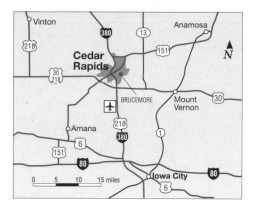

B rucemore, a classic Queen Anne–style mansion, was built in 1886 for Caroline Sinclair, the widow of Thomas Sinclair, who was the founder of the Sinclair Meat Packing Plant. Set amid a 26-acre estate, the elegant house offers insight into the lives of three generations of Iowa industrialists.

Caroline Sinclair spared no expense on this house for her six children. The red-brick-and-limestone mansion was constructed at a cost of $55,000—10 times that of the average dwelling in Cedar Rapids. Designed by the architectural firm Josselyn and Taylor, the three-story house was dubbed by many as "the finest residence this side of Chicago."

Among Brucemore's 21 rooms are a Great Hall, a grand staircase, 8 bathrooms, and 9 bedrooms. The house also boasts 14 fireplaces—which were an indulgence,

given that central heating had already been installed. The mansion's steep gabled roof, large chimneys, and porches are characteristic of Queen Anne architecture, as is the combination of smooth brick on the lower levels with decorative slate shingles on the upper story. The stylized relief decorations are also typical of the period.

HOUSE EXCHANGE

By 1906, Caroline Sinclair's children had grown up and she no longer needed to live in such a large house, so she exchanged it for the smaller residence of George Bruce Douglas. A founding partner of the Quaker Oats Company, Douglas also owned a linseed oil manufacturing company and the Douglas Starch Works.

Douglas renamed the Sinclair mansion Brucemore, a combination of his middle name and the Scottish word moor, from his ancestral home. Other nods to Douglas' heritage include a collection of family portraits and the rendering of Mary, Queen of Scots, that hangs in the Great Hall.

Douglas and his wife, Irene, added 26 acres to the property's original 10 or so, and remodeled the mansion at a cost of $30,000. The main entrance was moved from the north to the south facade and a north terrace, breakfast porch, and sunporch were added. They also put in a duck pond, gardens, and a swimming pool.

The couple filled the Great Hall with Renaissance-style furniture and installed butternut paneling and ceiling beams, and

later added a Skinner pipe organ. The room was further enhanced with a colorful mural depicting scenes from Richard Wagner's Ring cycle.

Mrs. Douglas' refined taste is on display in the 1935 Swan Room, where some 20 swans are carved on the furniture and the fireplace mantel. Used as a guest bedroom, the pretty room features a bay window that provides sweeping views of the lawn and Garden House.

The civic-minded Douglases sat on the boards of several local hospitals and churches and acted as benefactors for organizations, including a camp for handicapped children. The family tradition of community service was carried on by Margaret Douglas Hall, who inherited the house in 1937. In 1981 she bequeathed the property to the National Trust for Historic Preservation, stipulating that it be used as a community cultural center and museum.

Margaret and her husband, Howard, left their mark on Brucemore. They lightened the woodwork in the Great Hall, added picture windows in the library and dining room, and sold some of the land, reducing the grounds to its current 26 acres.

The Grizzly Bar and Tahitian Room were created by Howard Hall, an astute businessman with a penchant for movie stars and circuses. Paneled in material resembling bamboo, the Tahitian Room contains an amusing assortment of colored sea ferns, heads made from coconuts, shells, fishnets, artificial fruit, a wicker monkey, and ceramic palm trees. The Grizzly Bar is decorated with pictures of cancan girls, a collection of beer steins, and a wall covered with photographs of Mr. Hall with various celebrities and circus animals. The Halls were fond of animals and kept a pair of German shepherds and two pet lions at the estate. One of the lions is buried in the Brucemore pet cemetery with 20 other animals.

The Halls enjoyed entertaining guests in their spacious residence. In 1962 they hosted former presidents Herbert Hoover and Harry S. Truman, who were in Cedar Rapids for the dedication of the Herbert Hoover Presidential Library–Museum in nearby West Branch.

FOR MORE INFORMATION:
Brucemore, 2160 Linden Dr. SE, Cedar Rapids, IA 52403; 319-362-7375.

Brucemore's grand central staircase, left, reflects the solid yet elegant Queen Anne style.

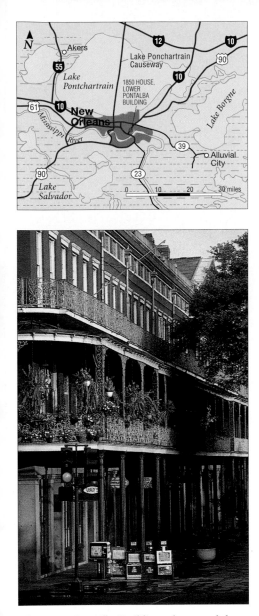

The Upper Pontalba Building, above, and the nearby Lower Pontalba Building were built between 1849 and 1851 and still house residences and retail businesses.

Flanking Jackson Square in New Orleans stand two rows of elegant town houses known as the Pontalba Buildings. The 1850 House, situated in the Lower Pontalba Building, has been opened to the public by the Louisiana State Museum, its rooms furnished in styles preferred by the Creole elite prior to the Civil War. Ongoing repairs by the museum are gradually restoring the National Historic Landmark to its antebellum splendor.

The Pontalba Buildings were the brainchild of Baroness Micaela Almonester de Pontalba, daughter of Don Andrés Almonester y Roxas, a wealthy Spaniard

who had financed a trio of buildings on Jackson Square in the 1790's, including the Saint Louis Cathedral. The baroness, described as obstinate by her contractors, scrutinized every detail of construction, even if it meant wearing men's pantaloons "to go up the ladders to examine the work herself."

While living in France, the baroness drew up a proposal for developing land she had inherited from her father. She persuaded city authorities to renovate New Orleans' Place d'Armes, which was then renamed Jackson Square after Gen. Andrew Jackson, hero of the Battle of New Orleans. To further revitalize the area, the baroness financed the construction of two block-long buildings, each containing 16 town houses and now known as the Upper Pontalba and Lower Pontalba Buildings. The second and third floors were rented to fashionable upper-middle-class tenants at high rates, the ground floor to posh retail establishments.

Their designer is unknown, but the baroness' hand can be seen in several touches, including the beautiful "AP" monograms of the Almonester-Pontalba names that are affixed to cast-iron railings on the exteriors. The buildings are a hybrid of Parisian-influenced Greek Revival and casual Creole styles. They represent one of the first American uses in a major project of industrially produced building materials, including New England granite, Baltimore pressed brick, English slate and roofing tiles, New York ornamental iron, and New Jersey window glass.

STAR ATTRACTION
The shrewd baroness attracted attention to her exclusive buildings by decorating an apartment in the Upper Pontalba for Jenny Lind, the renowned songstress who spent a month in New Orleans in 1851. Today a hand-painted lithograph of the Swedish Nightingale graces the wall of the gentleman's bedroom on the third floor of the Lower Pontalba's 1850 House. The room also contains a dresser with a mirror and a full tester bed, both of which were said to have been made by slaves who worked on a plantation that then occupied the Carrollton section of the city.

A complete set of Rococo Revival furniture in the 1850 House's master bedroom displays the profusion of bold curves and

A Rococo Revival bedroom ensemble, right, including a half tester bed, is on view in the 1850 House's master bedroom, located in the Lower Pontalba Building.

richly carved designs of that style. Paintings, sketches, and assorted needlework add decorative touches.

The parlor and a dining room on the second floor are equipped with marble mantels, coal grates, and reproductions of period carpets and window hangings. The era's penchant for bric-a-brac is displayed in the parlor in the form of games, figurines, musical instruments, religious objects, and numerous decorative trinkets.

The dining room is furnished with mahogany and rosewood pieces, a candelabrum, and upholstered chairs. A 75-piece set of Vieux Paris porcelain tableware is laid out on the sideboard and dining table.

After the Civil War, many of the Pontalba Buildings' shopkeepers went bankrupt. The baroness returned to France, leaving her handsome buildings to fall into decline. In 1921 her heirs sold the Lower Pontalba Building to philanthropist William Ratcliffe Irby, who bequeathed it in his will to the Louisiana State Museum in 1927.

FOR MORE INFORMATION:
1850 House, Louisiana State Museum, Box 2448, New Orleans, LA 70176; 504-568-6968 or 800-568-6968.

G ⌂ 🏛 ⌂

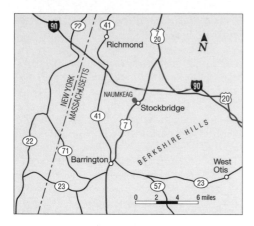

Carefully manicured trees grace the grounds of Naumkeag, above. The enclosure surrounds the Afternoon Garden, which contains Japanese holly, four small fountains, and a bronze statue.

The Entrance Hall, above, contains fine antique furniture and a portrait of Joseph Choate.

Naumkeag was constructed as a summer retreat by New York attorney and diplomat Joseph Hodges Choate. Naumkeag is an Algonquin word translated by the Choates as "Haven." The house's 26 rooms and sumptuous furnishings reflect the affluent lifestyle enjoyed by America's upper class in the decades after the Civil War.

In 1884 Choate and his wife, Caroline, purchased property in the Berkshire Hills of western Massachusetts and commissioned the New York firm McKim, Mead & White to design their home. The firm's other buildings included Madison Square Garden, the New York Herald Building, Pennsylvania Station, and the Washington Memorial Arch, all in New York City. Stanford White designed the house and

Frederick MacMonnies, a sculptor, was commissioned to create original works of art to complement it.

The exterior of Naumkeag combined the common American use of shingles as a building material, with European features such as brick and stone towers, two-toned brick patterns, and wrought-iron detailing. The gabled mansion was embellished with dormer windows, porches, and embossed chimneys, and was completed in 1886.

INSIDE THE MANSION

No expense was spared on Naumkeag's interior. The lavish rooms are paneled in cherry, oak, and mahogany, and feature ornate plasterwork, wood and tile floors, and lighting fixtures fashioned of brass, silver, and glass. The Choates filled their home with an impressive collection of Asian and European porcelain, early American furniture, and valuable carpets and draperies. Much of the fine china on display was acquired after the death of Joseph Choate in 1917. The china was purchased by his daughter Mabel, who spent the summer months at Naumkeag with her mother.

A three-story hand-carved oak staircase rises from the Entrance Hall, which is furnished with a 16th-century Flemish tapestry, an early American blanket chest, and an Ashton Macclefield grandfather clock.

The focal point of the drawing room is a marble bust of one of the Choate sons, Ruluff, sculpted in 1887 by Augustus Saint-Gaudens. Tin alloy foil was used to fashion the unusual dining room ceiling, and the

mahogany furniture includes a dining table and chairs made by Stanford White and a magnificent sideboard patterned on the style of the English furniture designer George Hepplewhite.

Nathan Barrett planned the original landscaping, which is built on two broad terraces to accommodate the property's steep grade. Mabel Choate inherited the estate upon her mother's death in 1929 and designed the splendid gardens. Her first project, in collaboration with landscape architect Fletcher Steele, was the Afternoon Garden, which is bordered with Venetian-style gondola poles, made of oak pilings dredged from the bottom of Boston Harbor and decked with garlands of woodbine. In 1938 Steele designed the Blue Steps, a series of sapphire fountain pools fringed with stands of birch trees and bordered by four flights of stairs leading down to Mabel's cutting gardens. A gravel path leads visitors through a rose garden featuring 16 beds of floribunda rosebushes.

In 1958 Mabel bequeathed the house and grounds to The Trustees of Reservations, stipulating that they preserve the "aura of good times and gracious living" enjoyed by the Choate family at Naumkeag.

FOR MORE INFORMATION:
Naumkeag, The Trustees of Reservations, Box 792, Stockbridge, MA 01262; 413-298-3239.

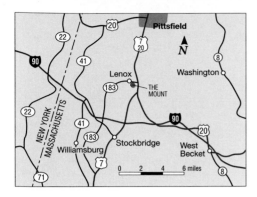

Crowning a hilltop in the Berkshires, The Mount was designed and built by Pulitzer Prize–winning author Edith Wharton in 1902. The noble white stucco manor within this 49-acre estate is an architectural expression of the design principles formulated by Wharton in her first book, *The Decoration of Houses,* co-written with Ogden Codman Jr. in 1897.

The publication of a later volume, titled *Italian Villas and Their Gardens,* coincided with her planning of The Mount. The influence of Renaissance landscaping is shown in Wharton's design of the terraces, woodland garden, and an Italian walled garden. Her adviser was her niece, Beatrix Jones Farrand, a renowned designer who belonged to the first wave of female landscape designers at the turn of the century.

Broad pathways connected a series of formal gardens bordered by clipped hedges and accented by fountains. Conceived as "outdoor rooms," the orderly gardens provided a transition between the clean lines of the house and the ruggedness of the surrounding New England landscape.

"Decidedly, I'm a better landscape gardener than novelist," Wharton wrote in 1911, "and this place, every line of which is my own work, far surpasses *The House of Mirth,*" her celebrated 1905 novel.

Seeking an escape from the "stuffy" confines of Newport, Rhode Island, where Wharton and her husband, Edward, owned a house, she purchased the property in Massachusetts when she was 39. Although Ogden Codman drew the initial plans for The Mount, Wharton objected to his fee and turned the work over to Francis Hoppin, formerly the chief draftsman in the office of McKim, Mead & White.

Wharton spent some of her most productive years at The Mount. She wrote perhaps her best work, *Ethan Frome,* here and also entertained a circle of literary friends, including Henry James, author of *The Turn of the Screw,* who referred to the house as "a delicate French château mirrored in a Massachusetts pond."

SYMMETRY AND BALANCE

The 35-room mansion, which was fashioned after a 17th-century English estate, maintains the sublime balance and proportion of its manicured lawns and gardens. The dining room, drawing room, and library flow seamlessly into one another, evoking the great houses of Europe, where the doors all opened on the same axis. Wharton valued symmetry and thought nothing of installing false windows, mirrors, or phony doors in order to achieve it.

Paintings of pastoral scenes along the main stairway create visual links to the exterior landscape—a trademark feature of Wharton's interior design. The graceful curving staircase leads to the gallery and the drawing room, where doors open onto an Italianate terrace with breathtaking views of Laurel Lake and the gentle slopes of the Berkshires beyond.

Wharton sold the property in 1912, divorced the following year, and moved to France, where she lived out the last 26 years of her life. The Mount changed hands twice and then a girls' school occupied it from the 1940's to the 1970's. In 1980, Edith Wharton Restoration, Inc., purchased the property with plans to restore the house as a center dedicated to the study of Edith Wharton's life and her literary works.

Although the house and grounds are currently undergoing extensive restorations, visitors can view the main rooms, including the library and drawing room, and watch matinee dramatizations of Wharton's stories, which are staged by the theater group Shakespeare & Co.

The Mount is one of the few National Historic Landmarks dedicated to a woman. To Wharton the estate was a place where she could retreat from the inhibiting world of New York society and discover her literary voice. In her 1934 autobiography, *A Backward Glance,* she wrote, "it was only at the Mount that I was really happy."

FOR MORE INFORMATION:

The Mount, P. O. Box 974, Lenox, MA 01240; 413-637-1899.

Edith Wharton spent many happy and relaxing hours in her library at The Mount, below. The design of the room, with matching doors and bookcases flanking a fireplace, is indicative of Wharton's innate feel for balance.

Meadow Brook Hall, a 100-room Tudor Revival–style mansion, was completed in Rochester, Michigan, in 1929 at a cost of $4 million. It is one of the most luxurious and architecturally stunning houses in America. The history of the house is a classic American success story. John and Horace Dodge, a pair of small-town boys with a talent for mechanics, set out to make their fortunes in the budding automobile industry in turn-of-the-century Detroit. They started up an auto parts company with $1,000 just as America's fascination with the motor car was beginning. Their fledgling enterprise, called Dodge Brothers, quickly prospered.

By 1914 Dodge Brothers had begun to expand into car manufacturing and rapidly became one of the Detroit auto successes. Tragically, the brothers both contracted a deadly influenza virus at a New York City auto show in 1920. John succumbed first and Horace, who had lost his lifelong companion, followed him to the grave 11 months later. Thus John's wife of 13 years, Matilda Rausch, and their two surviving children (a third had died of a childhood disease) became the heirs to one of the largest fortunes in the nation.

Matilda remarried Wisconsin lumber baron Alfred G. Wilson in 1925. Their European honeymoon inspired them to return to England with architect William E. Kapp to tour stately country estates and castles in search of designs for their home, which Matilda called Meadow Brook Hall.

A TOUCH OF ENGLAND

Construction of the brick-and-sandstone house began in 1926 and was completed three years later. Each of Meadow Brook's 39 chimneys has a distinct design, similar to those of Hampton Court in England.

Visitors enter the house through the Great Hall, the centerpiece of which is a long antique refectory table from England. The wood paneling in the hall is based on a design of a room of Cardinal Wolsey's in Hampton Court. The hall contains replicas of architectural details found in the Bromley Room of London's Victoria and Albert Museum, and the ceiling reflects the influence of England's Tudor showpiece, Knole House. A 15th-century English tapestry sofa and side chairs in the drawing room are offset by two green leather chairs.

The library is notable for its fine wood paneling, and the fireplace has a stone mantel carved with the seals of many American colleges and universities. The organ alcove is situated between the drawing room and the library. The alcove houses one of the largest residential organs in Michigan.

Diverse architectural styles are seen throughout. Matilda's study, which is considered by many to be the finest room in the house, was inspired by the Palladian designs of English architect Inigo Jones. The dining room features a carved ceiling reminiscent of the architectural style of Christopher Wren, and the Chinese breakfast room is decorated in a style known as chinoiserie. Matilda's bedroom, with its Louis XIV and XV furniture, pink marble fireplace, and rose-colored silk and velvet furnishings, is one of the most opulent rooms in Meadow Brook Hall.

The Grand Stairway features a 19th-century Chippendale clock on the landing, and needlework draperies frame the 20-foot-high windows with stained-glass panels of heraldic emblems. The second floor contains the family bedrooms as well as guest rooms. The young Danny Dodge's room has lighting fixtures and carvings in the shape of airplanes, cars, and characters from children's literature. A ladder in his closet leads to a playroom on the floor above. Frances Dodge's six-room brick playhouse, Knole Cottage, was built on the grounds in 1926 when she was 12 years old. The cottage is open to the public and is a favorite with young visitors.

In 1957 Matilda and Alfred Wilson donated the 1,400-acre estate plus a fund of $2 million toward the founding of Oakland University, provided that the Wilsons would continue to live at their beloved Meadow Brook Hall. Following their deaths—Alfred's in 1962 and Matilda's in 1967—ownership of the house was officially transferred to the university. Meadow Brook Hall was opened to the public in 1971 and offers tours year-round. A corps of volunteers helps preserve and interpret the mansion's glory years. During July and August visitors can lunch in the Christopher Wren dining room and every August Meadow Brook hosts the prestigious Meadow Brook Hall Concours d'Elegance antique and classic car show. A Landscape and Garden Show takes place here in June, and in December, a Holiday Walk allows visitors to view the house at its Christmas best.

FOR MORE INFORMATION:
Meadow Brook Hall, Oakland University, Rochester, MI 48309-4401; 248-370-3140.

Tables for pool and cards welcomed guests to the games room, left, at Meadow Brook Hall. The room was designed to resemble the interior of an English public house.

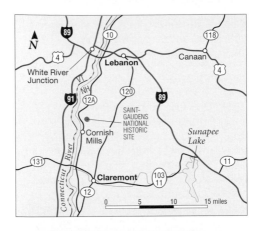

The inviting porch, above, which Saint-Gaudens called the piazza, looks out at the formal gardens. He often entertained guests here during the summer months.

The gilded bronze cast called Amor Caritas, *above, is by Saint-Gaudens. Another version is found at the Musée d'Orsay in Paris.*

Nestled in the high hills of Cornish, New Hampshire, the Saint-Gaudens National Historic Site preserves the Federal-style house, lush formal gardens, and studios of one of America's greatest sculptors.

The Irish-born Augustus Saint-Gaudens studied at the École des Beaux-Arts in Paris before spending five years perfecting his craft in Rome. His first major commission, an 1876 monument to Civil War admiral David Glasgow Farragut, unveiled in New York in 1881, was a huge success. Augustus Saint-Gaudens left New York in 1885 for Cornish, where he rented an old brick tavern from his friend Charles C. Beaman.

Enchanted by the area's white pines and sweeping meadows, Saint-Gaudens purchased a 150-acre estate there in 1892 and began to remodel the house and grounds to suit his needs. He named the house Aspet, after his father's ancestral village in France.

The artist added dormer windows and a pair of parapeted brick chimneys to the plain late 18th-century brick building, as well as a second-story porch off the master bedroom. The house's beauty rests on the simplicity of its overall design—the white exterior walls, the shuttered windows, a wide colonnaded veranda, and a front doorway with a semicircular fanlight.

Saint-Gaudens added a mezzanine study, a sunroom, and bedrooms to the two-story house. The first floor contains an entrance hall, dining room, double parlors, kitchen and pantries, and a wide curving staircase that leads to the second-floor bedrooms. Visitors can wander through four rooms furnished with Saint-Gaudens' possessions, including 17th-century Flemish tapestries, 18th-century American furniture, and paintings by the artist's wife, Augusta.

SCULPTURE GARDENS

The landscaping of the estate was a lifelong work in progress. For some 15 years, until his death in 1907, the artist refined his architectural and landscape design, and created monumental sculptures for a wonderland of picturesque pools and fountains, areas of dense woodlands, wide vistas, and formal gardens that served as settings for casts of his sculptures. These casts of earlier work include copies of the figure for the Adams Memorial in Washington, D.C., and the bronze relief of the Robert G. Shaw Memorial on Boston Common, which honors a colonel who died with his regiment of black soldiers during the Civil War.

Visitors can explore part of the 150-acre grounds along the Blow-Me-Down Trail, which descends through 80 acres of mature stands of white pine trees to a millpond. The Ravine Trail follows an old cart path through fern gardens, 100-foot-tall pines, and a hardwood forest of maple, birch, oak, ash, and beech trees.

Other buildings on the estate include the stable and icehouse, which was used to store blocks of ice cut from Blow-Me-Down Pond during the winter, and the New Gallery, existing outbuildings to which architect John Ames added a Roman-style atrium and a reflecting pool in 1948.

A marble temple marks the burial site of the Saint-Gaudens family. It was designed for a play by members of the Cornish Colony, a group of artists who lived here in the early part of the 20th century.

FOR MORE INFORMATION:
Saint-Gaudens National Historic Site, R.R. 3, Box 73, Cornish, NH 03745; 603-675-2175.

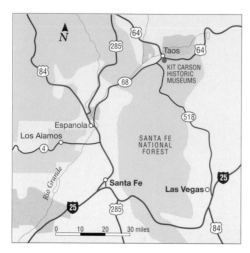

Carson's facility for languages and searing thirst for adventure drew him into all kinds of exploits over the next 42 years of his life. He became everything from a trapper, Indian fighter, and translator for settlers heading to Mexico to a scout on several mapping expeditions made by explorer John C. Frémont, an Indian agent and a Union officer in the Civil War.

Carson was known as a wide-ranging adventurer whose daring deeds in the saddle made him a legend. Trying his hand at ranching in the mid-1800's, he once drove 6,500 sheep from New Mexico to California through some of the most hostile Indian country in the nation.

Carson also entertained a steady stream of friends, admirers, and dignitaries, including Frémont and George Ruxton, a British writer who kept extensive records of his adventures in the United States.

VISITING THE HOMESTEAD

Only a portion of Carson's original four-room house is preserved as part of the museum. The U-shaped, 12-room structure underwent numerous alterations over the years, serving at various times as a home, stable, store, and saddle-making shop. By 1910 the local Masonic lodge had stepped in to take over the preservation of the house that once had belonged to one of its most famous members. Not much of the structure remained; in fact, only a few original walls and portals stand today. Though not part of the structure in Carson's time, the large timber beams, known as *vigas* in Spanish, are typical examples of the construction techniques of the Southwest.

The interior of the house is decorated with period pieces from the mid-1800's, including a spool bed, wooden organ, and Carson's rustic black desk. The living room, kitchen, and bedroom provide glimpses into the era in which Carson lived. The floors alternate between dirt and wooden planks and the kitchen is set up so authentically that it looks like Carson's large family might arrive any time and sit down to eat. One of the personal items on display is a brown silk dress that was among Josefa's favorites. Other exhibits illustrate Carson's larger-than-life story with displays of his personal effects, including a Spencer carbine rifle and a beaded rifle bag.

The museum also provides visitors with a better understanding of the contributions that diverse groups of people made to the development of the region. Displays of guns, weathered saddles, Native American artifacts, settlers' household utensils, and Hispanic artwork all form part of the rich cultural mosaic that make up the history of northern New Mexico.

The Carsons lived in their beloved adobe home until they died, within a month of each other, in 1868. Josefa's death resulted from complications in childbirth, and Kit died from an aneurysm. They are buried in the cemetery at nearby Kit Carson Park, just a few blocks north of the house in which they raised their family.

A garden with fragrant lilac bushes, tulips and towering aspen trees surrounds the rambling adobe building where Kit Carson and his large family lived, above.

In 1826 a weary 17-year-old boy named Christopher Carson arrived in Taos, New Mexico, as a member of a wagon train that had been traveling along the Santa Fe Trail. Just weeks earlier, he had been an apprentice at a Missouri saddle-maker's shop when the wagon train passed by. Acting on impulse, he quit his job and signed on with the pioneers. At the time, the impetuous Carson was just another unknown young man who had been coaxed into the journey westward by the promise of exciting adventure and a better standard of living. By the time he died in 1868, Kit Carson, as he was then known, had become one of the most famous characters in the history of the Old West.

What many people don't realize is that this great frontiersman was also a doting husband and father. Visitors to the Kit Carson Historic Museums in Taos, New Mexico, can explore the house where Carson lived out many of his happiest days—as a homebody. Originally built in 1825, the long, low adobe building with 30-inch-thick walls was bought by Carson in 1843 as a wedding present for his new bride, Maria Josefa Jaramillo, the daughter of a prominent family in the region. Carson had been married previously to an Arapaho woman, but she died shortly after the wedding. His marriage to Josefa lasted 25 years, and the couple lived happily in the house where six of their eight children were born.

FOR MORE INFORMATION:

Kit Carson Historic Museums, Drawer CCC, Taos, NM 87571; 505-758-0505.

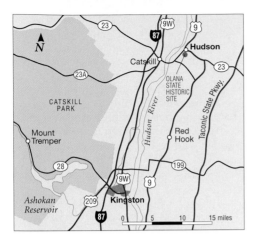

When artist Frederic E. Church built Olana, he designed the windows and doorways as frames for the breathtaking landscape surrounding his house. Set on a lofty hill overlooking the Hudson River, the fanciful structure is an architectural collage of patterned brickwork, Islamic arches, balconies, and high towers. After acquiring the hilltop property, Church wrote: "About an hour this side of Albany is the center of the world. I own it."

Widely considered the finest of the Hudson River School painters, Church first purchased land in the area in 1860. Seven years later, he traveled to Europe and the Middle East with his wife, Isabel, where the two were smitten by Islamic architecture. The Italianate villa they had planned for the Hudson River property was abandoned in favor of an Eastern-style building. In 1879 the Churches named the estate Olana, after an ancient Persian fortress.

Church constructed the house between 1870 and 1876 consulting with New York architect Calvert Vaux. The two-story house borrows freely from Persian, Italian, and Moorish architectural design. The exterior is faced with yellow, red, and black bricks arranged in a decorative array above a mosquelike entryway.

Church embellished the interior with zeal, painting the baseboards, spandrels, and borders with stencils of Maltese crosses, fleurs-de-lis, and other floral designs. The home is filled with Oriental rugs, Shaker rockers, Mexican religious statuary, mounted birds from South America, Arab spears, ornamental Persian filigreed peacocks, and other souvenirs from his travels.

The principal rooms open off the court hall, which offers a stunning view through the Moorish-arched ombra, a shaded, recessed porch. The hall features the most unusual furnishings in the house, including an Indian chair and a pair of bronze cranes

from Asia. Church established the palette for the entire villa here, dipping his brush liberally into plum, peacock blue, lemon yellow, terra cotta, russet, and claret tints.

Vibrant colors enliven the parlor, sitting room, library, and combined dining room and picture gallery. The 18-foot-high walls of the dining room were painted in maroon, and many of the paintings from Church's collection of Old Masters hang on the walls. The extensive collection includes works dating from the 14th to the 19th centuries. In the sitting room, the color scheme takes its cue from Church's painting above the fireplace called *El Khasné, Petra*, which depicts the ruins of an ancient biblical city.

NATURE'S CHANGING EXHIBITION

The 250-acre grounds were conceived as a great natural composition, one that Church continued to refine until his death in 1900. Here, the artist created a rich mélange of contrasting textures using thousands of trees, including birch, hemlock, chestnut, and oak. Dark woodlands alternate with meadows, manicured lawns, and mirrorlike waters. The farm resembled a pastoral tableau composed of tilled fields, orchards, and grazing lands. Church wrote, "I can make more and better landscapes in this way than by tampering with canvas and paint in the studio."

FOR MORE INFORMATION:

Olana State Historic Site, R.D. 2, Hudson, NY 12534; 518-828-0135.

Frederic Church's love of the exotic is shown in the colorful tile work and pointed arch of the Moorish-style doorway at Olana, above. In 1868 Church wrote to a friend that he had "plenty of capital ideas and new ones about house building." Middle Eastern influences are dramatically displayed on the exterior of the house, below. Church and his architect, Calvert Vaux, made many sketches for Olana before a final design was chosen.

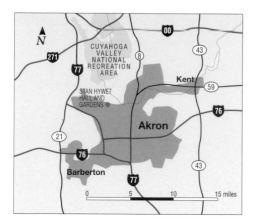

Frank A. Seiberling, cofounder of the Goodyear Tire and Rubber Company, lived for 40 years in Stan Hywet Hall, the largest private residence in Ohio. Overlooking the Cuyahoga Valley and crowned with crenellated towers, the sprawling 65-room brick mansion is a rich showcase for fine-carved paneling, molded plaster ceilings, Oriental and English rugs, and stained-glass windows.

In 1912 Seiberling and his wife, Gertrude, commissioned Cleveland architect Charles S. Schneider to build a house of distinction on their vast estate of several thousand acres. Enamored of Tudor architecture, the couple invited Schneider and decorator H. F. Huber to accompany them to Great Britain, where they toured grand English manors in search of inspiration and interesting architectural details.

Built between 1912 and 1915, the mansion was designed as a rectangle with wings at each end. The Tudor-style elements of the house include numerous bay windows, assorted chimneys, and half-timbered gables, which imbue it with a look of nobility. The front entranceway is modeled after a medieval portcullis, and bears the Latin motto *Non Nobis Solum,* "Not for Us Alone." Heirs of the Seiberlings' perpetuated the family motto by donating the beautifully preserved house to the public in 1956.

The mansion was constructed mainly of sandstone quarried on the grounds, and the name, Stan Hywet, is a derivative of the Middle English word for stone quarry. The quarry now holds a placid lagoon.

The interior rooms of Stan Hywet Hall are trimmed with lustrous woods such as American oak, chestnut, black walnut, sandalwood, teak, and rosewood. Doors feature wrought-iron hardware, and windows are enhanced with leaded-glass panes.

The magnificent house was designed with state-of-the-art technology but to preserve its Old World, Tudor-Revival elegance, Schneider concealed unsightly radiators, telephones, and closets behind decorative grillwork and carved panels. Although the mansion was designed with a central heating system, the large fireplaces in almost every room evoke a bygone era when families gathered around the hearth for warmth and fellowship.

THE GREAT HALL

A massive fireplace of hand-cut stone in the three-story Great Hall extends from the blue flagstone floor almost to the medieval-style timbered ceiling. The walls are covered with luxurious 16th-century Flemish tapestries, paintings by George Romney and Sir Thomas Lawrence, and the mounted heads of various game animals. A colored lithograph by Joseph Nash depicts Ockwells Manor, the English mansion that was the model for the Great Hall.

An 18th-century harpsichord from Ockwells Manor now graces the Music Room, where the Seiberlings hosted performances by such famed musicians as violinist Fritz Kreisler, composer Ernest Bloch, and conductor Leopold Stokowski. Widely considered one of the most beautiful chambers in America, the room is lit by crystal chandeliers with amber and amethyst hanging prisms, 18th-century English paintings from the famous Blakeslee collection, and an Indo-Persian rug bearing the tree of life design.

The walls of the Dining Room are painted with characters and scenes from Geoffrey Chaucer's *Canterbury Tales.* The silver tea set was custom-made to match an antique urn fashioned in 1763 by Thomas Whipman and Charles Wright.

After touring the house, visitors can stroll through gardens and meadows designed by Warren Manning, a founding member of the American Society of Landscape Architecture. Stone walls enclose a quiet reflecting pool in the English garden, and a stately fountain is the centerpiece of the West Terrace. A Japanese garden is composed of a gentle waterfall, picturesque rocks, and a stone lantern that was presented as a gift by the government of Japan.

FOR MORE INFORMATION:
Stan Hywet Hall and Gardens, 714 North Portage Path, Akron, OH 44303-1399; 330-836-5533.

The Boys' Suite consisted of the Red Room, right, which features decorative crenellation on the walls and fireplace, and the Blue Room. The rooms shared a connecting bath and a sleeping porch, and are furnished primarily with made-to-order furniture and rugs.

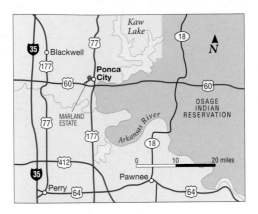

The biography of oil tycoon Ernest Whitworth Marland is a a rags-to-riches story filled with romance, controversy, and tragedy. Befitting the dramatic tale, Marland lived in a castle, known as the Marland Mansion and often referred to as the Palace on the Prairie.

Marland was born outside Pittsburgh, Pennsylvania, in 1874 and graduated from law school at the age of 19. Working as an oil prospector, he made his first million before his 30th birthday—only to lose it all in a matter of days when three of his banks went under during the Great Panic of 1907. Hoping that their luck would change, Marland and his wife, Mary Virginia, moved to the Ponca City area of Oklahoma in 1908. Three years later, literally down to his last few dollars, the oil man struck the first in a long succession of gushers that by the mid-1920's gave him control of about 10 percent of the world's entire oil supply.

Having amassed a fortune of nearly $100 million, Marland engaged the master architect John Forsythe in 1924 to draw up plans for a spectacular mansion in Ponca City. The design of the 55-room mansion was influenced by that of the Davanzati Palace in Florence, which Marland had fallen in love with during an excursion to Italy. Three years and $ 5.5 million later, the estate was completed.

When Ernest Marland moved into his Oklahoma castle in 1928, Mary Virginia wasn't at his side. She had died suddenly in 1926. Two years later, Marland shocked the nation by annulling his adoption of his wife's niece, Lydie, and then marrying her. Following a honeymoon in Canada and California, Marland brought his young bride back to Ponca City, Oklahoma, where he presented her with the mansion as a wedding present.

Marland and his second wife came home to a sprawling estate that included not only the opulent mansion, but also a game preserve, five lakes, a T-shaped swimming pool, and polo grounds.

Soaring arches and vaulted ceilings with intricately painted designs, above, are found throughout Marland Mansion. A detail of the wrought-iron stair railing, left, displays the careful attention that was paid to the smallest ornamental feature of the house.

Visitors enter the Italian Renaissance house through the carriage entrance. The mansion's severe exterior gives little hint of its rich interior. The wood paneling in the dining room is made of rare Pollard oak, felled in the royal forests in England by permission of a special grant. The hand-painted ceiling of the inner lounge depicts the history of this part of Oklahoma.

MARLAND'S MICHELANGELO

Many of the ceilings were designed and painted by the renowned Italian mural artist Vincent Margoliotti, who lived in the mansion's basement during its construction. Perhaps Margoliotti's most exquisite work is exhibited on the ballroom ceiling, with its paper-thin 24-karat gold detailing that is worth more than $1.4 million. The massive galleries also display two chandeliers made of sterling silver and Waterford crystal.

In October 1928 Marland was replaced as president of the Marland Oil Company after a hostile takeover by bankers who had financed his previous business ventures. Severing all ties with the oil company, Marland and Lydie moved into one of the outbuildings, no longer able to afford the palatial lifestyle they had enjoyed for so short a time.

FOR MORE INFORMATION:

Marland Mansion and Estate, 901 Monument Rd., Ponca City, OK 74604; 405-767-0420.

The multilevel structure of Fallingwater, above, was designed by Frank Lloyd Wright as a counterpoint to the waterfall and precipice upon which it was built. The musical sound of falling water is audible throughout the house.

Fallingwater is less a house than a sculpture composed of poured reinforced concrete, stone, and glass. Designed by the groundbreaking American architect Frank Lloyd Wright, the building hovers above a waterfall, its cantilevered terraces projecting like extensions of the stream's rocky ledges.

Wright designed the house in 1936 for department store magnate Edgar J. Kaufmann, who wanted to build a weekend residence for his family near the 20-foot-high waterfall on his country property at Bear Run. When the 67-year-old architect presented his drawings to Kaufmann, he said, "E.J., I want you to live with the waterfall, not just to look at it, but for it to become an integral part of your lives."

WATER AND STONE

Fallingwater is considered an architectural masterpiece largely because of the way Wright integrated the structure with its setting. Bear Run's flowing waters are audible in many areas of the house and represent a unifying theme. Its twisting stairways and multiple levels echo the water's course, and the flagstone floors are polished to resemble stones in the stream.

A stone outcropping, once used by the Kaufmann family for sunbathing and as a place to listen to the falls, juts from the living room floor and is now incorporated into the hearth. The boulder serves as a base for a four-story sandstone chimney that anchors the house to the riverbed's rocky cliffs. Terraces of reinforced concrete extend like rocky ledges over the chilly, tumbling stream.

A Pittsburgh engineering firm advised Kaufmann against Wright's design, criticizing the choice of site and questioning the stability of the terraces. Although there have been occasional problems with leaky roofs due to the deflection of the cantilevers, the structure has proved remarkably sound, requiring only minor repairs during the time the Kaufmanns lived there.

Tours of Fallingwater offer insight into Frank Lloyd Wright's original architectural ideas. Besides designing the house, Wright customized the furniture and decorative features, down to a Venetian red metal kettle that swings from a welded steel pivot near the hearth in the living room and was used to heat mulled wine.

Wright regarded furnishings and decor as part of the total architectural composition and pondered every aspect of the interior. The beds, desks, and wardrobes were built in, as were the couches. Wright offset the room's beige walls with accent colors of vivid red and yellow. The Kaufmanns had to ask Wright's permission before making any changes to the design, such as erecting bookshelves in a bedroom or adding an annex to the house for their staff.

The living room merges with the dining room to form an expansive living area that is surrounded by large windows on three sides. Low ceilings and stone building materials create a cavelike ambience, which opens up to the living area's two terraces out over the waterfall. Terraces branch off each of the four small bedrooms as well, offering a variety of perspectives on the forest and stream.

Wright's exhaustive attention to detail extended to the design of the wardrobe drawers, which have cane insets to allow air to circulate through the garments, and the choice of wood veneers, which feature strong grains that emphasize the horizontal lines of the house.

In 1963 Edgar Kaufmann Jr. presented Fallingwater to the Western Pennsylvania Conservancy. It is now the only major house by Frank Lloyd Wright within its original setting that has retained its furnishings and artwork intact. The house looks much as it did when the Kaufmanns lived here: the beds are made, the dining table set, and the shelves filled with books.

FOR MORE INFORMATION:
Fallingwater, P.O. Box R, Mill Run, PA 15464; 412-329-8501.

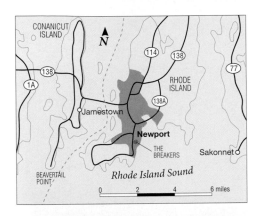

A series of archways, decorated with statuary, overlooks the lawns and gardens landscaped by Ernest Bowditch, a student of Frederick Law Olmsted.

C ornelius Vanderbilt II, for all that he was the patriarch of America's wealthiest family, was reputedly a modest man of simple tastes. When he decided in 1893 to build a summer cottage at Newport, he asked architect Richard Morris Hunt to design a two-story Italianate villa. What he got instead was a four-story palace that encompassed nearly an acre and contained 70 rooms—33 of which were set aside for servants. The house, called The Breakers because of its position on the cliffs above the Atlantic, represents the epitome of the Gilded Age.

Cornelius was born in 1843, the grandson of the shipping and railroad magnate Cornelius "Commodore" Vanderbilt, whose consolidation of the Harlem, Hudson, and New York Central railway lines had made him the wealthiest man in the United States. Cornelius II followed the family tradition and worked his way up through the ranks. By the time The Breakers was built, he had become the director of 49 railroads and the chairman of the New York Central, which owned property estimated to be worth $200 million.

MILLIONAIRES' ARCHITECT

To build The Breakers, Vanderbilt turned to Richard Morris Hunt, who had already earned a reputation as the architect to millionaires with his grand houses in Newport, on Fifth Avenue in New York City, and elsewhere. He spent a year working on the design for The Breakers, which was inspired by the palazzos of the Italian merchant princes of 16th-century Genoa and Turin. Hunt was also influenced by the work of the Italian architect Andrea Palladio, who built his palaces around open courtyards. In his design, Hunt roofed over the central courtyard of The Breakers and arranged the first- and second-floor rooms around a lofty Great Hall.

The Breakers was the second house by that name built on the Atlantic cliffs of Ochre Point. The first one, a wood-and-brick Queen Anne–style mansion, had been the Vanderbilts' summer cottage for seven years before it burned to the ground in 1892. Cornelius had a version of it built on the grounds of The Breakers as a playhouse for his seven children.

It took the builders two years to complete the second Breakers. Parts of the house, such as the Renaissance-style paneling, pilasters, and cornice work in the Morning Room, were made in France and then taken apart and shipped to Newport, where they were then reinstalled.

For many visitors, the Great Hall symbolizes the extravagance of the entire project. Its 45-foot-high ceilings are painted to simulate the open sky. A wall made almost completely of glass offers a breathtaking view of the Atlantic. The grand staircase, illuminated by a 33-foot-long stained-glass skylight by John LaFarge, climbs past an Italian fireplace to a balcony displaying a tapestry designed by the Flemish artist Karl van Mander the Younger in 1619.

The carved and gilded walls and ceilings of the ornate public reception rooms on the first floor were decorated by the Parisian firm of Allard et Fils. The bedrooms on the second and third floors were designed by Ogden Codman Jr., a Bostonian whose restrained touches strike a more subdued and intimate note. Codman's work on The Breakers led him to formalize his ideas, which he later published in his groundbreaking book on interior design, *The Decoration of Houses,* written in collaboration with the great American writer Edith Wharton. The 30-year-old Codman was introduced to Cornelius Vanderbilt II by Wharton at her Newport cottage, known as Land's End, which had been remodeled for her by Codman.

FOR MORE INFORMATION:

The Preservation Society of Newport County, 424 Bellevue Ave., Newport, RI 02840; 401-847-1000.

After his first Newport cottage burned down, Cornelius Vanderbilt insisted that The Breakers, below, be made as fireproof as possible. It was built entirely of masonry and steel, and the heating plant was installed some distance away, beneath the caretaker's cottage.

Drayton Hall's riverside entrances, above, and front roadside entrances are perfectly aligned so that the roadside greenery is visible when both doors are open.

Drayton Hall exudes quiet authority from its commanding position on the banks of the Ashley River. Its imposing brick facade, anchored by white-painted pedimented windows and doors, bestows a classical symmetry on the house.

Built at the behest of John Drayton between 1738 and 1742, Drayton Hall was designed to impress. Raised above a high basement, the house possesses a double set of stone steps, which lead to a pediment-ed two-story front portico, facing the road.

The house dates to a period when rice and indigo plantations ruled the Carolina Low Country's economy. Drayton, who owned plantations elsewhere, wanted a country estate that would proclaim his wealth and position. Like many Southern merchants and planters in the 18th century,

he aspired to be an English country gentle-man. He bought the land in 1738 after an advertisement appeared in the *South Carolina Gazette* that described the proper-ty as having "350 acres, whereof 150 acres of it is not yet clear'd, with a very good Dwelling-house, kitchen and several out houses, with a very good orchard, consist-ing of all sorts of Fruit Trees."

DELICATE CRAFTSMANSHIP

The non-profit National Trust for Historic Preservation has restored Drayton Hall and maintains it for the public. The house is shown unfurnished, and tours focus on the architecture and craftsmanship of the struc-ture. The house's symmetrical design, hip roof, and bold use of classical features dis-tinguish it as one of the oldest examples of Georgian Palladian architecture in the South. Georgian architecture, which was the first true architectural style to appear in America, is a style that flourished during the reigns of England's first three King Georges, from about 1700 to the American Revolution. The epitome of this style was the Palladian country house, modeled after the designs of the 16th-century Italian architect Andrea Palladio. The style made its way to England and then to the colonies.

No one knows who designed Drayton Hall, but it has been shown that much of the labor that went into the house was car-ried out by the Draytons' slaves, as well as European craftsmen. Nowhere is the skill of these workers more in evidence than on the delicately hand-molded ceiling in the draw-ing room, which was executed in plaster. Many of the materials employed in the construction of Drayton Hall were native

to America, with the exception of the mahogany used for the Stair Hall, which came from the Caribbean, and the English limestone used for the portico steps.

Fortunately Drayton Hall survived the devastations of the Civil War that destroyed most of the other plantation homes along the Ashley River. Today visitors are guided through the empty rooms, where neither electricity nor plumbing has been installed to spoil its original features.

A French aristocrat who visited the house on a trip to North America in 1796 described the landscape surrounding Drayton Hall as "better laid out, better cul-tivated, and better stocked with good trees than any I have hitherto seen." Although most of the gardens have vanished, a walk through the grounds conjures up the grandeur of Drayton Hall's glory days.

FOR MORE INFORMATION:
Drayton Hall, 3380 Ashley River Rd., Charleston, SC 29414-7105; 803-766-0188.

The walls of the second floor Great Hall, below, were originally cream, but were painted blue after 1874. Uncluttered by furnishings, Drayton Hall reveals its architectural details.

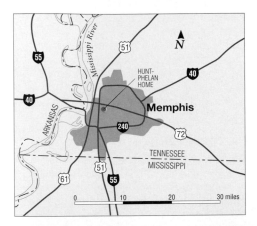

and 1832, was designed by the architect Robert Mills for a prominent Virginian surveyor, engineer, and land speculator named George Hubbard Wyatt. Mills, America's first native-born architect, received much of his training on the job, working with James Hoban, who designed the White House. Mills also served as a draftsman on Thomas Jefferson's home, Monticello, in Virginia, and he worked with Benjamin H. Latrobe, the father of Greek Revival architecture in America, when Latrobe made several additions to the Executive Mansion.

Eli Driver, the owner of the Hunt-Phelan Home, stipulated in his will that a Greek Revival portico with two-story Ionic columns, above, should be substituted for the original Federal-style front porch. The porch was moved to the east side of the house.

The east end of Beale Street in Memphis, Tennessee, is a far cry from its western end. Once crowded with honky-tonk bars that resonated with the strains of the Mississippi Delta blues, the east end dates back to a time when butlers shooed away loiterers who had wandered into affluent neighborhoods from the seedier part of town, and wealthy Memphis families entertained their friends in elegant antebellum mansions, well out of earshot of the new blues sound.

One of these elaborate mansions is the Hunt-Phelan Home, now one of the oldest houses in Memphis. The handsome Federal-style house, built between 1828

From 1836 to 1851, Mills acted as the federal government's architect of public buildings and the Hunt-Phelan Home reflects the formal, restrained style for which he is renowned. This type of architecture reached its height with the Greek Revival style, a favorite with Southern plantation owners during the antebellum period. As with many pre–Civil War houses, the Hunt-Phelan Home was built by slaves and Chickasaw Indians.

Wyatt installed Memphis' first built-in gaslights, hot-air furnace, swimming pool, and indoor bathroom. Fearing attacks by local rowdies and the Chickasaw, who resented the loss of their lands, he also had an escape tunnel dug under the house. During the 15 years Wyatt lived in the house, he sank further and further into debt. Finally, he left for California in search of gold. The house was sold to a cousin, Eli Driver, and later passed into the hands of Col. William Richardson Hunt, who

had married Driver's 15-year-old daughter, Sarah Elizabeth. Hunt was a staunch supporter of the Southern cause and a close friend and his frequent guest was the Confederate president, Jefferson Davis.

CIVIL WAR HEADQUARTERS

In 1861 Confederate general Leonidas Polk made Hunt a captain and set up headquarters in the house. The following year, when Memphis fell to Union soldiers, Gen. Ulysses S. Grant commandeered the Hunt-Phelan Home. Grant and his staff planned the second campaign to take Vicksburg in the Hunts' elegant, book-lined library, a successful mission that gave control of the Mississippi River to the Federal side. Later, house and grounds were used as a Union hospital; some 2,500 soldiers died here.

After the war, Pres. Andrew Johnson pardoned Colonel Hunt on the condition that he not seek payment for the years the federal government had used his home and he returned the house to him. For a few short years, a group of freed African-Americans were given their first opportunity for an education in a schoolhouse built behind the house. The school was part of the Freedmen's Bureau, a federally funded reconstruction program that was set up to provide education and medical help for America's ex-slaves.

More recently the mansion was occupied by Stephen Rice Phelan, a reclusive descendant of Colonel Hunt. Phelan spent many of his 87 years developing a red, white, and blue rose (for which he held a patent) and painstakingly documenting the history of his home and family. When he died in 1993, his cousin and heir, Bill Day, found hundreds of boxes of old documents, letters, photographs, and ephemera stashed in the house—a treasure trove of historical information. "Fortunately, my ancestors saved everything, and Stephen Rice Phelan in particular was passionate about documenting the history of our home, our family and our community," he said. Among the artifacts was a sword that had been relinquished by a Confederate soldier when the Southern army surrendered at the Battle of Vicksburg during the Civil War.

Opened to the public in 1996, the Hunt-Phelan Home has undergone extensive restoration, and work is still being carried out on the Freedmen's schoolhouse.

FOR MORE INFORMATION:
Hunt-Phelan Home, 533 Beale St., Memphis, TN 38103; 901-344-3166 or 800-350-9009.

The Bishop's Palace of Galveston, a four-story architectural marvel, has been designated as one of the hundred outstanding buildings in the country by the American Institute of Architects. The house incorporates a variety of styles, taken from Moorish, Tudoresque, French Renaissance Revival, and Richardsonian Romanesque architecture.

Constructed between 1886 and 1893 for wealthy Galveston attorney Col. Walter Gresham, his wife, Josephine, and their nine children, the house is known locally as Walter Gresham's Castle. At one time it was the hub of the city's social life. After Colonel Gresham's death in 1923, the 25-room mansion was purchased by the Diocese of Galveston as a residence for Christopher E. Byrne, who served for 32 years as Galveston-Houston's bishop, giving the house its name.

Walter Gresham commissioned stonecutter turned architect Nicholas J. Clayton to design the High Victorian home. Not surprisingly, Clayton chose a varied palette of stone for the exterior, including limestone, pink and blue granite, and red and gray sandstone. Highly skilled craftsmen sculpted the Assyrian winged horses that were mounted atop the house's turrets and the gargoyles at the front entrance. The face of a child carved into the keystone over the front door is reputed to be a likeness of the Greshams' youngest daughter, Beulah, and the capitals of the pillars flanking the front door are decorated with Mrs. Gresham's favorite flower, the calla lily.

The mansion's interior displays even more extravagant touches than its exterior. The calla lily motif reappears on an elaborate Venetian glass chandelier that hangs in the entranceway. Every room on the main floor is finished in a different wood. The focal point of the main entrance hall is a monumental staircase made of stained oak with the Texas state seal prominently displayed on its pulpitlike balcony. The stairway took 61 craftsmen three years to carve. Natural light through several large stained-glass windows illuminates the stairs.

A rotunda, featuring a decorative skylight, rises 55 feet above the staircase. The rotunda served a practical purpose as a Victorian-era air conditioner that channeled hot air up and out of the house. In 1900 a terrible storm struck Galveston, but fortunately the Greshams' home did not incur any damage. In fact, it provided sanctuary to many residents of the Galveston area who were left homeless. The view of the delicately wrought rotunda is said to have brought peace of mind to the people who had suffered through this devastating act of nature.

VICTORIAN PHILOSOPHY

For Colonel Gresham, as for most house-proud Victorians, practical necessities had to be beautiful as well as functional. This philosophy is evident in the home's 14 fireplaces. For his study, the colonel decided on a fireplace made of Numidian marble imported from what is now Algeria. An elaborately carved mahogany mantel from Santo Domingo graces the front parlor. It won first-prize at the 1876 Philadelphia Centennial Exposition. A statue of the risen Christ that now rests on the mantelpiece was added during Byrne's time. Perhaps the most spectacular fireplace in the house is found in the Music Room. Made of Mexican onyx, silver, pewter, and satinwood, it was the winner of the first prize at the 1886 New Orleans Exposition. The Greshams paid $10,000 for it.

Josephine Gresham, who was an artist, set up her studio on the top floor inside the house's castlelike turret, a round room with seven large windows. Her artistic touches can be seen throughout the house. The top shelf of the massive sideboard in the dining room houses her hand-painted chinaware, and the room's ceiling features a portrait on canvas of her four sons depicted as angels. Mrs. Gresham also painted cherubs on some of the plaster moldings of the second-floor level of the rotunda.

When Bishop Byrne moved into the house, he left most of it in its original condition, including the house's chandeliers—among them a 350-pound bronze and gold caprice that hangs from the ceiling in the dining room. The bishop made some modifications to reflect the residence's new ecclesiastical purpose. The most important of these changes was the conversion of one of the children's bedrooms into a chapel. The room was decorated with stained-glass depictions of religious themes that were produced in Munich, Germany. A large painting of the crucifixion hangs over the white marble mantelpiece.

The castlelike exterior of the Bishop's Palace, left, was made of sandstone, limestone, and granite, all of which were quarried at Marble Falls, Texas. Mrs. Gresham's studio was located in the tower.

FOR MORE INFORMATION:
The Bishop's Palace, 1402 Broadway, Galveston, TX 77550; 409-762-2475.

An ornate crystal chandelier, left, illuminates the hall to the central staircase.

When Mamie McFaddin, the heir to a Texas oil fortune, married Carrol Ward in 1919, the young newlyweds moved into her parents' home in Beaumont, Texas. For the next 63 years Mamie lavished her attention on the care and upkeep of the gracious Southern Colonial mansion. The couple never had any children and upon Mamie's death in 1982, their home was turned into a museum at her behest.

Mamie's home was built in 1906 with oil money. Her father, W.P.H. "Perry" McFaddin, had made a small fortune from his cattle business, rice farming and milling, and real estate interests. When oil was discovered on Spindletop Hill, which was partly owned by Perry, both his personal wealth—and that of all the residents of Beaumont—flourished.

Henry Conrad Mauer designed the house for the family. The first formally trained architect to set up practice in Beaumont in the wake of the boom, Mauer chose the impressive Beaux-Arts Colonial style for this ambitious project and proudly displayed his design in the window of a local jewelry store. He employed mail-order architectural plans and used many custom-made architectural elements, such as plaster columns, wood paneling, colorful stained glass, and oak flooring. Other design elements were custom-made for the house.

To ensure that the interior of the house remained cool in those days before air conditioning, Mauer sited the building with the majority of its large windows facing south to take advantage of prevailing breezes. High ceilings, transomed doorways,

The substantial McFaddin-Ward property, right, encompasses four and a half acres. The three-story house boasts a wide, wraparound porch on the first floor and a large second-floor veranda, where family members sometimes slept during extremely hot nights.

double-sash windows, and ceiling fans also helped keep the house comfortable during the long Texan summers.

The house was wired for electrical power and the original knob-and-tube wiring system still functions, and push-button light switches turn the lights on and off. An internal telephone system allowed the McFaddins and then the Wards to communicate with their domestic servants.

The Carriage House, built in 1907, originally contained the servants' quarters, a stable, hayloft, gymnasium, and car garage. Mamie's parents never learned how to drive and preferred to be shepherded about by chauffeurs, but Mamie picked up the skill, and her parents bought her a car in 1912.

AVID COLLECTORS

Parts of Mamie and her mother's collections of decorative objects are on display in the house, including silver, furniture, linen, rare oriental carpets, and antique chinaware and glassware. Of particular note are a silver punch bowl engraved with the McFaddin monogram and an unusual jack-in-the-pulpit vase from the early 1900's that was made by the Quezal Art Glass and Decorating Company.

Some personal items of the McFaddin and the Ward families are also on exhibit, including their tennis rackets, golf clubs, phonographs and records, ice skates, and roller skates. Perry McFaddin's pocket watch is perhaps the most intriguing of these. Made in the 1890's, the watch face shows a wedding photograph of his wife and is inscribed with his name.

The McFaddin-Ward House officially opened its doors to the public in 1986. The all-white, three-story structure encompasses 12,800 square feet of interior space and has been carefully restored. The entrance hall, formal parlor, and upstairs bedrooms contain their original furnishings. As they walk through the front doors, visitors enter an era when Beaumont's wells were gushing with oil and Mamie and her family lived the high life in their beautiful home.

FOR MORE INFORMATION:

McFaddin-Ward House, 1906 McFaddin Ave., Beaumont, TX 77701; 409-832-1906.

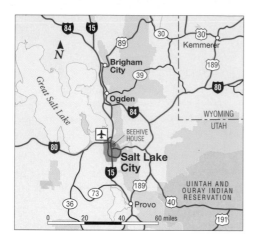

Brigham Young stares out from a portrait, above, in the dining room on the first floor of the Beehive House. The dining table seats 30, and is always set for dinner with gold-monogrammed china.

The Beehive House in Salt Lake City was the official residence of Brigham Young, a leader of the Mormon Church and Utah's first territorial governor. Young worked with architect Truman Angell to design a building that would serve as a comfortable home for his very large family, a dignified setting for his official duties, and a suitable place to entertain his many distinguished visitors.

Erected in 1854 in the Great Salt Lake valley, the three-story house featured the stately columns, green-shuttered windows, and porches common to buildings in Young's native Vermont. The name Beehive comes from the Mormon symbol of industry and could not have been more appropriate, for this was a center of constant activity. A sculpted beehive is perched on the house's gilded cupola.

Young was the patriarch of a polygamous family that is believed to have numbered 27 wives and 56 children. Only one wife, Lucy

Decker Young, and her seven children lived in the Beehive. His other wives and children occupied either the Lion House next door or had private homes.

The interior of the 35-room Victorian house is both practical and attractive. The front hall contains intricately carved pine paneling and plastered walls that are painted to resemble Tennessee marble. A skilled carpenter by trade, Young designed intricate carved-leaf patterns for many of the door frames. He also made some of the pieces of furniture in the house.

Young's bedroom/office was located to the left of the main entrance hall so that he could be reached easily, day or night, by anyone who might call. The room contains his swivel chair and cherrywood secretary, and his hat and cane rest on top of a massive mahogany bedstead. Not far away is the sitting room, where the family gathered each evening to sing, read, and pray. The Victorian furniture in the sitting room includes a floor-to-ceiling walnut bookcase, and a piano. The parlor's muted green walls are offset by Nottingham lace–curtained windows and a paisley cloth on the table.

The parlor on the second floor was the center of the fledgling community's social activities. The 32-foot-long room called the

Long Hall is decorated with heavy red silk drapes and carpeting that replicate the original pattern. Young entertained an assortment of notable guests here, including Pres. Ulysses S. Grant, Gen. William Sherman, author Mark Twain, and the circus sensation Tom Thumb.

Young's involvement in the lives of his family members is reflected in the design of the residence. For example, the furniture in the children's schoolroom and the playroom has been scaled down to size. A cozy but efficient pantry and kitchen equipped with an 1854 cast-iron stove was designed to turn out as many as 25 pies in a single day. The family store, perhaps the most unusual room of all, was always kept well stocked with a variety of dry goods, cheeses, dried fruit, and candy. Oil lanterns, bolts of 100-year-old cloth, and old-fashioned hat pins are displayed on its shelves.

In 1961 the exterior of the Beehive House was restuccoed to match its original straw color and the rooms were restored to their appearance in Young's time. Even the front door was restored, and its silver doorknob bearing the symbol of a bee on the ornamental plate now has a gleaming sheen.

FOR MORE INFORMATION:
Beehive House, 67 East South Temple, Salt Lake City, UT 84111; 801-240-2672.

Hollyhock and morning glory bloom profusely in the front garden of Beehive House, left, Young's family home in Salt Lake City.

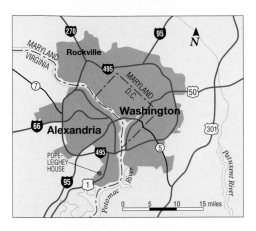

designed. It pleased him that the word begins with the initials of the United States. Without ever visiting the site and using only a contour map as a guide, Wright designed one of his first Usonian houses for the Popes' one-and-a-half-acre property in Falls Church, Virginia.

In addition to his architectural genius, Wright was also a great amateur inventor in the Jeffersonian tradition. He brought both of these talents to his Usonian houses. With a total budget, including land and furnishings, of only $7,000 in pre–World War II terms, the house had to be modest. It would

the bedroom wing at the entrance. The bedrooms are small, but outfitted with built-in furniture that increases the sense of space and orderliness. The living space is also designed as an open concept. Wright reasoned that for Usonian families who had neither maids nor downstairs kitchens, the cooking and dining areas should be free-flowing. He combined the two rooms into one large space, introducing another architectural innovation.

CONTAINMENT AND RELEASE

The ceiling heights in the Pope-Leighey House vary from 7 to 11 feet, creating a sensation of containment and release. The living room, the largest and highest room in the house, is the central gathering place for the family. It features a two-sided fireplace that faces both the living and dining areas. For Wright, the hearth had a unifying effect.

The exterior has a flat overhanging roof and clerestory windows that were not visible from street level to assure privacy. The house was originally oriented so that the occupants could look out without being seen by passersby. The front door was—and still is—hidden from view by the shadows cast by the overhanging carport.

In the kitchen, Wright's dual interests in function and aesthetics are clear. The cabinets open toward the window in order to take advantage of the natural illumination, and a tall slot window was positioned above the stove as a vent to the outdoors for cooking odors.

When the Popes offered their little house for sale in 1947 they received 100 responses to a three-line classified ad. They sold it to Robert and Marjorie Leighey, and as Loren Pope said later, they chose the new owners well. When the house was threatened by highway construction in 1964, Mrs. Leighey persuaded the National Trust for Historic Preservation to step in. She donated the funds to help pay the cost of moving it to its current site on Woodlawn Plantation.

The combination of Loren Pope's wish, Frank Lloyd Wright's talent, and Marjorie Leighey's generosity ensures that today visitors can continue to appreciate this monument to the humble American home. Loren Pope once described the house as having "a great and quiet soul."

The exterior of the Pope-Leighey House, above, reveals the signature style of its architect, Frank Lloyd Wright. The overhanging eaves of the flat roof and the horizontal board-and-batten walls give the house the overall appearance of greater space.

In August 1939 a struggling young journalist named Loren B. Pope wrote a letter to Frank Lloyd Wright, the famed American architect, that began with the following words: "There are certain things a man wants during life, and, of life. Material things and things of the spirit. The writer has one fervent wish that includes both. It is for a house created by you." Two weeks later came the reply: "Dear Loren Pope: Of course I am ready to give you a house."

Wright designed a house for Pope, who was not a wealthy man, out of the utopian ideal that affordable and beautiful housing should be available to every citizen. Wright borrowed the term Usonian, which was coined by Samuel Butler, to describe this and the other modest homes that he

be small—only 1,200 square feet—and built all on one level without a basement or attic. But Wright made the house feel big.

He saved space by using a heated floor—a Japanese idea—for all of his Usonian homes, eliminating the clutter of radiators. He devised a wooden wall that could be prefabricated and erected as a complete unit. It was an ingenious method of putting up both an exterior and interior wall at the same time, thus saving both time and money in construction and labor. Natural cypress wood was used as a wall covering throughout the interior, bringing the feel of nature into the house.

Using an L-shaped plan, Wright joined the living wing—which included the kitchen, living, and dining rooms—and

FOR MORE INFORMATION:

Pope-Leighey House, c/o Woodlawn Plantation, 9000 Richmond Hwy., Alexandria, VA 22309; 703-780-4000.

INDEX

Bold numerals indicate map reference.
Italic numerals indicate an illustration.
State abbreviations are in parentheses.
NF = National Forest
NHL = National Historic Landmark
NHS = National Historic Site
NM = National Monument
NP = National Park
NRA = National Recreation Area
NWR = National Wildlife Refuge
SHM = State Historical Monument
SHS = State Historic Site
SP = State Park

A-B

Adams, John, 37, 39
Adams, John Quincy, 37
Alabama
 Gaineswood NHL, **119**, *119*
Alexandria (VA), **40**, *41*, **141**, *141*
Allard et Fils, 135
American Clock and Watch Museum
 (CT), **18**, 18, *19*
Angell, Truman, 140
Architects
 Angell, Truman, 140
 Bulfinch, Charles, 19
 Clayton, Nicholas J., 138
 Codman, Ogden, Jr., 127, 135
 Dakin, James, 74
 Eastlake, Charles, 94
 Forsythe, John, 133
 Hardenbergh, Henry Janeway, 76, 78
 Heuck, Theodore C., 112
 Hoban, James, 30, 32, 34, 35, *36*
 Hoffman, F. Burall, 122
 Hoppin, Francis, 127
 Hunt, Richard Morris, 56, 58, 59-60,
  61, 135
 Jefferson, Thomas, 37, 38, 42-51
 Josselyn and Taylor, 124
 Kapp, William E., 128
 Latrobe, Benjamin Henry, 38
 Mauer, Henry Conrad, 139
 McKim, Mead & White, 123, 126, 127
 Mills, Robert, 137
 Morgan, Julia, 98, 100, 101, 102, 104
 Palladio, Andrea, 42-43, 47, 135, 136
 Petit, A. P., 94
 Potter, Edward Tuckerman, 10, 12
 Richardson, Henry Hobson, 123
 Schneider, Charles S., 132
 Thorp, Alfred H., 14
 Vaux, Calvert, 131
 Wall, Charles J., 108-109
 Whitfield, Nathan Bryan, 119
 Wright, Frank Lloyd, 87-93, 134, 141
  See also Landscape architects
Arizona
 Arizona Military Museum, **94**, 95
 Arizona State Capitol Museum, **94**, 94
 Desert Botanical Garden, **94**, *95*
 Mystery Castle, **94**, 95
 Phoenix, **94**, *94-95*
 Pueblo Grande Museum and Cultural
  Park, **94**, 95
 Rosson House, **94**, *94*
 Taliesin West, **89**, *86-93*
Arizona Military Museum (AZ), **94**, 95
Arizona State Capitol Museum (AZ),
 94, 94
Armstrong-Lockett House (TN), **64**, 64
Asheville (NC), *54-63*, **64**, 65

Ash Lawn–Highland (VA), **52**, *52*, 53
Barrett, Nathan, 126
Baton Rouge (LA), **74**, *74*
Beehive House (UT), **140**, *140*
Bighorn Canyon NRA (MT/WY), **84**, *85*
Billings (MT), **79**, *76-83*, **84**
Biltmore Estate (NC), **57**, *54-63*
The Bishop's Palace (TX), **138**, *138*
Blue Ridge Parkway (NC/VA), **64**, *64*, 65
Bougère, Achille D., 72
Brandywine River Museum (PA),
 28, 29
The Breakers (RI), **135**, *135*
Brucemore (IA), **124**, *124*
Bulfinch, Charles, 19
Byrne, Christopher E., 138
California
 Hearst San Simeon SHM, **99**, *96-105*
 Helen Moe's Antique Doll Museum,
  106, 106
 Larkin House, **120**, *120*
 Mission San Luis Obispo, **106**, *107*
 Morro Bay SP, **106**, *106*, 107
 Pismo Beach, **106**, *107*
 Rios-Caledonia Adobe, **106**, 106
 San Simeon, *96-105*, **106**
 Santa Maria Museum of Flight,
  106, 107

C-D

Carson, Kit, 130
Cecil, William, 61
Chalfin, Paul, 132
Chalmette Battlefield Site (LA), **74**, 75
Choate, Joseph Hodges and Caroline,
 126
Choate, Mabel, 126
Church, Frederic E. and Isabel, 131
Clayton, Nicholas J., 138
Clemens, Samuel Langhorne, 9-17
 See also Twain, Mark
Cleveland, Grover, 34
Codman, Ogden, Jr., 127, 135
Coffin, Marian Cruger, 22
Colman, Samuel, 14
Connecticut
 American Clock and Watch Museum,
  18, 18, *19*
 Connecticut Historical Society
  Museum, 11
 Gillette Castle SP, **121**, *121*
 The Harriet Beecher Stowe Center, 11
 Hartford, 11, *8-17*, **18**, *18*, 19
 Lutz Children's Museum, **18**, 19
 The Mark Twain House, 11, *8-17*
 Menczer Museum of Medicine
  and Dentistry, **18**, 19
 New England Air Museum, **18**, 19
 Nook Farm, 9, 10, 16
 Old State House, **18**, *18*, 19
 Stanley-Whitman House, **18**, *18-19*
 State Capitol, 11
Connecticut Historical Society Museum
 (CT), 11
Coolidge, Calvin, 32
Coronel, Ygnacio, 106
Crista, Heloise, *89*, 92
Custer NF (MT/SD), **84**, 85
Dakin, James, *74*
Damien Museum (HI), **116**, 116
DAR Museum (DC), 33
Deering, James, 122
de Forest, Lockwood, 14
de Pontalba, Baroness Micaela
 Almonester, 125

Delaware
 Eleutherian Mills, **28**, *28-29*
 Fort Delaware SP, **28**, 28, *29*
 Hagley Museum and Eleutherian
  Mills, **28**, *28-29*
 Nemours Mansion, **28**, 29
 Wilmington, **28**, *28*, 29
 Winterthur Museum, Garden and
  Library, **23**, *20-27*
Desert Botanical Garden (AZ), **94**, *95*
Designers. *See* Architects; Interior
 decorators; Landscape architects
District of Columbia
 DAR Museum, 33
 Explorers Hall, **40**, 40-41
 Freer Art Gallery, 33
 Jacqueline Kennedy Garden, 32
 Jefferson Memorial, 33, *37*, *41*
 Lincoln Memorial, 33, 41
 National Air and Space Museum,
  40, 41
 The National Museum of Natural
  History, 33
 Old Stone House, **40**, 40
 Rose Garden, 32
 U.S. National Arboretum, **40**, *40*, 41
 Vietnam Veterans Memorial, 33, 41
 Washington, 33, *30-39*, **40**, *40-41*, 141
 Washington Monument, 33, *37*, 41
 West Potomac Park, **40**, *41*
 The White House, 33, *30-39*
 Woodrow Wilson House, **40**, 40
Dole Cannery Square (HI), **116**, 117
Douglas, George Bruce and Irene, 124
Drayton, John, 136
Drayton Hall (SC), **136**, *136*
Driver, Eli, 137
du Pont, Alfred Irénée, 29
du Pont, Eleuthère Irénée, 29
du Pont, Henry Francis, 21-27
du Pont, Pierre, 29

E-F-G-H

Eastlake, Charles, 94
1850 House (LA), **125**, *125*
Eisenhower, Dwight D., 32, 35
Eisenhower, Mamie, 36
Eleutherian Mills (DE), **28**, *28-29*
Elkins, Frances Adler, 120
Explorers Hall (DC), **40**, 40-41
Fairview-Riverside SP (LA), **74**, 74
Fallingwater (PA), **88**, **134**, *134*
Farrand, Beatrix Jones, 127
Florida
 Vizcaya Museum and Gardens,
  122, *122*
Forsythe, John, 133
Fort Delaware SP (DE), **28**, 28, *29*
Fort Pike State Commemorative
 Area (LA), **74**, 74, *75*
Foster Botanical Garden (HI), **116**,
 116, 117
Fredericksburg (VA), **52**, 52, *53*
Freer Art Gallery (DC), 33
Gaineswood NHL (AL), **119**, *119*
Gillette, William, 121
Gillette Castle SP (CT), **121**, *121*
Glessner, John J. and Frances M., 123
Glessner House (IL), **123**, *123*
Grant, Ulysses S., 37
Great River Road (LA), 69
Great Smoky Mountain NP (NC/TN),
 64, 65
Gresham, Walter and Josephine, 138
Guinness World Records Museum

(TN), **64**, 64-65
Gulley, Boyce Luther, 95
Hagley Museum and Eleutherian Mills
 (DE), **28**, *28-29*
Hailstone NWR (MT), **84**, 84
Hall, Howard and Margaret
 Douglas, 124
Hardenbergh, Henry Janeway, 76, 78
The Harriet Beecher Stowe Center
 (CT), 11
Harrison, Benjamin, 32, 35
Harrison, Caroline, 35
Hartford (CT), 11, *8-17*, **18**, *18*, 19
Hawaii
 Damien Museum, **116**, 116
 Dole Cannery Square, **116**, 117
 Foster Botanical Garden, **116**, *116*, 117
 Honolulu, **111**, *108-115*, **116**, *116-117*
 Iolani Palace, **111**, *108-115*
 Japanese Cultural Center, **116**, 117
 Kamehameha I Statue, 111
 Kawaiahao Church, 111
 Polynesian Cultural Center, **116**,
  116, *117*
 Queen Emma Summer Palace, **116**,
  116, *117*
 Waikiki Aquarium, **116**, 116-117
 Washington Place, 111
Hayes, Rutherford B., 35
Hearst, William Randolph, 97-105
Hearst San Simeon SHM (CA), **99**,
 96-105
Helen Moe's Antique Doll Museum
 (CA), **106**, 106
Heuck, Theodore C., 112
Hoban, James, 30, 32, *34*, 35, *36*
Hoffman, F. Burall, 122
Honolulu (HI), **111**, *108-115*, **116**,
 116-117
Hoppin, Francis, 127
Huber, H. F., 132
Hunt, Richard Morris, 56, 58, 59-60,
 61, 135
Hunt, William Richardson, 137
Hunt-Phelan Home (TN), **137**, *137*

I-J-K

Illinois
 Glessner House, **123**, *123*
Interior designers
 Allard et Fils, 135
 Chalfin, Paul, 132
 Colman, Samuel, 14
 de Forest, Lockwood, 14
 Elkins, Frances Adler, 120
 Huber, H. F., 132
 Louis Comfort Tiffany and Associated
  Artists, 14, 16, *17*
 Tassinari & Chatel, *62*
 Tiffany, Louis Comfort, 14
 Wheeler, Candace Thurber, 14
 W. P. Nelson Company, 80, 81
Iolani Palace (HI), **111**, *108-115*
Iowa
 Brucemore, **124**, *124*
Jackson, Andrew, 32, 37
Jacqueline Kennedy Garden (DC), 32
Japanese Cultural Center (HI), **116**, 117
Jaramillo, Maria Josefa, 130
Jefferson, Martha, 42, 47
Jefferson, Thomas, 37, 38, 42-51
Jefferson Memorial (DC), 33, *37*, *41*
J. K. Ralston Studio and Gallery
 (MT), 79
Johnson, Lyndon B., 35

Johnson, Robert F., 120
Josselyn and Taylor, 124
Kalakaua, King David Laamea, 109-115
Kamehameha I Statue (HI), 111
Kapiolani, Queen, *114*
Kapp, William E., 128
Kaufmann, Edgar J., 134
Kawaiahao Church (HI), 111
Kennedy, Jacqueline Bouvier, 32, *34*, 35, 36, 37
Kennedy, John F., 34, 35, 37
Kit Carson Historic Museums (NM), **130**, *130*

L-M
Landscape architects
  Barrett, Nathan, 126
  Coffin, Marian Cruger, 22
  Farrand, Beatrix Jones, 127
  Manning, Warren, 132
  Olmsted, Frederick Law, 56, 58, *60*, 62-63
  Pinchot, Gifford, *60*
  Schenck, Carl, *60*
  Steele, Fletcher, 126
  Suarez, Diego, 122
Langdon, Olivia, 10-17
Larkin, Thomas Oliver, 120
Larkin House (CA), **120**, *120*
Latrobe, Benjamin Henry, 38
Leese, Jacob P., 120
Leighey, Robert and Marjorie, 141
Levy, Jefferson M., 48
Levy, Uriah P., 48
Lincoln, Abraham, 37, 38
Lincoln, Mary Todd, 38
Lincoln Memorial (DC), 33, 41
Little Bighorn Battlefield NM (MT), **84**, 84-85
Longwood Gardens (PA), **28**, *29*
Louis Comfort Tiffany and Associated Artists, 14, 16, *17*
Louisiana
  Baton Rouge, 74, *74*
  Chalmette Battlefield Site, **74**, 75
  1850 House, **125**, *125*
  Fairview-Riverside SP, **74**, 74
  Fort Pike State Commemorative Area, **74**, *74*, *75*
  Great River Road, 69
  Lower Pontalba Building, **125**, *125*
  New Orleans, 74, **125**, *125*
  Oak Alley Plantation, **74**, *75*
  San Francisco Plantation, **69**, *66-73*
  Southdown Plantation, **74**, 75
  Upper Pontalba Building, **125**, *125*
Lower Pontalba Building (LA), **125**, *125*
Lutz Children's Museum (CT), **18**, 19
Madison, Dolley, 38
Madison, James, 34, 37, 53
Manning, Warren, 132
The Mark Twain House (CT), **11**, *8-17*
Marland, Ernest Whitworth, 133
Marland Mansion and Estate (OK), **133**, *133*
Marmillion, Antoine Valsin, 66-73
Marmillion, Louise Von Seybold, 66-73
Mary Washington House (VA), 52
Massachusetts
  The Mount, **127**, *127*
  Naumkeag, **126**, *126*
Mauer, Henry Conrad, 139
McFaddin, Mamie, 139
McFaddin-Ward House (TX), **139**, *139*
McKim, Mead & White, 123, 126, 127

McKinley, William, 34
Meadow Brook Hall (MI), **128**, *128*
Menczer Museum of Medicine and Dentistry (CT), **18**, 19
Michigan
  Meadow Brook Hall, **128**, *128*
Mills, Robert, 137
Minor, William, 75
Mission San Luis Obispo (CA), **106**, *107*
Monroe, James, 37, 38, *39*, *52*, 53
Montana
  Bighorn Canyon NRA, **84**, *85*
  Billings, 79, *76-83*, 84
  Custer NF, **84**, 85
  Hailstone NWR, **84**, 84
  J. K. Ralston Studio and Gallery, 79
  Little Bighorn Battlefield NM, **84**, 84-85
  Montana Centennial Cattle Drive Statue, 79
  The Moss Mansion, 79, *76-83*
  Oscar's Dreamland, **84**, *84*
  Pryor Mountain Wild Horse Range, **84**, *85*
  Western Heritage Center, 79
Montana Centennial Cattle Drive Statue (MT), 79
Monticello (VA), **45**, *42-51*
Montpelier (VA), **52**, *53*
Morgan, Julia, 98, 100, 101, 102, 104
Morro Bay SP (CA), **106**, *106*, 107
Moss, Mattie, 76-83
Moss, Melville, *81*, 83
Moss, Preston Boyd, 78-83
The Moss Mansion (MT), **79**, *76-83*
The Mount (MA), **127**, *127*
Mount Mitchell SP (NC), **64**, 65
Mystery Castle (AZ), **94**, 95

N-O-P-Q
National Air and Space Museum (DC), **40**, 41
National Geographic Society (DC), 36, 40-41
The National Museum of Natural History (DC), 33
Naumkeag (MA), **126**, *126*
Nemours Mansion (DE), **28**, 29
New England Air Museum (CT), **18**, 19
New Hampshire
  Saint-Gaudens NHS, *118*, **129**, *129*
New Mexico
  Kit Carson Historic Museums, **130**, *130*
New Orleans (LA), 74, **125**, *125*
New York (state)
  Olana SHS, **131**, *131*
Nixon, Patricia, 34, 37
Nixon, Richard, 32
Nook Farm (CT), 9, 10, 16
North Carolina
  Asheville, *54-63*, **64**, 65
  Biltmore Estate, **57**, *54-63*
  Blue Ridge Parkway, **64**, *64*, 65
  Great Smoky Mountain NP, **64**, 65
  Mount Mitchell SP, **64**, 65
  Thomas Wolfe House, 65
Oak Alley Plantation (LA), **74**, *75*
Ohio
  Stan Hywet Hall and Gardens, **132**, *132*
Oklahoma
  Marland Mansion and Estate, **133**, *133*
Olana SHS (NY), **131**, *131*
Old State House (CT), **18**, *18*, 19
Old Stone House (DC), **40**, 40
Olmsted, Frederick Law, 56, 58, *60*,

62-63
Ory family, 72
Oscar's Dreamland (MT), **84**, *84*
Palladio, Andrea, *42-43*, 47, 135, 136
Peirce–du Pont House (PA), 29
Pennsylvania
  Brandywine River Museum, **28**, 29
  Fallingwater, 88, **134**, *134*
  Longwood Gardens, **28**, *29*
  Peirce–du Pont House, 29
  Philadelphia, **28**, 29
Petit, A. P., 94
Phelan, Stephen Rice, 137
Philadelphia (PA), **28**, 29
Phoenix (AZ), **94**, *94-95*
Pinchot, Gifford, *60*
Pismo Beach (CA), **106**, *107*
Polynesian Cultural Center (HI), **116**, *116*, *117*
Pope, Loren B., 141
Pope-Leighey House (VA), **141**, *141*
Potter, Edward Tuckerman, 10, 12
Prince Michel Vineyard (VA), *52*, 52
Pryor Mountain Wild Horse Range (MT), **84**, *85*
Pueblo Grande Museum and Cultural Park (AZ), **94**, 95
Queen Emma Summer Palace (HI), **116**, 116, *117*

R-S-T-U
Reagan, Nancy Davis, 35
Rhode Island
  The Breakers, **135**, *135*
Richardson, Henry Hobson, 123
Rios-Caledonia Adobe (CA), **106**, 106
Roman, Jacques Telesphore, 75
Roosevelt, Eleanor, 34, 35
Roosevelt, Franklin Delano, 36
Roosevelt, Theodore, 34, 35, 37, 38-39
Rose Garden (DC), 32
Rosson, Roland Lee, 94
Rosson House (AZ), **94**, *94*
Saint-Gaudens, Augustus, 129
Saint-Gaudens NHS (NH), *118*, **129**, *129*
San Francisco Plantation (LA), **69**, *66-73*
San Simeon (CA), *96-105*, 106
Santa Maria Museum of Flight (CA), **106**, 107
Schenck, Carl, 60
Schneider, Charles S., 132
Seiberling, Frank A. and Gertrude, 132
1752 Carlyle House (VA), 41
Shenandoah NP (VA), **52**, 52
Sinclair, Caroline, 124
South Carolina
  Drayton Hall, **136**, *136*
South Dakota
  Custer NF, **84**, 85
Southdown Plantation (LA), **74**, 75
Stan Hywet Hall and Gardens (OH), **132**, *132*
Stanley-Whitman House (CT), **18**, *18-19*
State Capitol (CT), 11
Staunton (VA), **52**, 53
Steele, Fletcher, 126
Stewart, Andrew and Josephine, 75
Suarez, Diego, 122
Taliesin West (AZ), **89**, *86-93*
Tassinari & Chatel, *62*
Tennessee

Armstrong-Lockett House, **64**, 64
Great Smoky Mountain NP, **64**, *65*
Guinness World Records Museum, **64**, 64-65
Hunt-Phelan Home, **137**, *137*
Texas
  The Bishop's Palace, **138**, *138*
  McFaddin-Ward House, **139**, *139*
Thomas Wolfe House (NC), 65
Thompson, Mrs. Clark, 72
Thorp, Alfred H., 14
Tiffany, Louis Comfort, 14
Toulmin, Alice Larkin, 120
Truman, Harry S., 32, 34, 39
Twain, Mark, 9-17
Tyler, John, 38
Upjohn, Richard, 10
Upper Pontalba Building (LA), **125**, *125*
U.S. National Arboretum (DC), **40**, *40*, 41
Utah
  Beehive House, **140**, *140*

V-W-X-Y-Z
Van Buren, Martin, 38
Vanderbilt, Cornelius, II, 135
Vanderbilt, Edith Stuyvesant, 60-62
Vanderbilt, George Washington, III, 54-63
Vaux, Calvert, 131
Vietnam Veterans Memorial (DC), 33, 41
Virginia
  Alexandria, **40**, *41*, **141**, *141*
  Ash Lawn–Highland, 52, *52*, 53
  Blue Ridge Parkway, **64**, *64*, 65
  Fredericksburg, 52, *52*, *53*
  Mary Washington House, 52
  Monticello, **45**, *42-51*
  Montpelier, **52**, *53*
  Pope-Leighey House, **141**, *141*
  Prince Michel Vineyard, *52*, 52
  1752 Carlyle House, 41
  Shenandoah NP, **52**, 52
  Staunton, 52, 53
Vizcaya Museum and Gardens (FL), **122**, *122*
Waikiki Aquarium (HI), **116**, 116-117
Wall, Charles J., *108-109*
Ward, Carrol, 139
Washington (DC), 33, *30-39*, **40**, *40-41*, **141**
Washington Monument (DC), 33, *37*, 41
Washington Place (HI), 111
Western Heritage Center (MT), 79
West Potomac Park (DC), **40**, *41*
Wharton, Edith, 127
Wheeler, Candace Thurber, 14
The White House (DC), 33, *30-39*
Whitfield, Nathan Bryan, 119
Wilmington (DE), **28**, *28*, 29
Wilson, Alfred G. and Matilda, 128
Wilson, Woodrow, 32, 35, 40
Winterthur Museum, Garden and Library (DE), **23**, *20-27*
Woodrow Wilson House (DC), **40**, 40
W. P. Nelson Company, 80, 81
Wright, Frank Lloyd, 87-93, **134**, 141
Wright, Olgivanna, 87, 90, 91, 92
Wyatt, George Hubbard, 137
Wyoming
  Bighorn Canyon NRA, **84**, *85*
Young, Brigham and Lucy Decker, 140

143

PICTURE CREDITS

Cover photograph by Paul Rocheleau
2 Fred Hirschmann
5 John Elk III

MARK TWAIN'S HOUSE
8, 9 The Mark Twain House
10 The Mark Twain House
11 The Mark Twain House
12 Robert Kern
13 *(upper left)* The Mark Twain House
13 *(lower right)* Robert Benson
14 *(upper)* Lee Snider/Photo Images
14 *(lower)* Robert Benson
15 Robert Kern
16 *(upper)* Robert Benson
16 *(lower)* The Mark Twain House
17 Robert Kern
18 Robert Benson
19 *(upper)* Robert Perron
19 *(lower)* Robert Benson

WINTERTHUR
20, 21 Courtesy of Winterthur Museum
22 Courtesy of Winterthur Museum
23 Courtesy of Winterthur Museum
24 *(upper)* Lee Snider/Photo Images
24 *(lower)* Carol Betsch
25 Courtesy of Winterthur Museum
26, 27 *(all)* Courtesy of Winterthur Museum
28 Lee Snider/Photo Images
29 *(upper left)* James P. Rowan
29 *(lower right)* Lee Snider/Photo Images

THE WHITE HOUSE
30, 31 Phyllis Picardi/Stock Boston
32 The White House Historical
   Association
33 Robert Llewellyn
34 *(upper)* Robert Llewellyn
34 *(lower)* The White House
   Historical Association
35 *(upper left)* ChromoSohm/
   Sohm-Stock Boston
35 *(lower right)* The White House
   Historical Association
36 *(upper)* The White House
   Historical Association
36 *(lower)* Robert Llewellyn
37 Robert Llewellyn
38 *(both)* The White House
   Historical Association
39 The White House Historical
   Association
40 Linda Bartlett
41 *(upper right)* Linda Bartlett
41 *(lower left)* Wolfgang Kaehler

MONTICELLO
42, 43 Kevin Shields
44 *(upper)* Lee Snider/Photo Images
44 *(lower)* Robert Lautman/Monticello
45 Linda Bartlett
46 *(upper)* Linda Bartlett
46 *(lower)* Robert Lautman/Monticello
47 Robert Lautman/Monticello
48 *(upper right)* Robert Llewellyn
48 *(lower left)* Robert Lautman/Monticello
49 Robert Llewellyn
50 *(upper)* Robert Lautman/Monticello
50 *(lower)* Kevin Shields
51 Robert Lautman/Monticello
52 Lee Snider/Photo Images
53 *(upper left)* Paul Rocheleau
53 *(lower right)* Lee Snider/Photo Images

BILTMORE ESTATE
54, 55 J. Faircloth/TRANSPARENCIES, Inc.
56 The Biltmore Company
57 Jim & Diane Morris/
   TRANSPARENCIES, Inc.
58 *(upper)* The Biltmore Company
58 *(lower)* Mike Booher/
   TRANSPARENCIES, Inc.
59 *(upper left)* Mike Booher/
   TRANSPARENCIES, Inc.
59 *(lower right)* The Biltmore Company
60 *(left)* Kevin Shields
60 *(upper right)* Tim Thompson
60, 61 Index Stock Photography, Inc.
62 *(lower left)* John Elk III
62 *(upper right)* The Biltmore Company
63 *(upper left)* John Elk III
63 *(lower right)* The Biltmore Company
64 Laurence Parent
65 *(upper right)* Laurence Parent
65 *(lower)* Tom Till Photography

SAN FRANCISCO PLANTATION
66, 67 Les Riess
68 D. Donne Bryant
69 Bernard Boutrit/Woodfin
   Camp & Associates
70 *(upper right)* Bernard Boutrit/Woodfin
   Camp & Associates
70 *(lower left)* Courtesy of San Francisco
   Plantation
71 Courtesy of San Francisco Plantation
72 *(upper left)* Courtesy of San Francisco
   Plantation
72 *(lower right)* Bernard Boutrit/Woodfin
   Camp & Associates
73 *(upper)* Philip Gould

73 *(lower)* Bernard Boutrit/Woodfin
   Camp & Associates
74 John Elk III
75 *(upper left)* James P. Rowan
75 *(lower right)* Laurence Parent

THE MOSS MANSION
76, 77 John Reddy
78 Donnie Sexton
79 Donnie Sexton
80 Michael Degnan Photographic
81 *(upper left)* Donnie Sexton
81 *(lower right)* Michael Degnan Photographic
82 *(upper)* Larry Mayer
82 *(lower)* Donnie Sexton
83 Michael Degnan Photographic
84 Donnie Sexton
85 *(upper left)* David Muench
85 *(lower right)* John Reddy

TALIESIN WEST
86, 87 Kerrick James/Adstock Photos
88 *(upper)* Richard Maack/Adstock Photos
88 *(lower)* David H. Smith
89 Richard Maack/Adstock Photos
90 *(upper left)* Tom Bean
90 *(lower right)* Richard Maack/Adstock Photos
91 *(upper)* Sally Weigand
91 *(lower)* Tom Bean
92 Sally Weigand
93 *(upper)* John Elk III
93 *(lower)* Richard Maack/Adstock Photos
94 John Elk III
95 *(both)* Tom Bean

HEARST CASTLE
96, 97 John Elk III
98 Dickerson Fotographics, Halcyon, CA.
99 John Elk III
100 *(left)* Tim Thompson
101 Dave G. Houser
102, 103 *(upper)* John Blades/Hearst Castle,
   Hearst San Simeon State Historical
   Monument
102 *(lower)* Frank Balthis
104 *(lower left)* John Elk III
104 *(upper right)* A. Ramey/Unicorn
   Stock Photos
105 A. Ramey/Unicorn Stock Photos
106 John Elk III
107 *(lower right)* Terry Donnelly
107 *(upper right)* Dickerson Fotographics,
   Halcyon, CA.

IOLANI PALACE
108, 109 The Friends of Iolani Palace
110 *(upper left)* Rob D. Tringali Jr. &
   Geneviève Monette
110 *(lower right)* Kay Shaw
111 Alan Seiden
112, 113 Milroy/McAleer for the Friends
   of Iolani Palace
113 The Friends of Iolani Palace
114 The Friends of Iolani Palace
115 *(upper)* Alan Seiden
115 *(lower)* The Friends of Iolani Palace
116 Wolfgang Kaehler
117 *(upper)* James P. Rowan
117 *(lower)* John Elk II

GAZETTEER
118 Kevin Shields
119 *(both)* Paul Rocheleau
120 Lee Foster
121 *(upper)* Kay Shaw
121 *(lower)* Manrico Mirabelli/Index
   Stock Photography
122 *(upper)* Paul Rocheleau
122 *(lower)* Lee Snider/Photo Images
123 Robert Perron
124 Tim Thompson
125 *(upper left)* John Elk III
125 *(lower right)* Alan Briere
126 *(both)* Paul Rocheleau
127 Paul Rocheleau
128 Oakland University's Meadow Brook
   Hall, Rochester, Michigan
129 *(both)* Kevin Shields
130 Judith Bronner/Courtesy of
   Kit Carson Historic Museum
131 *(both)* Lee Snider/Photo Images
132 H. K. Barnett/Stan Hywet Hall
   and Gardens
133 *(upper)* Tim Thompson
133 *(lower)* John Elk III
134 Christopher Little
135 *(upper left)* Mae Scanlan
135 *(lower right)* Lee Snider/Photo Images
136 *(upper right)* Jonathan Wallen
136 *(lower left)* Paul Rocheleau
137 Hunt-Phelan Home
138 John Elk III
139 *(upper)* Tim Thompson
139 *(lower)* John Elk III
140 *(upper right)* Tim Thompson
140 *(lower left)* John Elk III
141 Rodney Todt

Back cover photograph by Linda Bartlett

ACKNOWLEDGMENTS

Cartography: Dimensions DPR, Inc.; map resource base courtesy of the USGS.

The editors would also like to thank the following: Lorraine Doré, Pascale Hueber, and Valéry Dumas-Pigeon.

GREAT AMERICAN HOMES

Please note that the addresses and/or telephone numbers for the following sites have changed since GREAT AMERICAN HOMES *went to press:*

page 11

Mark Twain House
Insert zip code:
06105

page 57

Biltmore House
Spelling change: One
North Pack Square

page 89

Taliesin West
New mailing address:
Taliesin West
P.O. Box 4430
Scottsdale, AZ 85261

page 99

Hearst Castle
New mailing address:
Hearst Castle
Dept. of Parks and
Recreation/San
Simeon District
750 Hearst Castle Rd.
San Simeon, CA
93452-9741

page 134

Fallingwater
New area code:
(724) 329-8501

page 136

Drayton Hall
Leave out last four
digits of area code:
BEFORE: 29414-7105
NEW: 29414

page 139

McFaddin-Ward House
Change street address to:
725 Third Street

page 141

Pope-Leighey House
New mailing address:
Pope-Leighey House
Woodlawn Plantation
P.O. Box 37
Mount Vernon, VA 22121